THE MASTER REFERENCE COLLECTION

POCKET GUIDE

TO THE

BIBLE

CYRIL BRIDGLAND
FRANCIS FOULKES

INTERVARSITY PRESS
DOWNERS GROVE, ILLINOIS 60515
LEICESTER, ENGLAND

Inter-Varsity Press
38 De Montfort Street, Leicester LE1 7GP, England
P.O. Box 1400, Downers Grove, Illinois 60515, U.S.A.

*Inter-Varsity Press, England is the publishing division of the Universities and Colleges
Christian Fellowship, a student movement linking Christian Unions in universities and
colleges throughout the United Kingdom and the Republic of Ireland, and a member
movement of the International Fellowship of Evangelical Students. For information about
local and national activities write to UCCF, 38 De Montfort Street, Leicester LE1 7GP.*

*InterVarsity Press, U.S.A., is the book-publishing division of InterVarsity Christian
Fellowship, a student movement active on campus at hundreds of universities, colleges and
schools of nursing. For information about local and regional activities, write Public
Relations Dept., InterVarsity Christian Fellowship, 6400 Schroeder Rd., P.O. Box 7895,
Madison, WI 53707-7895.*

*Distributed in Canada through InterVarsity Press, 860 Denison St., Unit 3, Markham,
Ontario L3R 4H1, Canada.*

Cover illustration: Roberta Polfus

ISBN 0-8308-1401-9

Printed in the United States of America

Library of Congress Cataloging in Publication Data

Bridgland, Cyril.
    Pocket guide to the Bible/Cyril Bridgland, Francis Foulkes.—
*Rev. ed./by InterVarsity Christian Fellowship of the United States
of America.*
        p.   cm.
    *Rev. ed. of: Pocket guide to the Old Testament/Cyril Bridgland,
1982, and Pocket guide to the New Testament/Francis Foulkes, 1978.*
    Bibliography: p.
    Includes index.
    ISBN 0-8308-1401-9: $12.95 (U.S.)
    *1. Bible—Introductions.   I. Bridgland, Cyril. Pocket guide to
the Old Testament.   II. Foulkes, Francis. Pocket guide to the New
Testament.   III. InterVarsity Christian Fellowship of the United
States of America.   IV. Title.*
BS475.2.B67 1988   *88-1389*
220.6'1—dc19   *CIP*

16	15	14	13	12	11	10	9	8	7	6	5	4	3	2	1
99	98	97	96	95	94	93	92	91	90	89	88				

PART ONE □ THE OLD TESTAMENT

General Articles

The Pentateuch

History

Poetry and Wisdom

Major Prophets

Minor Prophets

PART TWO ☐ THE NEW TESTAMENT

General Article

The Four Gospels

Paul

The General Epistles

Introduction

The aim of this pocket guide is to provide the basic help needed to study the books of the Bible effectively, and to understand their message for today. Many Christians are very familiar with portions of the Bible, whether it be the Gospels or the Psalms, but when it comes to the Old Testament as a whole or even the New Testament epistles, there are huge gaps in our knowledge. How many of us have given up halfway through Leviticus or even begun to understand the images of Zechariah? How many of us have struggled with the thought of Paul in Romans or have groped our way through the strange world of Revelation? Yet these are all part of the literary tapestry that is God's Word.

This *Pocket Guide to the Bible* is a combination and revision of two volumes formerly published as *Pocket Guide to the Old Testament* by Cyril Bridgland and *Pocket Guide to the New Testament* by Francis Foulkes. Now, in one comprehensive guide, you have the main purpose of each book, what is in it, its historical background and how it "hangs together." In many cases the books of the Bible tell us nothing of their authors and provide nothing to show us how or when they came into being. In such cases we have tried to consider different opinions with an open mind; but we have always proceeded with the view that the content of the books is of far greater importance than the study of dates and authors. As you use this book you will notice that the summaries of each book do not follow a

consistent pattern. This is because the books of the Bible
vary in their literary type and construction and it would be
misleading to impose an artificial uniformity on them.

Of course a pocket guide aims to deal with the basics.
If you want to study the Bible in more depth, or pursue a
subject introduced in this guide, you will need to go to the
larger reference books and commentaries. We recommend five books that you will find useful throughout your
study of the Bible:

The New Bible Commentary Revised (IVP, 1970; Eerdmans,
1970)

The International Bible Commentary (Marshall Pickering,
1986; Zondervan, 1986)

The New Bible Dictionary Revised (IVP, 1982; Tyndale-USA,
1982)

The Illustrated Bible Dictionary (IVP, 1980; Tyndale-USA,
1980)

Handbook of Life in Bible Times (IVP, 1986)

These and other books will be referred to by their abbreviations (see the list of books and their abbreviations
following the table of contents), and where we suggest a
book for further reading in most cases you will find the
British, followed by the United States, publisher (unless
IVP has published the book in both countries) as well as
the date of publication. There are also series of study
books of various kinds which give more detail on individual books. Many of these will appear in the lists of books
for further reading at the end of chapters. At a basic level
there are:

The Bible Speaks Today (IVP, USA)

Bible Commentary for Laymen (Regal/Gospel Light)

At a more advanced level you might consider:

Tyndale Old Testament Commentaries (IVP)

Tyndale New Testament Commentaries (IVP, UK; Eerdmans)

The New International Commentary on the Old Testament

(Hodder; Eerdmans)

The New International Commentary on the New Testament (Hodder; Eerdmans)

The Expositor's Bible Commentary (Marshall Pickering; Zondervan)

If we're honest, none of us finds that learning comes naturally—it's too easy to let what we read just wash over us. That is why we have included study questions on each book of the Bible. Writing answers down is a help, and you might consider keeping a notebook for this purpose. The questions will help you look more closely at particular passages and also build up your knowledge of the Bible.

A Word about Translations

English translations are so numerous today that the student is often perplexed over which translation to use. Some stick with the Authorized Version (King James Version) of 1611 because it has meant so much to so many people for so long. But our increased knowledge of the ancient manuscripts and the ancient languages in which the Bible was written make it wise for us to use a more recent translation for study purposes. The Revised Version of 1885 is a careful and accurate translation. But the Revised Standard Version of 1952 shows the influence of a further half-century of biblical studies and removes many of the archaic terms that remained in the Revised Version. The New American Standard Bible of 1963 has enjoyed great success, but more and more Evangelicals are adopting the New International Version (1978) for personal reading and study.

Other translations such as the Roman Catholic Jerusalem Bible and the New English Bible have many things to commend them. The latter is often very beautiful in its rendering of the text, but it is a freer translation than the others mentioned and its English is not always that of the common person. For many English speakers the Good News Bible (Today's English Version) cannot be bettered for its colloquial expression, but the student should realize that its rendering is not as precise as translations which allow for the use of a larger English vocabulary. The Living Bible is a paraphrase rather than a translation, often interpretive, but valuable for its purpose of bringing the message of the Bible into plain, contemporary speech. But it is not a study Bible. The many translations by individual translators such as Moffatt, Knox, Phillips and others all have their own advantages, but in general they lack the excellence of translations over which many dedicated minds have worked.

For purposes of studying God's Word it is best to choose one of the more precise translations into contemporary English such as the RSV, NASB or NIV. These are available in a wide range of sizes and formats, as well as in study versions with copious notes, introductions, maps and other study aids.

But above all, we need to remember that we are handling God's Word, and to do it right we need the help of the Holy Spirit. We have written this book from the conviction that behind all that men have done to produce these books there has been the work of the Holy Spirit. He has guided men's minds and overruled their efforts. So we may speak of the whole of the Scriptures as 2 Timothy 3:16 speaks of the Old Testament, as inspired Scripture. It is God's Word, given to lead us to faith in him through Jesus Christ, given to teach us how we, individually and with our fellow Christians, should walk in his ways. God's Word in both Old and New Testaments is given to us not only so that we may *know,* but that we may be *changed* by his truth. May God use this pocket guide as a small part of that great transformation.

Table of Maps, Figures and Charts

Maps

Figures and Charts

Table of Abbreviations

Abbreviations for the Books of the Bible

The following abbreviations have been used for the books of the Bible:

Old Testament		Micah	: Mi.
Genesis	: Gn.	Nahum	: Na.
Exodus	: Ex.	Habakkuk	: Hab.
Leviticus	: Lv.	Zephaniah	: Zp.
Numbers	: Nu.	Haggai	: Hg.
Deuteronomy	: Dt.	Zechariah	: Zc.
Joshua	: Jos.	Malachi	: Mal.
Judges	: Jdg.		
Ruth	: Ru.	**New Testament**	
1 & 2 Samuel	: 1, 2 Sa.	Matthew	: Mt.
1 & 2 Kings	: 1, 2 Ki.	Mark	: Mk.
1 & 2 Chronicles	: 1, 2 Ch.	Luke	: Lk.
Ezra	: Ezr.	John	: Jn.
Nehemiah	: Ne.	Acts	: Acts
Esther	: Est.	Romans	: Rom.
Job	: Jb.	1 & 2 Corinthians	: 1, 2 Cor.
Psalms	: Ps. (Pss.)	Galatians	: Gal.
Proverbs	: Pr.	Ephesians	: Eph.
Ecclesiastes	: Ec.	Philippians	: Phil.
Song of Solomon	: Ct.	Colossians	: Col.
Isaiah	: Is.	1 & 2 Thessalonians	: 1, 2 Thes.
Jeremiah	: Je.	1 & 2 Timothy	: 1, 2 Tim.
Lamentations	: La.	Titus	: Tit.
Ezekiel	: Ezk.	Philemon	: Phm.
Daniel	: Dn.	Hebrews	: Heb.
Hosea	: Ho.	James	: Jas.
Joel	: Joel	1 & 2 Peter	: 1, 2 Pet.
Amos	: Am.	1, 2 & 3 John	: 1, 2, 3 Jn.
Obadiah	: Ob.	Jude	: Jude
Jonah	: Jon.	Revelation	: Rev.

What Use Is the Old Testament?

What use is the Old Testament today? If you were ship-wrecked on a desert island, and were allowed only one book of the Bible, which would you take, Ecclesiastes or the Gospel of John? Almost everyone would choose the Gospel, and rightly. Certainly most people would choose a New Testament rather than an Old Testament book. We feel that the New Testament is more important than the Old, and that the Old Testament is difficult, full of contradictions, a book of wrath and irrelevant to everyday life.

It has, of course, educational value in terms of general knowledge, history and literature. But the Old Testament is more than ancient literature. We are concerned in this pocket guide with the importance of the Old Testament for practical day-to-day Christian living.

Incidentally, the popular idea that the Old Testament is the book of God's wrath, whereas, in contrast, the New Testament is the book of his love, does not bear investigation. The love of God is constantly emphasized in the Old Testament, and God's wrath also features in the New Testament.

Jesus' use of the Old Testament
The overwhelming argument for the usefulness of the Old Testament is its commendation by Christ. 'And beginning with Moses and all the prophets, he interpreted to them in all the scriptures (*i.e.* the Old Testament) the things concerning himself' (Lk. 24:27, *cf.* 24:44). He was well acquainted with it. He showed by quotation or reference

that he knew most of the thirty-nine books.

Jesus understood himself and his ministry in terms of the Old Testament. At his baptism the voice from heaven joined Psalm 2:7, which speaks of Messiah as a conquering king, with Isaiah 42:1, which is about God's suffering servant 'Thou art my beloved Son; with thee I am well pleased' (Lk. 3:22). This confirmed to Jesus that he was to be the Lord's king by the way of the cross, and the temptations which followed were Satan's attempt to turn him from this way (Lk. 4:1–13). Soon after, in the synagogue at Nazareth, he chose to read from Isaiah, and defined his ministry with the words, 'The Lord . . . has anointed me to preach good news to the poor . . . to proclaim the acceptable year of the Lord' (Lk. 4:18–19, *cf*. Is. 61:1–2). His death was to be in fulfilment of the Scriptures (Mk. 9:12; 14:49) and was the sealing of the new covenant of which Jeremiah wrote (Je. 31:31–34; Lk. 22:20). He used the story of Jonah and the big fish when speaking of his resurrection (Mt. 12:40).

He regarded it as the Word of God and as historically reliable. He referred to its stories as though he believed them: David and the bread of the presence (Lk. 6:3–4); the Queen of Sheba and King Solomon (Lk. 11:31); and Jonah and the fish (Mt. 12:39–41).

The precision of the text was important to him ' . . . till heaven and earth pass away, not an iota, not a dot, will pass from the law . . . ' (Mt. 5:18). The iota is the smallest Hebrew letter and the dot is a small ornament added to a letter.

He quoted the words of the Old Testament as though they were the actual words spoken by God himself. Genesis 2:24, 'Therefore a man leaves his father and his mother and cleaves to his wife, and they become one flesh', is quoted as the very word of God. Genesis does not say that God spoke it, but Jesus says he did, because it is written in the Old Testament (Mt. 19:5). The words of the Old Testament given with the authority of God are the Word of God.

In the life and thinking of Jesus, the Old Testament was of supreme importance. 'What was indispensable to the Redeemer must always be indispensable to the redeemed' (G. A. Smith).

The first Christians' use of the Old Testament

The Old Testament was the handbook of the early Christians. They understood Jesus in terms of it. The letter to the Hebrews begins by saying that the God who had spoken by the prophets has now spoken to us by a Son who bears the very stamp of God's nature (Heb. 1:1–3), and goes on to demonstrate from the book of Psalms the superiority of Jesus to angels and even to Moses (Heb. 1–2; Pss. 2:7; 97:7, *etc.*). The tabernacle and its sacrifices find their completion and fulfilment in Jesus (Heb. 8–10). The pattern for Christian living is that of the servant in Isaiah perfectly exemplified in Christ (1 Pet. 2:21–25).

They, too, regarded it as God's Word. For the apostle Peter 'no prophecy ever came by the impulse of man, but men moved by the Holy Spirit spoke from God' (2 Pet. 1:21). What the Old Testament teaches is what God teaches.

They preached the gospel from it even while the New Testament was being written. On the day of Pentecost Peter takes Joel 2:28–32, Psalm 16:8–11 and Psalm 110:1 as his texts to proclaim that God has made Jesus both Lord and Christ (Acts 2:36). Stephen gives a long résumé of Israel's history to explain why he preaches that Jesus is the Righteous One (Acts 7:1–53). The Ethiopian is reading Isaiah 53 when Philip meets him and it is from this chapter, written hundreds of years before Jesus was born, that Philip 'told him the good news of Jesus' (Acts 8:26–38).

They imitate their Master by quoting the Old Testament as though they believe it (1 Cor. 10:1–4, *cf.* Ex. 13:21, 14:22, 29; 2 Pet. 2:5–7, *cf.* Gn. 8:18; 6:6–8; 19:24; 19:16, 29), and by quoting its words as though they were spoken by God himself (Heb. 3:7, *cf.* Ps. 95:7–8; Acts 13:34–35, *cf.* Is. 55:3, *etc.*). They identify the Old Testament with the voice of God, so that the apostle Paul calls it 'the oracles of God' (Rom. 3:2).

Our use of the Old Testament

It is useful to bring us to faith in Christ. The apostle Paul is referring to the Old Testament when he writes to Timothy, ' . . . from childhood you have been acquainted with the sacred writings which are able to instruct you for salvation through faith in Christ Jesus. All scripture is inspired by God and profitable for teaching, for reproof, for correction, and for training in righteousness, that the man of God may be complete, equipped for every good work' (2 Tim. 3:15–17).

The early Christians were fortunate to have the apostles' teaching about Jesus and his fulfilment of the Old Testament by word of mouth. That teaching is written for us in the New Testament. It gives us a fuller revelation of God and expands and enlarges the message of the Old Testament. Nevertheless, we should remember that the essentials for bringing us to faith in Christ are to be found in the Old Testament.

It teaches us that sin is a failure to attain the standard God has set, a perversion of our nature (Is. 53:6), a breaking of God's holy law (Ex. 32:7–8, 15–16, 19) and rebellion against our Creator (Gn. 3:3–6). His law is given to show what he requires of us (Lv. 18:1–5), to convince us of our inability to meet his requirements (Rom. 7:7–12), and of our need of his grace (Ex. 34:6–7; N.B. the three categories: iniquity, transgression, sin). The Old Testament teaching about sacrifice and deliverance is fundamental to an understanding of the cross and of our salvation in Christ. The Israelites were brought out of slavery, each family by the blood of a lamb. So 'Christ, our paschal lamb, has been sacrificed' (1 Cor. 5:7). The New Testament references to 'the blood of Christ' are understood with the help of Leviticus 17: 'the life is in the blood' (v. 11). Blood taken from a body produces death. The blood of Christ means the death of Christ. To be cleansed in the blood of Christ means to appropriate all that Christ accomplished by his death. The book of Leviticus and the letter to the Hebrews are to be read side by side if we would understand either of them.

All this sets the stage for Christ and helps us to understand his mission.

Having brought us to Christ, the Old Testament can be used to help us to grow into mature Christians. We are to use it so that it can instruct us, reprove and correct us, and train us in righteousness. How can we use it so that it may do this?

We need to get to know it generally. Each Christian must learn to do this for him- or herself, but we may give some general hints.

Begin to gain a broad sweep of the Old Testament. Do this by reading selected passages rather than by starting at the beginning and reading to the end. A few people have the tenacity to keep on to the end this way, but most will do better to select chapters from the outline of each book given in this pocket guide. Get a bird's-eye view of the Old Testament.

Use the study questions. Set aside a weekly time for this, and use the questions either for personal study or in a group. Always remember that, by definition, a Christian cannot be a lone wolf. He or she is a member of the church and the Scriptures yield their fullest benefit when they are used within its fellowship.

Use both Testaments for personal daily Bible reading. We recommend *Food for Life* (IVP, 1977), *Search the Scriptures* (IVP, 1967), Scripture Union Notes, or *The Daily Bible Commentary* (Scripture Union). The commentary is especially useful for intelligent devotional study of the Old Testament.

It is helpful to mark the verses or phrases which speak powerfully to you. This is for many the best way of getting to know the Bible. We need to remember, however, that if words and phrases are lifted out of their context, they can be made to teach anything. Nevertheless, it is the experience of thousands that God sometimes speaks through a single verse or phrase. Indeed it was the experience of Christ himself.

When he was tempted to avoid the cross by going the way of popularity, or of materialism, or of expediency, he resisted by arguing rationally from the teaching of the Old Testament. He was unable to be a kind of welfare-state Messiah because the Old Testament said that man needs more than bread to live. He was unable to be merely a popular Messiah because the Old Testament said that we must not put the Lord to the test. He was unable to embrace expediency as a way of winning loyalty, because the Old Testament said that only the Lord was to be worshipped and only he was to be served (Mt. 4:1–11; Lk. 4:1–13).

The Bible is not made up of two contrasting parts. It is one consistent Word from the one unchanging God. It is his will that we use both Testaments, Old and New. Obviously we do not argue for the neglect of the New Testament, but for the use of the Old along with it. Often what is said here about using the Old Testament applies to the use of the whole Bible. 'The New is in the Old concealed. The Old is in the New revealed.'

No Christian grows to full maturity until he or she has learnt to use the whole Bible.

Useful books

On the Old Testament:

B. W. Anderson, *The Living World of the Old Testament* (Longman, 1978); *Understanding the Old Testament* (4th ed. Prentice Hall, 1986)

J. Bright, *A History of Israel* (2nd ed. SCM, 1981; 3rd. ed. Westminster, 1981)

W. Dyrness, *Themes in Old Testament Theology* (Paternoster, 1980; IVP, 1979)

H. L. Ellison, *The Message of the Old Testament* (Paternoster, U.K., 1969)

R. K. Harrison, *Introduction to the Old Testament* (IVP, 1970; Eerdmans, 1969)

R. K. Harrison, *Old Testament Times* (Eerdmans, U.S.A., 1970)

E. A. Martens, *Plot and Purpose in the Old Testament* (IVP, 1981); *God's Design* (Baker, 1981)

G. Treasure, *The Book that Jesus Read* (IVP, U.K., 1981)

L. J. Wood and D. O'Brien, *A Survey of Israel's History* (rev. ed. Zondervan, U.S.A., 1986)

For general reference:
Cruden's Complete Concordance
Oxford Concise Concordance to the RSV
Oxford Bible Atlas

The Books and Divisions of the Old Testament

It is a serious mistake to regard the Bible as one book. It is not. It is composed of sixty-six books, or booklets or leaflets, bound into one volume for convenience. It is divided into Old Testament books, written whilst the old covenant was in force, and the New Testament books, written after Christ had sealed the new covenant with his blood.

Thirty-nine books make up the Old Testament and they have five main divisions in the English Bible. It is helpful to mark these divisions in the index of one's personal copy of the Bible. They are:

The Pentateuch:	from Genesis to Deuteronomy
The history books:	from Joshua to Esther
The poetry books:	from Job to the Song of Solomon
The major prophets:	from Isaiah to Daniel
The minor prophets:	from Hosea to Malachi

This arrangement was taken from the Latin Vulgate version which, in turn, took it over from the Greek Old Testament, the Septuagint. The Hebrew Bible is arranged differently. It has three main divisions:

The Torah:	from Genesis to Deuteronomy

The Prophets:

Former:	Joshua, Judges, 1 and 2 Samuel, 1 and 2 Kings
Latter:	Isaiah, Jeremiah, Ezekiel, The Book of the Twelve
The Writings:	Psalms, Proverbs, the Scrolls, Daniel, Ezra, Nehemiah, and 1 and 2 Chronicles

In Hebrew thinking what we would call history is included in prophecy because Hebrew history is written prophetically. It contains a message from the Lord. History is his story.

The minor prophets are treated as one book, the Book of the Twelve, and so also are Canticles (Song of Solomon), Ruth, Lamentations, Ecclesiastes and Esther (the Scrolls).

| GENESIS | EXODUS | LEVITICUS | NUMBERS |
| | | | DEUTERONOMY |

LAW

JOSHUA	JUDGES	RUTH	1 & 2 SAMUEL	1 & 2 KINGS	1 & 2 CHRONICLES	ESTHER
					EZRA	
					NEHEMIAH	

HISTORY

| JOB | PSALMS | PROVERBS | ECCLESIASTES | SONG OF SOLOMON | LAMENTATIONS | ISAIAH | JEREMIAH | EZEKIEL | DANIEL |

POETRY AND WISDOM   **PROPHETS**

| HOSEA | JOEL | AMOS | OBADIAH | JONAH | MICAH | NAHUM | HABAKKUK | ZEPHANIAH | HAGGAI | ZECHARIAH | MALACHI |

PROPHETS

The Canon

How were the books of the Old Testament collected together? How did they become part of the canon of Holy Scripture? The Greek word *kanōn* means a reed, a rod, a mason's plumbline, and so a pattern to guide the artisan. It came to be used in the technical sense of a list of sacred writings which possessed special divine authority. It describes the collection of books making up the Bible. The books in the canon constitute the required standard by which other things may be measured.

The Pentateuch (Genesis to Deuteronomy) is the foundation of the Old Testament and indeed of the whole Bible. We do not know how long it took to reach its present shape. Conservative scholars accept a basic Mosaic authorship of the Pentateuch even if they allow for later editing and addition. All agree that it was complete and canonical by the time of Ezra and Nehemiah in the fifth century BC.

Probably the second and third parts of the Hebrew Bible, the Prophets and the Writings, were organized into their separate sections about 165 BC. The Greek Old Testament (the Septuagint) indicates that all the books of the Hebrew Bible were complete by 150 BC at least. This means that the Hebrew Bible was complete when Jesus was born in Bethlehem, and he speaks of the Old Testament canon when he says 'everything written about me in the law of Moses and the prophets and the psalms must be fulfilled' (Lk. 24:44). He is referring to the threefold division of the Old Testament: the Law, the Prophets and the Writings (called the Psalms because the Psalter is the first and longest book in the Writings). He quotes frequently and widely from it and often so as to set his seal upon an entire collection and not only upon the book from which he quotes. It is this imprimatur of Christ upon the Old Testament which makes it authoritative for Christians today.

It is certainly true that after Christ's ascension discussion continued among the rabbis about the canonicity of some books. With the destruction of Jerusalem in AD 70, a centre for scriptural study grew up at Jamnia (near Joppa) and, from time to time, discussion took place about the canonicity of Ezekiel, Esther, Canticles, Ecclesiastes and Proverbs. It is doubtful whether the 'councils' held at Jamnia (*c.* AD 90) were councils in our modern sense. The frequent assertion that they were decisive in canonizing the thirty-nine books of our Old Testament is conjectural. Certainly the upshot of the debates was the acknowledgment of these books as canonical. From the little we know of the discussions, it seems that they were concerned about whether some books should be excluded from the canon rather than whether any should be added. The council (if it was a council) did not *make* Holy Scripture. They did not form it. They accepted what the people of God in the Old Testament already accepted and they rejected what was already rejected. Canon Stafford Wright's words should be heeded: 'The Council of Jamnia was the confirming of public opinion, not the forming of it.'

Reference has been made above to the Greek Old Testament (the Septuagint). This translation from Hebrew into Greek was begun in Alexandria, Egypt (*c.* 250 BC), presumably with the Pentateuch. Eventually the rest of the Old Testament was also translated into Greek and so is an early witness to the existence of a canon of Scripture. When completed, it contained all the thirty-nine books of the Hebrew canon. It also included the books which came to be called apocryphal (see section The Apocrypha).

The Dead Sea Scrolls found at Qumran (near Masada) in

southern Israel include parts of all the books of the Old Testament, and a scroll containing the whole of Isaiah is specially important. They have given us manuscripts one thousand years earlier than any of the oldest previously surviving copies of Old Testament books, and have made a great contribution to the textual history of the Old Testament. Other scrolls show that the Essenes regarded some of the Writings at least as canonical since the second century BC.

The Scrolls also enable scholars to get behind the work of the Massoretes. Hebrew, as originally written, contains only consonants. Vowels are not represented in writing. There were various stages by which the vowels came to be written. Four consonant letters were given a secondary function as vowels before the Christian era. Then other methods were devised to give guidance when the Scriptures were read in public. Between AD 100 and AD 900 a school of Jewish scholars called Massoretes ('transmitters') established first a standard consonantal text and, in succeeding generations, invented a complicated system of signs which included vowel points and punctuation marks. Their work has been invaluable in transmitting an accurate text through the centuries. But to have today scrolls which pre-date their work by a thousand years is little short of a miracle.

For further study
NBCR; IBD
F. F. Bruce, *The Books and the Parchments* (Marshall Pickering, 1972; Revell, n.d.)

Authority, Inspiration, Revelation

Technical terms used with discrimination are helpful in any discipline which requires the use of the mind. The doctrine of Scripture is no exception to this rule, and these terms, *authority, inspiration, revelation,* are often used in defining it.

Authority has to do with the final court of appeal where matters of faith and conduct are concerned. Some look to the church, some to tradition, and some to reason, as their final authority. Evangelical Christians will assert that Holy Scripture is their final authority. They will not lightly turn their backs on what all Christians at all times and in all places have believed, and they will firmly maintain that Christ's command to love with the mind means that they must bring the best mental equipment and use the finest scholarship available as they study the Scriptures. But they dare not allow these things to stand in judgment over 'the sacred letters'. They will maintain this attitude to the Bible because they are convinced that it is the attitude of Christ, the Lord of the Church. If it can be demonstrated that Christ did not so regard Holy Scripture, then, and only then, will they regard them differently. It is not that Christians desire to elevate the Bible, the written Word of God, but that they are eager to emulate Christ, the living Word of God.

Inspiration refers to the Holy Spirit's control of the speakers or writers of Holy Scripture so that they wrote only what he willed them to write. He neither superseded their personalities nor nullified their mental processes. He did not use them as typewriters, but he did mould their faculties so that they produced what he wished to be produced. Sometimes he led them to speak and write things they did not fully comprehend or understand. He is the author of the Scriptures and they are its writers.

Often, in ordinary speech, 'inspiration' means 'inspiringness'. We talk of an inspired poet, or of being inspired by poetry or music. But in 2 Timothy 3:16, the phrase 'inspired by God' translates the Greek word *theopneustos*, which means 'God-breathed'. Hence when it refers to the Holy Spirit's action as the originator of Holy Scripture, it does not mean that the writers were inspired, nor that what they wrote was inspiring, but that what they wrote was 'God-breathed'. The apostle Peter makes the same point in different words when he says that 'men moved by the Holy Spirit spoke from God' (2 Pet. 1:21).

Distinguish carefully between inspiration and revelation. Whereas the former refers to God's control of the writers, the latter describes what he shows or reveals of himself in what they wrote. It is correct to speak of degrees of revelation, but not of degrees of inspiration. All Scripture is God-breathed, but some, by his sovereign will, reveals more of him and some less. This is the difference, for instance, between Ecclesiastes and the Gospel of John. Biblically speaking, they are equally 'God-breathed', for both writers recorded what God willed them to record for the purpose he willed, but they are not equally revealing of God. We shall learn more about him, of his holiness and his love, of his transcendence and of his immanence, in the Gospel of John than we shall in the book of Ecclesiastes. Nevertheless, Ecclesiastes is a part of his total revelation. Indeed, we shall be better prepared and more receptive to what God wants to show of himself in John's Gospel if we have understood first what he is saying in Ecclesiastes.

Christ taught that Holy Scripture was God-breathed, Old Testament as well as New (this is the reason for his promises to the apostles in John 14–16), so that in it God might reveal himself and his only Son, and thus he stamped his imprimatur upon it.

Revelation is a dynamic process because God is a God who acts in the history of his world. It is in the dramatic narratives of the Old Testament that we see God mightily at work. It is there that we also see his explanation of these events; words of warning and blessing spoken through his prophets. His people's response to this twofold revelation is at once the most depressing and encouraging story ever told. It is a constantly repeated sequence of rebellion and repentance on the Hebrews' part, and faithful love on God's part. We find our own story of redemption mirrored in the Old Testament revelation.

For further study

J. F. Balchin, *Let the Bible speak* (IVP, 1981)

B. Edwards, *Nothing but the Truth* (Evangelical Press, 1978)

Survey of Old Testament History

New discoveries constantly force us to revise our chronologies of Israel's history and so we cannot be precisely accurate with Old Testament dates. The sharpest differences arise in assigning dates to the period prior to the rise of Israel's kings. The chart below reflects the differences in chronologies for that period between the generally accepted dates (GAD) among scholars and the literal biblical chronology (LBC). The rest of the dates are based on those in the IBD. Both systems have adherents among evangelical scholars, though some recent studies have tended to substantiate the literal biblical chronology for this period.

(GAD) BC	(LBC)	
2000-1825	2166-1191	Abraham
1900-1720	2066-1886	Isaac
1800-1700	2006-1859	Jacob
1750-1640	1915-1805	Joseph
1710/30-1280/60	1876-1446	Israel in Egypt
1200-1050	1375-1050	The Judges (Ruth fits into this period)
1200	1367-1327	Othniel
1170	1309-1229	Ehud
1125	1209-1169	Deborah
1100	1162-1122	Gideon
1070	1075-1055	Samson
1075-1035		Samuel, Judge and Prophet
1050		The Monarchy: Saul
1011		David
971		Solomon
931		The Divided Kingdoms:

BC	JUDAH	ISRAEL	
931	Rehoboam	Jeroboam I	
913	Abijam (Abijah)		
911	Asa		
910		Nadab	
909		Baasha	
900			Ben-hadad I of Syria
886		Elah	
885		Zimri	
		Omri (Tibni, rival till 880)	
874		Ahab	Elijah
870	Jehoshaphat		
853		Ahaziah	Battle of Qarqar
852		Jehoram (Joram)	Elisha
848	Jehoram (Joram)		
843			Hazael of Syria
841	Ahaziah	Jehu	
	Athaliah		
835	Jehoash (Joash)		
814		Jehoahaz	
798		Jehoash (Joash)	
796	Amaziah		
782		Jeroboam II	
767	Azariah (Uzziah)		
760			Jonah to Nineveh
			Amos to Israel
755			Hosea to Israel
753		Zechariah	
752		Shallum	
		Menahem	
750			Rezin of Syria
745			Tiglath-pileser III of Assyria
742		Pekahiah	Micah to Judah
740	Jotham	Pekah	Isaiah to Judah
732	Ahaz	Hoshea	Damascus falls to Assyria
727			Shalmaneser of Assyria

BC	JUDAH	ISRAEL	
722		Fall of Samaria	Sargon II of Assyria Deportation to Assyria
716	Hezekiah		
705			Sennacherib of Assyria
701	Sennacherib's invasion		
687	Manasseh		
681			Esarhaddon of Assyria
669			Ashurbanipal of Assyria
664			Nahum to Nineveh
642	Amon		
640	Josiah		Zephaniah to Judah
626			Nabopolassar of Babylon
621			Jeremiah to Judah
612			Fall of Nineveh to Babylon
609	Jehoahaz (Shallum) Jehoiakim (Eliakim)		Battle of Megiddo End of Assyria
605			Battle of Carchemish Pharaoh Neco of Egypt defeated by Babylon Habakkuk
604			Daniel taken to Babylon
597	Jehoiachin (Coniah, Jeconiah) Zedekiah (Mattaniah)		Ezekiel taken to Babylon
593			Ezekiel begins to prophesy
587	Fall of Jerusalem to Nebuchadnezzar of Babylon		Deportations to Babylon Obadiah
556			Nabonidus of Babylon (Belshazzar acts as regent)
539			Fall of Babylon to Cyrus of Persia

BC	JUDAH	ISRAEL	
538	Zerubbabel returns to Jerusalem		
537	Temple foundation laid		
530			Cambyses of Persia
522			Darius I of Persia
520	Temple building resumed		Haggai and Zechariah
516	Temple completed		
486			Xerxes I of Persia (Ahasuerus)
464			Artaxerxes I of Persia
460			Malachi
458	Ezra goes to Jerusalem		
445–433	Nehemiah at Jerusalem		
423			Darius II of Persia

Jesus in the Old Testament

'Everything written about me in the law of Moses and the prophets and the psalms must be fulfilled', said Jesus in the greatest Bible study of all time (Lk. 24:44, *cf.* verse 27; Jn. 5:39).

He was talking about the three divisions of the Hebrew Scriptures. All of it, he was saying, pointed forward to him.

'The Law' referred to the first five books of the Old Testament, the Pentateuch. They record man's creation and fall into sin, and God's gracious choice of one people whom he delivers or 'redeems' from slavery. He establishes his covenant with them and provides a system of sacrifice and an anointed priesthood to deal with their sins. Early in their history God teaches his people that he is their Redeemer, and that sin cannot be forgiven without sacrifice and a mediating priesthood.

'The Prophets' included the history books Joshua, Judges, Samuel and Kings as well as what we call the prophets. In the first book God fulfils his promise to bring his people into their own land under the leadership of Joshua, whose name, like 'Jesus', means 'the Lord saves'. In Judges God is continually providing deliverance for his wayward people. And in Samuel and Kings we are introduced to his covenant with King David and his descendants – even the best of whom fall short of God's requirements.

The prophets such as Isaiah and Jeremiah focus on the people's disobedience and unfaithfulness, which provoke God's judgment. Many of them, however, catch a glimpse of a future restoration. Some have more than a glimpse and speak of a 'new covenant' in which God will grant complete forgiveness for sin and the ability to keep his commands. There will be a faithful remnant which will fulfil God's intentions for Israel.

Isaiah goes further. His title for the remnant is 'the servant of the Lord', who in perfect obedience will die a criminal's death, bearing the people's sins, and then be vindicated. Though the 'servant' at first seems to be a collective term, it eventually appears to signify one man.

Central to the idea of a new covenant with a renewed people was the new Davidic king who would rule them righteously and whose kingdom would extend over the whole earth. When God had made his covenant with David he had promised, 'I will establish the throne of (your son's) kingdom for ever. I will be his father, and he shall be my son' (2 Sa. 7:13–14). The subsequent 'sons of David' had failed – but the prophets looked forward to *the* Son of David, the Messiah or anointed king, who would fulfil all God's will.

Further light is shed on this by 'the Writings' comprising the Psalms and the rest of the Old Testament. Many of the Psalms focus on the Lord's relationship with David and hence with his successors. By extension they also speak of the Messiah who was to come.

The book of Daniel (part of the Writings and not the Prophets) contains an important passage about another figure, the 'son of man'. Representing the 'saints of the Most High', he comes to God and receives the kingdom on their behalf (Dn. 7).

So the Old Testament is about redemption, sacrifice, priesthood, salvation, a new covenant, a son of David, a Messiah, a suffering servant and a son of man. Some of these may have referred to specific historical situations and may in some way or other have been partially fulfilled then. But the writers were writing about something – or Someone – greater than they knew. 'They bear witness to *me*', said

Jesus (Jn. 5:39).

If this is so, why did the Jews fail to recognize their Messiah when he came?

They had concentrated on the passages that appealed to them and ignored others. They gloried in the fact that they were God's chosen people, and looked forward to the prospect of becoming a great world power under the rule of a mighty king. They overlooked passages about judgment, the Messiah's humility and the servant's suffering.

Their example is a warning to us to study carefully the whole of the Old Testament in order to gain a rounded understanding of God's nature and purposes and indeed of Christ himself.

Prophecies of the Messiah

Here are some of the various types and metaphors by which the conception of the Messiah was given to the people of God; some of them had for long been so regarded by the Jews, others were explained to the disciples by Christ himself (Lk. 24:27):

The prophet	Dt. 18:15
Immanuel	Is. 7:14
The suffering servant	Is. 42:1–9; 49:1–13; 50:4–9; 52:13–53:12
The branch (a shoot from a tree stump)	Is. 11:1; Je. 23:5; 33:15; Zc. 3:8; 6:12
The son of man	Dn. 7:13–14
The son of David	2 Sa. 7:12–13; Ps. 2:7; *cf.* Gn. 49:10; Ezk. 34:23; 37:24
The cornerstone	Ps. 118:22–23; Is. 28:16; *cf.* 1 Pet. 2:4–7

Genesis 3:15 speaks of the Messiah as the woman's seed (Mt. 1:23; Gal. 3:16; 4:4). Micah 5:2 foretells his birthplace. Psalm 22 and Isaiah 53 speak of his crucifixion and resurrection.

The Pentateuch

The first five books of the Bible, Genesis, Exodus, Leviticus, Numbers and Deuteronomy, are collectively called the Pentateuch. Traditionally, the Jews regarded it as one book, and it is known to them as the Law (Hebrew *torah*). Frequently when the Bible refers to the Law, it indicates not merely the collections of laws given in Exodus or Leviticus but the whole Pentateuch (*e.g.* Ps. 119).

Here is to be found a record of God's dealings with mankind from creation, on to the call of Abraham to become father of a chosen nation, to the day when that nation, after slavery in Egypt and wanderings in the wilderness, was poised to enter the promised land of Canaan.

Traditionally, authorship has been ascribed to Moses, and today too there are able Old Testament scholars who maintain the essential Mosaic authorship of the Pentateuch whilst allowing for editorial emendations, interpolations and additions after his time.

Early in the eighteenth century a theory was propounded which was taken up nearly a hundred years later by two German scholars and grew into what is sometimes called the 'documentary theory', or the Graf-Wellhausen theory of the Pentateuch. Graf and Wellhausen were partly influenced by the evolutionary presuppositions of the nineteenth century, and their theory is based on the idea that religion also 'evolved' from a primitive animism to a sophisticated monotheism.

This theory is based on alleged differences of style and emphasis in various parts of the Pentateuch. Graf and Wellhausen, and many scholars since their day, argue that these differences point to a number of sources underlying the Pentateuch as we know it. These sources come from different writers and different periods of Israel's history.

Each scholar has his own variation on the theme, but its basic form (if we may oversimplify) is as follows.

Early in the period of the monarchy (c. 950–850 BC), someone wrote down the stories of the patriarchs and Moses in such a way as to justify Israel's present occupation of Canaan and the supreme position of the tribe of Judah. This author referred to God as YHWH (English Jehovah, Yahweh or the LORD), for which the German is Jahveh; so this writer was called 'J' (the Yahwist).

A hundred years later, someone in the northern kingdom of Israel also wrote about the patriarchs. He, however, emphasized matters of particular interest to the northern tribes. Because he called God simply *Elohim* (God), he was designated 'E' (the Elohist). After a century or so, J and E were merged by an editor or 'redactor'.

A third source originated when moral and spiritual life in Judah was at a low ebb during the reign of the evil Manasseh in the seventh century BC. This document, roughly corresponding to our Deuteronomy, was written in order to bring about a reformation, which it did in the reign of Josiah (621 BC). This writer was labelled 'D' (the Deuteronomist), and his work was soon added to J E.

Eventually, another source was woven in. This had a priestly emphasis (and so is known as 'P'), concerning itself with genealogies and the origins of legal and ritual practices. Since these were also the main concern of the Jews who returned after the exile, P must belong to that date (c. 500–450 BC). Hence the mysterious letters J E D P with which some readers may be acquainted.

In its more radical form, the theory seriously undermined the historical value of the Pentateuch. In the 1950s, however, H. H. Rowley, Professor of Hebrew Language and

Literature in the Victoria University, Manchester, an outstanding Old Testament scholar and, at that time, the leading British exponent of the documentary theory, said, 'it is
widely rejected in whole or in part . . . it is only a working
hypothesis, which can be abandoned with alacrity when a
more satisfying view is found, but which cannot with profit
be abandoned until then'.

Indeed, the middle decades of the twentieth century saw
considerable modification of the original theories. Over-
simplified ideas of an 'evolution' of Hebrew religion within
the five books did not accommodate all the evidence. 'Yahweh' and 'Elohim', for example, occur together in some
texts; scholars have argued that the P material is older than
D; the role of Moses as the great lawgiver has been re-
affirmed. Archaeologists such as the outstanding W. F.
Albright have questioned the 'evolutionary' theories on
archaeological grounds and more recent findings have cor-
roborated the basic authenticity of the patriarchal stories.
Some modern scholars have seen each document as representing the work of a 'school', with a particular emphasis,
and it has been proposed that these operated in parallel
rather than consecutively, as ancient elements can be found
in each document. More attention is being paid to the forms
of the narrative, to material reflecting a background in
liturgy, law or contractual agreements. Nevertheless, the
old-style theory is still taught, sometimes as though it were
fact, in colleges and schools today.

Since no-one knows with certainty, or even beyond
reasonable doubt, how the Pentateuch or other books of
the Old Testament were first written and compiled, it is
surely wise, accepting Christ's endorsement of them, to use
them to make us 'wise to salvation' and to train us in
godliness. The ordinary layman does well to pay attention
to what the biblical books actually say rather than to theories of authorship which are always changing and must
remain unproven.

According to the book of Joshua, when Moses died he left the Pentateuch complete. Referring to it, the Lord commissioned Joshua: 'This book of the law shall not depart out of your mouth, but you shall meditate on it day and night, that you may be careful to do according to all that is written in it; for then you shall make your way prosperous, and then you shall have good success' (Jos. 1:8).

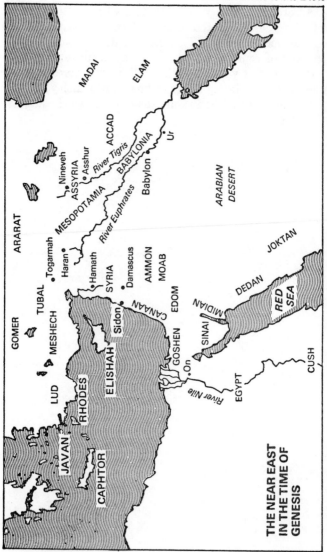

THE NEAR EAST
IN THE TIME OF
GENESIS

Genesis

As the English and Greek names imply, Genesis is the book of beginnings. Here is recorded the beginning of life, man, the sabbath, marriage, of sin, sacrifice, nations, covenant, of music, art, civilization, languages and of salvation.

The book sets the stage and records the opening events which will lead through many centuries to the great climax of history when God sent his Son. Beginning with the creation of the universe, the account moves to this earth and creation on it. The story of the descendants of the first human pair becomes restricted to those in the 'salvation line'. Of Noah's three sons it is Shem, not Ham or Japheth, who is important; of Terah's, Abraham not Nahor or Haran; of Abraham's, Isaac not Ishmael; of Isaac's, Jacob not Esau; of Jacob's, Judah not the other eleven. It is through these chosen representatives that God will reveal his plan to save mankind.

Genesis, and indeed the whole Bible, is about salvation. That is its theme and purpose and it quickly becomes apparent as we read the book. In this sense, we should read it as 'salvation history' (although the phrase needs to be used with care because it sometimes is used to mean that events did not really happen).

Summary

The opening chapters of Genesis are specifically designed to answer questions about origins. Where did this world come from? Who is man? Why is there sin, unhappiness, death? So chapters 1–11 set the scene for the story of God's chosen people, the Hebrews, who are to be his instrument in bringing salvation to mankind. The subsequent chapters of Genesis, indeed the rest of the Bible and human history, are the continuation of this story.

We begin, however, at the beginning, with the creation of a perfect world marred by man's wilful rebellion which produces sin, misery and death. The account of the flood shows God's determination to cleanse and recreate his earth, and man within it. The hostility, misunderstanding and alienation in the world are also shown, in the story of the tower of Babel, to be the result of man's rebellion against his Creator. All this is a reconstruction, under the Spirit of God, of the primeval world. It is prehistory and we should not attempt to date individual events (1–11).

At the end of Genesis 11 we reach (roughly) datable history, when God calls Abraham to leave his birthplace, the city of Ur at the head of the Persian Gulf. With his family he travels via Haran (in southern Turkey today) through Canaan and because of famine there on into Egypt. When they return to Canaan, Lot his nephew leaves him but later has to be rescued when he is caught up in a war between a southern Canaanite alliance and Chedorlaomer of Elam and his allies. He is met and blessed by the strange king of Salem, Melchizedek. The Lord promises that Abraham's heirs shall inherit Canaan. Abraham takes Hagar as his concubine and Ishmael is born. God makes a covenant with Abraham renewing his promise that Sarah, Abraham's wife, shall have a son, and giving him the covenant sign of circumcision. God destroys the cities of Sodom and Gomorrah but, for Abraham's sake, allows Lot to escape. Isaac is born and years later Abraham's faith is tested with the command to offer him as a sacrifice. At the last minute the Lord provides a substitute. Before his death Abraham makes sure that Isaac is married to Rebecca, a distant relative from the old home in Haran (12–24).

God chooses Isaac's second son, Jacob, to be the heir,

and he is Rebecca's favourite. He is also a natural cheat and persuades the first son, Esau, to sell his birthright, and then, by trickery when Isaac is old and blind, obtains the heir's blessing from him. Fearful of Esau's revenge, he escapes and has an awesome meeting with God at Bethel At Haran he marries his uncle Laban's daughters, Leah and Rachel. Laban tries to keep him at Haran but eventually he breaks away, again with trickery. Before a dreaded meeting with Esau, the Lord wrestles with him at Peniel and, with a prospective change in his character, changes his name also, to Israel. At Bethel God renews to him the covenant made with Abraham (25–36).

Jacob has twelve sons, the progenitors of the twelve tribes. But two of them are favourites: Joseph and, later in life, Benjamin, the youngest. Jacob's partiality for Joseph and the latter's unctuous naivety provoke the hostile jealousy of the other brothers and they sell Joseph to travelling Ishmaelites. He becomes a slave in the house of the Egyptian Pharaoh and is put in prison on the lying evidence of Pharaoh's lustful wife. The jailer gives him responsibility and after several years in prison (40:1; 41:1) he foretells the coming famine and advises the Pharaoh on action to meet it. Pharaoh makes him Governor of Egypt. The famine envelops Canaan and Joseph's brothers go to Egypt to buy food. They meet Joseph, who eventually arranges for Jacob and the whole extended family to settle in Goshen in north-eastern Egypt. Both Jacob and Joseph die there. Jacob is taken to Canaan for burial and Joseph orders that when God keeps his promise to lead them out of Egypt they shall take his body with them (37–50).

The patriarchs

From Genesis 12 onwards, and beginning with the story of Abraham, we are given a series of 'potted' life-stories of individuals used by God to unfold his message of salvation from sin and destruction. These men are called the patriarchs (Abraham, Isaac, Jacob and Joseph) and their lives span something like 700 years.

But the Genesis accounts are much more than biographies of individual men of God. The word patriarch is connected to the idea of fatherhood, and from the first promise to Abraham that he would be 'the father of a multitude of nations' (Gn. 17:4) the sense increases that God is working out his plan of salvation not only through individuals but through families, tribes and a nation. Abraham is told that God 'will make of you a nation' and it is the story of the people of God, the 'covenant community', which unfolds through the pages of the Old Testament and is continued in the worshipping community of the church in the New Testament.

Covenant

The word 'covenant' is one of the most significant in the Old Testament, and the wonder of the 'loving bond' which God graciously effects with his people runs through the Bible from Genesis onwards. The idea of a covenant between two parties, whether equals or a commanding power and a subordinate, was common enough. From the beginning, and right through the turbulent history of the children of Israel, it is a sheer work of grace on God's part. Even with the early patriarchs we are given ample evidence of man's inability to keep his part of the bargain. Time and again they doubt, they forget the only, almighty God and they are unfaithful to him. But God is faithful and constant; he loves, he disciplines and he restores. Not only is this a wonderful prefiguring of his saving love in the Lord Jesus Christ, but the chequered history of the covenant people of God, our forerunners in the faith, is a constant encouragement and reminder that, despite our weakness and failure, God remains faithful. He has committed himself to us, through thick and thin, as he did to the patriarchs.

There are, in fact, four distinct covenants in the Old

Testament: through Noah (Gn. 9:9), through Abraham (Gn.15:18; 17:4), through Moses at Sinai (Ex. 24:7) and, closely related to this, the Davidic covenant (2 Sa. 7:8–16). The 'new covenant' established by Jesus Christ fulfils and supersedes all the Old Testament covenants.

Genesis and science
How was the universe created?

The question 'How was the universe created?' raises the subject of evolution versus special creation. The clash between science and religion on this matter in the last century is notorious and still today the strength of convictions on both sides of the debate must not be underestimated. Suffice it to say that, among high-ranking scientists, the evidence for a complete, water-tight evolutionary system is regarded as far from conclusive. We must remember, too, that Genesis, with its poetry and its panoramic sweep, is not concerned with 'How did it happen?', but with the theological truth of God, the almighty ruler of the universe. Let the biologist continue to work on the 'how' of creation. Let the Christian expound the opening chapters of Genesis to teach the 'why'.

Genesis tells us about God. He is the Personal Ultimate; Eternal, outside of time, outside of space, Almighty, Creator, Love. Creation took place at his command. His will is the cause, and creation the effect.

It tells us about man. Created in the image of God, *i.e.* able to have fellowship with God; a physical-spiritual being; given intellectual, moral and spiritual responsibility, with freedom of choice; not forced to do right but able to choose between good and evil (2:17); created male and female, biologically and psychologically complementary; made to be lord of creation; rebelling against the Creator and so needing retribution, discipline and redemption. For his happiness and God's glory he was given four creation ordinances: marriage, procreation, work and sabbath; a properly regulated sexual relationship, children to be brought up in the fear and nurture of the Lord, the satisfaction and joy of creative work which subdues and dominates sea, earth and space, and a controlled rhythm of work and leisure so that re-creation may take place.

It tells us about creation. Not part of God (pantheism), not of itself evil (manichaeism); in God's intention, good and not to be rejected; subservient to man, not his master; inferior to man, not his equal.

The more one reads the opening chapters, the more one is delighted, excited, humbled by their profundity. At every reading there come fresh hints of depths unplumbed and meanings unperceived before.

It is worth asking the question, 'If I had to produce an account of creation and human origins to teach all this and much more to men of every kind and of every time, educated and totally illiterate, how would I do it?' One turns back to the Genesis accounts convinced that they cannot be improved.

The antiquity of man

The burgeoning sciences of archaeology, astronomy, palaeontology and geology seem to demonstrate an immense antiquity both for the universe and for early man. So palaeontologists suggest that our ancestors were roaming this planet a million or more years ago.

By contrast, the early chapters of the Bible, with their lists of genealogies, seem to imply that Adam was created only a few thousand years ago. There is obviously a vast difference between these two views of man's antiquity and various attempts have been made to explain that difference.

Some say that the genealogical lists of the Bible are not complete and that when the word 'son' is used it often means 'descendant'. These lists, therefore, cannot be used to calculate a date for Adam. Others point out that there is little consensus among the scientists themselves, that many of the methods of dating fossils are questionable, and their interpretations of fossil evidence are highly speculative. Some Christians insist that to be faithful to the Bible we must maintain that Adam was created by a special act of God in relatively recent history, say *c.* 10,000 BC. Others argue that the biblical evidence does not rule out the possibility of the evolution of man over a much greater period of time. (For further discussion see the introduction in *Genesis* (IVP, 1967) by Derek Kidner.)

Genesis 1–11 and 'myth'

'Myth' is the word often used to describe the first eleven chapters of Genesis. But this needs explanation. The Christian theologian who uses the word will insist that he intends it to mean timeless spiritual truth which may or may not be based on events that actually happened. In popular use, for the ordinary person, of course, the word is synonymous with untruth, fiction, a fairy tale, and therefore it is not helpful when discussing Genesis 1–11.

We have already said that the chapters are concerned with prehistory. They give a sweeping panorama of God's creation. We are dealing with enormous theological truths and to express them properly the account uses poetry and perhaps symbol. Whether or not, under the inspiration of God, the writer recording the prehistorical events intended all the details to be understood literally, there is no doubt of the actual *truth of the events* in the primeval account. *God created* the world and man. They were perfect, but man was a free agent. *Man chose* the way of selfishness and not obedience, and all mankind is tainted with this same inclination to serve his own ends and disregard his Creator. This pervading spirit of rebellion, disobedience and self-centredness inevitably produces a far from perfect world. But *God is still involved* in his creation, in punishment and in restoration.

With this section of the Bible it is valuable to keep clear

the distinction between 'historical' and 'literal'. Most people confuse them. We would want to insist that the events of chapters 1–11 are historical. They happened, but they may not all be narrated, or not wholly narrated, in literal terms. It is surprising that some people who constantly speak in idiom find this difficult to grasp. Having talked to a friend for too long, we say, 'We must fly'. We do not expect our friend to understand that we are about to make a dash for the airport. We do not mean to be taken literally, but we do mean to be understood historically. At this point in time we intend to hurry. A good biblical example of the difference will be found by comparing 2 Samuel 11 with 2 Samuel 12:1–6.

The selective principle

As we have already seen, Genesis rapidly narrows down from the whole world to the 'salvation line' through Abraham and his descendants. This selective principle, in fact, runs throughout the Bible. The twelve tribes, descended from Jacob's twelve sons, occupied the promised land. But eventually ten tribes are rejected because of their faithlessness, leaving only the southern kingdom of Judah. Then Judah's inhabitants are taken into exile, and attention focuses on the 'remnant' which later returns to the land. Finally, just one man, Jesus Christ, is the one in whom God's will is perfectly fulfilled.

But this process of selection was never meant to be restrictive and élitist. Abraham was chosen so that in him and his descendants 'all the families of the earth shall bless themselves' (Gn. 12:3). Prophets from Isaiah onwards declared that the chosen nation was to be the Lord's witness among the Gentiles, who would thus be drawn to Israel's God (*e.g.* Is. 11:10; 42:6; 60:3, *etc.*; Je. 16:19; Mal. 1:11). In Christ and the Christian mission this has been fulfilled: 'Go therefore', he said, 'and make disciples of all nations' (Mt. 28:19). God's people have always been chosen to be his servants, never to be his favourites. General William Booth, founder of the Salvation Army, summed it up well in the slogan 'saved to serve'.

Writer and date
See 'The Pentateuch' for consideration of how Genesis was compiled and 'the documentary problem'.

Structure and contents
 I. Prehistory 1–11
    1. The creation and the fall 1–3
    2. From the fall to the flood 4–8
       Cain and Abel 4   Descendants of Adam 5   Noah and the flood 6–8
    3. From the flood to Babel 9:1–11:26
       Noah after the flood 9   The nations 10   Tower of Babel 11:1–26
 II. The patriarchs 11:27–50:26
    1. Abraham 11:27–25:10
       From Ur to Canaan 11:31–13:18   Settlement to the birth of Isaac 14:1–21:7   Isaac to Abraham's death 21:8–25:10
    2. Isaac 21–35
       Birth to marriage 21–24   Marriage to camp at Beersheba 25–26   Beersheba to Isaac's death 27–35
    3. Jacob 25:26–50:14
       Birth to Bethel 25:26–28:22   Bethel to Gilead 29:1–31:55   Gilead to Egypt 32:1–45:28   Egypt to Mamre 46:1–50:14
    4. Joseph 30:22–50:26
       Birth to Egypt 30:22–37:36   Egypt to power 39:1–41:45   Power to his death 41:46–50:26
N.B. The latter part of one patriarch's life overlaps with the opening years of his son, *e.g.* Joseph's birth is noted in chapter 30 but he does not become dominant until chapter 37.

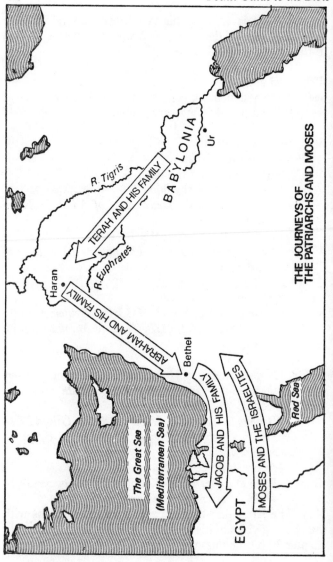

THE JOURNEYS OF
THE PATRIARCHS AND MOSES

Study questions

1. What teaching about a) God, b) creation, and c) man, do you find in chs. 1 and 2?

2. What teaching about the relationship between male and female do you find in 1:27–28 and 2:18–24 (*cf.* Mt. 19:4–6)?

3. What do you learn about temptation, sin and its results from ch. 3 (*cf.* 1 Jn. 2:16)?

4. Paul wrote that Christians are 'those who share the faith of Abraham' (Rom. 4:16). From Genesis 12–24, summarize the ways in which Abraham demonstrated faith in the Lord. What lessons and principles do you find for Christian life today?

5. From Genesis 27–33, 35 and 48 write a personality profile of Jacob. Notice what effects his encounter with God in chapter 32 had on him. What does Jacob's story teach you about God and his ways?

6. Genesis 50:20. Illustrate the truth of this verse at each of the various stages in Joseph's life (37–50).

7. If you have a Bible atlas or maps in your Bible, trace Abraham's movements from the references in Genesis 11–25.

Reference books

G. Ch. Aalders, *Genesis,* 2 vols. (Zondervan, 1981)

J. G. Baldwin, *The Message of Genesis 12-50* (IVP, 1986)

H. L. Ellison, *Fathers of the Covenant: Studies in Genesis and Exodus* (Paternoster, U.K., 1978)

D. Kidner, *Genesis* (IVP, 1971; 1968)

A. W. Pink, *Gleanings in Genesis* (Moody, U.S.A., 1922)

R. S. Wallace, *Abraham: Genesis 12—23* (Nelson, U.S.A., 1983)

Exodus

This is the book of redemption – freedom secured by payment of a price. The highlight of the book, the exodus from Egypt, is the highlight of Israelite and Jewish history. Since it foreshadows Calvary, it is a highlight of Christian theology also.

It speaks not only of individual redemption, but of the nation's corporate deliverance. The book of Exodus shows us the line which began with Abraham given by God the solidarity of a nation. There is a national consciousness about it. Its initial purpose was to tell Israel the story of her redemption and of God's demands upon her. For the Christian it sets down in embryo God's plan to offer salvation through 'the blood of the Lamb'. The Passover (1 Cor. 5:7), the manna (Jn. 6:31–33), the smitten rock (1 Cor. 10:4) and the tabernacle (Heb. 9:11–12) all speak of Christ and his atonement. Moses foreshadows Jesus, the Son of God (Heb. 3:1–6). Here are recorded the birth, life, call and part of the work of Moses, the builder of a nation, giver of the great law of God, first in the line of the prophets, and prophetic forerunner of the Messiah (Dt. 18:15). From the account of his birth (Ex. 2:1–10), to that of his death (Dt. 34:1–12), his person and character dominate the narrative.

The exodus from Egypt, which was accomplished through Moses, is the supreme example of God's gracious favour to, and deliverance of, his people. Time and time again in the Hebrew writings preserved for us in the Old Testament, God's people look back to this magnificent victory of the Lord on their behalf. When they are tempted to despair, when they are being led astray to other gods and by selfish concerns, when they are conscious of their weakness and sin, they call to mind the exodus and the God who redeemed them. No other image has the same powerful meaning for the Israelites as does the exodus.

Summary

About 400 years after Jacob with his sons and their families had emigrated to Goshen in Egypt, they have become a people so numerous that the Pharaohs believe they threaten the security of Egypt. Persecution follows, but Moses is born and called by God to be their deliverer (1–4).

Pharaoh is unwilling to co-operate, and after the merciful judgments of the nine plagues (merciful because less severe than the last, and offering the possibility of avoiding it), the first Passover is kept and the terrible tenth plague compels Pharaoh to 'let my people go' at last (5:1–12:36).

The exciting and sometimes traumatic trek of thousands of men, women and children from north-eastern Egypt to the extreme south of the Sinai peninsula begins, and with it the story of a people constantly oscillating between disobedience, pagan worship and repentance. Hemmed in by the Sea of Reeds in front and the pursuing Egyptian army behind, the Lord rescues them with an east wind which makes a way through the waters (12:37–15:27).

The manna, quail and water are provided for them and they are given victory over the Amalekites. Jethro, Moses' father-in-law, visits them and gives wise advice about delegating authority (16:1–18:27).

At Sinai the Law is given, the core of which is the Ten Commandments, an event influential for the whole of future human history. Parts of the Law, including the Ten Commandments, are written in a book, and there is a solemn sealing of what is now known as the old covenant (19:1–24:18, *cf.* Je. 31:31–34). The Lord tells Moses to collect

voluntary gifts from the people to construct a sanctuary and
gives him directions for making the tabernacle, its furniture
and the priests' vestments, and for appointing craftsmen to
supervise the work (25:1–31:18).

Suddenly the narrative is broken. The people have turned
to the idolatry of the golden calf. Moses pleads for them
and the covenant is renewed (32:1–34:35). The gifts are
collected, Bezalel and Oholiab are appointed as supervising
craftsmen, the tabernacle is constructed and erected and
the work is crowned as 'the glory of the Lord filled the
tabernacle' (35:1–40:38).

The exodus

Certainty has not yet been reached concerning the date of
the exodus and there is still much discussion. Probably the
general consensus favours a date *c*. 1300 BC and that will be
adequate for our purpose.

There is some doubt about the exact route of the exodus.
The coastal route was the most direct, but it was avoided
because it might have provoked a clash with Philistine
forces. From Rameses, the Israelites went south to Succoth
and then turned north before crossing the sea. The Red
Sea, or more correctly the Sea of Reeds, may refer to the
Gulf of Suez or to the region of the Bitter Lakes. Probably
the sea was crossed somewhere between Qantar (30 miles
south of Port Said) and Suez. They then journeyed south
along the Sinai peninsula to Mount Sinai, which is also
called Horeb, and from there north to Kadesh-barnea. The
discussion about the details of the route of the exodus is
complicated. The interested reader is referred to R. A.
Cole's commentary on Exodus for a fuller treatment of the
subject.

The Ten Commandments

In the Ten Commandments, the revelation of the character
of God is crystallized. They are given in the form of com-

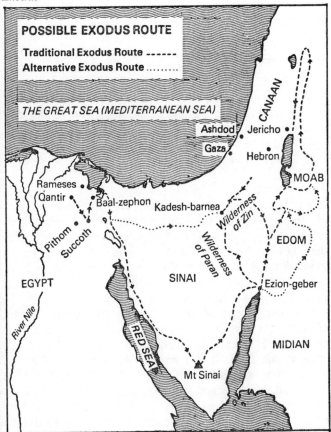

mandments to Israel because the people of God are to reproduce the character of God. 'You shall be holy; for I the LORD your God am holy' (Lv. 19:2). It is necessary to distinguish between the moral law, epitomized by the Ten Commandments, and the ceremonial and civil laws which were fulfilled by Christ and, therefore, are not binding under the new covenant. For this reason, it is worth noting

that the Ten Commandments were the only part of the
Law:

1. Spoken in the hearing of the people (Dt. 5:4);
2. Of which it is written 'and he added no more'
   (Dt. 5:22);
3. Delivered under circumstances of singular solemnity
   accompanied by thunder, lightning and earthquake
   (Dt. 5:22);
4. Said to be written 'with the finger of God' (Ex. 31:18);
5. Placed in the covenant box (Dt. 10:5).

The tabernacle

It was while the people of Israel were camped at the foot
of Mount Sinai that this 'tent of worship' was constructed
to God-given, detailed instructions, as a constant reminder
that God was 'in the midst of his people'. While they were
living in tents, he, too, would be present in a tent, right in
the middle of the camp. The eternal, almighty God had
made his home with them.

We cannot attempt here to look at the details of the
construction. The interested reader will gain much insight
on the biblical text by the use of modern reference books
such as the *IBD*. It was around the tabernacle that the
people met, celebrated God's passover in Egypt, heard the
Law read, and pledged their obedience to their Lord. At
the very heart of the tabernacle stood the ark of the covenant, containing the two tablets of stone engraved with
the Ten Commandments. This symbolized the fact that
God who was living with his people was a holy God who
made demands on them. The covenant was not without
commitment on man's side, too (see note on 'Covenant' on
p. 46).

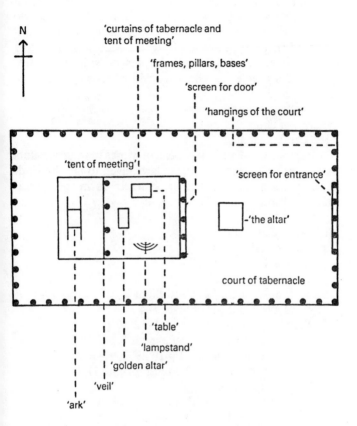

'curtains of tabernacle and tent of meeting'

'frames, pillars, bases'

'screen for door'

'hangings of the court'

'tent of meeting'

'screen for entrance'

'the altar'

court of tabernacle

'table'

'lampstand'

'golden altar'

'veil'

'ark'

'I am who I am'

In Exodus 3 God reveals to Moses his plan to rescue his people from Egypt. So that he may be able to answer questions from his fellow Israelites, Moses asks for more information about the 'name'. The name stands for the character of the God who has promised to save them. The Lord replies with the mysterious words, 'I AM WHO I AM . . . Say this to the people of Israel, "I AM has sent me to you" ' (3:14). The great I AM is the eternal fount of all being; always present, never past or future. 'I the LORD do not change; therefore you, O sons of Jacob, are not consumed' (Mal. 3:6). So when God tells Moses, 'I AM WHO I AM', he is saying that he will be present with, and active among, his people; his character will be shown in what he is about to do.

Writer and date
See 'The Pentateuch'.

Note that 17:14 and 24:4 speak of Moses writing accounts of at least one event and of the laws given to him by God. It may also be presumed that he wrote down the specifications for the tabernacle.

Structure and contents
I.   Moses, the deliverer 1–4
     1. Israel's increase 1:1–7
     2. Slavery 1:8–22
     3. Moses' birth, fight and flight 2
     4. His call and his excuses 3–4
II. Preparing for the exodus 5:1–12:36
     1. Two interviews with Pharaoh 5:1–7:13
     2. The nine plagues 7:14–10:29
     3. The passover and the tenth plague 11:1–12:36
III. The exodus 12:37–18:27
     1. Rameses to Succoth 12:37–13:19
     2. Succoth to Etham 13:20–22
     3. Crossing the Sea of Reeds 14
     4. The song of Moses 15:1–21
     5. The Sea of Reeds to Marah 15:22–26
     6. Elim to Sinai 16–18
IV. At Sinai 19–40
     1. Ten Commandments 19–20
     2. Rights of persons, property, piety 21:1–23:19
     3. Promise of the presence 23:20–33

Study questions

1. Read Exodus 1:6–4:17. How would you describe the character of Moses? How did God's control of events in his early life prepare him for the special work God wanted him to do? In the episode of the burning bush, how did God deal with Moses on a personal level?

2. Why do you think Paul described Christ as 'our paschal (*i.e.* passover) lamb'? (See Ex. 12 and 1 Cor. 5:1–8.)

3. Assuming that the holding up of Moses' hands symbolizes prayer, what lessons do you learn from Exodus 17:8–16?

4. Paraphrase the Ten Commandments (Ex. 20:1–17), replacing terms drawn from Hebrew culture with their modern western equivalents (*e.g.* for the 'servants' in verse 17 you could substitute various household gadgets).

5. Commencing with Exodus 24:1–8 and moving to Jeremiah 31:31–34, Luke 22:7–23 and Hebrews 8:1–10:18, study the similarities and the differences between the old and new covenants.

6. If you have a concordance, spend some time looking up references to the exodus in other Bible books. What does this show you of the meaning of the event to the Israelites and the early Christians?

Reference books

R. A. Cole, *Exodus* (IVP, 1973)

J. H. Dobson, *A Guide to the Book of Exodus* (SPCK, 1977; Judson, 1978)

H. L. Ellison, *Exodus* (St. Andrew, 1982; Westminster, 1982)

H. L. Ellison, *Fathers of the Covenant: Studies in Genesis and Exodus* (Paternoster, U.K., 1978)

W. H. Gispen, *Exodus* (Zondervan, 1982)

G. A. F. Knight, *Theology as Narration: A Commentary on the Book of Exodus* (Eerdmans, 1976)

A. W. Pink, *Gleanings in Exodus* (Moody, U.S.A., 1964)

B. L. Ramm, *God's Way Out* (rev. ed., Regal, U.S.A., 1987)

Leviticus

Once the Christian has experienced the new life in Christ and has grasped the essentials of basic Christianity, Leviticus can broaden his understanding of the need for atonement and sacrifice. It should be read in conjunction with the letter to the Hebrews, especially 4:11–10:25.

However, it gives the lie to those who recommend the beginner to read his Bible straight through. Genesis and Exodus with their enthralling narratives will give little trouble but the beginner may be perplexed when he reaches this book of Old Testament priests and sacrifices.

The break between Exodus and Leviticus is artificial, for both are part of the Torah (Law) and Leviticus continues the story of Israel's redemption and God's expectations of her.

It is in Leviticus that a substantial foundation is laid for the coming sacrifice of Christ. It is hard for us to understand how a death 2,000 years ago can have anything to do with God forgiving our sin today. The whole idea of atonement, of a price being paid to reconcile us to God, and the use of a substitute (under the old covenant usually an animal), is illustrated in the details of the levitical laws. Sin is a continuing fact of life which we are powerless to do anything about on our own. As God sent Jesus, so he laid down the instructions for Old Testament sacrifice.

The reason for all this is the central fact of Leviticus that Israel's God is a holy God. Israel, on the other hand, is a sinful nation. So how can the two have a covenant relationship? Israel's sin is bound to make a barrier, to cut the people off from God. God, therefore, gives explicit and detailed laws for them to obey, which will keep them on the right track. Hence we have what is sometimes called the 'Holiness Code' in chapters 16–27. But God knows they will be unable even to approach his standard of perfection and so he institutes a wealth of ceremony and ritual which symbolizes their need of forgiveness. Thus Leviticus sets out the basic details of Israel's worship, their need of forgiveness and the fact that a price must be paid for sin.

This emphasis on the need for purification and the way of sacrifice obviously makes Leviticus, in many ways, a forerunner of accounts of Christ's complete atonement for sin. The principles behind the laws are most instructive for us as Christians, but we should beware of pushing the ideas too far and finding a 'Christian' meaning for every detail, as some 'typology' tries to do.

The book also demonstrates God's concern for his people's health and well-being, for many of the laws, though somewhat obscure at first sight, have been shown to be excellent hygienic precautions for a nomadic people. It shows too that the people must reflect God's character in all they do; in marriage (ch. 18), in daily life (ch. 19), in holidays (ch. 20) and in the use of money (ch. 27).

Summary

The book paints a detailed picture of the ceremonial law of the Hebrews. This includes sacrifices and their performance (1–7); the consecration and duties of the priests and the laws of cleansing (8–15); the ritual of the Day of Atonement and the meaning of blood (16–17); social and priestly laws and details of the special seasons (18–25); the dangers of disobedience and the rewards for obedience; and regulations for giving gifts to the Lord (26–27).

Leviticus is the old covenant priests' book. It shows the principles of atonement and purification in a particular situation and gives many illustrations of the work of our Lord

Jesus Christ. 'His atoning death on the cross is the reality of which the rituals of Leviticus are but pictures and symbols' (*Search the Scriptures* (IVP, 1967), p. 146).

Sacrifice

The very idea of sacrifice seems foreign, distasteful and barbarous. We know that many 'primitive' peoples practised it, but it was removed with the coming of 'civilization'. So how are we to look at Israel's sacrificial system, which has been preserved for us in the Word of God?

To begin with, Israel's sacrifices were not just man's attempts to appease an angry god. They were part of their covenant relationship. They were also different from other systems in that they were based on a law, God's law, and were therefore very strictly regulated. They were different, too, in the emphasis given to a right inward attitude on the part of those offering the sacrifice. The external performance was not enough.

Nor were the sacrifices random or arbitrary. They usually symbolized some part of the covenant relationship between God and his people. The burnt offering, for instance (Lv. 1), where a whole animal, the most perfect that could be found, was sacrificed, represented a total, wholehearted attitude of worship. The peace offering (Lv. 3) was marked by the fact that everyone shared in the sacrifice, part being burnt as an offering to God, and the rest being eaten by the priests and the family concerned. The emphasis here was clearly on fellowship, while in the sin and guilt offerings (Lv. 4:1–6:7) the focus was on the sin itself and the need for forgiveness. The Day of Atonement was the climax of this (Lv. 16).

Just as today we look back retrospectively to the cross and are saved by the sacrifice of the Christ who died there, so the people of God in Old Testament days looked forward to the supreme sacrifice which would save them from God's judgment. The sacrifices helped them to know in experience the saving grace of the Christ who was yet to come. Though they only faintly comprehended it, the sacrifices represented to them 'the Lamb of God, who takes away the sin of the world' (Jn. 1:29). The writer to the Hebrews explains that the old sacrifices covered sins until the sacrifice of Calvary bore them away (Heb. 9:6–28).

In all the sacrifices prescribed, it was God who had taken the initiative and he had sole right, through his priests, to accept or reject the offering made. Nothing was automatic and Israel's God could not be blackmailed. But because the prerogative lay with God, the sacrifices had a real, if incomplete, effect in dealing with the problem of sin. Christ's death, in contrast, was not only 'superior' (Heb. 9:23–24) but, as the *Book of Common Prayer* expresses it, 'a full, perfect, and sufficient sacrifice, oblation, and satisfaction, for the sins of the whole world'.

Blood

An important element in the sacrificial regulations is the shedding of blood, concerning which detailed instructions are given. The point of this is that 'the life of the flesh is in the blood' (17:11) and blood drained from the body symbolizes death, violent death.

For the Hebrew the blood sacrifices would speak of at least three things. First, life, especially human life, is sacred to God, for man is made in his image. Since God created life, only he may take it away. Secondly, forgiveness is costly. The writer to the Hebrews sums up this aspect of the Old Testament blood sacrifices when he writes 'without the shedding of blood there is no forgiveness of sins' (Heb. 9:22). Thirdly, God is holy. This is especially brought out in the ceremonies of the Day of Atonement (ch. 16). It requires the substitutionary death of a sacrificial victim before a sinful people can approach a perfect and holy God. Phrases about 'the blood of Christ' in the New Testament always stand for the death of Christ and the benefits which accrue to believers because of it.

Festivals and fasts
Israel's year was divided up by a number of festivals and fasts which are set down in Leviticus 23: the Sabbath, God's institution of one day in seven to be given to rest and communal worship; Passover (together with the Feast of Unleavened Bread) which recorded Israel's deliverance from Egypt; Pentecost (the Feast of Weeks) which was a harvest thanksgiving and was associated in later Judaism with the giving of the Law; Tabernacles, which commemorated the forty years in the wilderness when the people lived in crude shelters and God provided all their physical needs. There was also the Day of Trumpets which later became known as Rosh Hashana (head of the year) and marked the beginning of the Jewish civil year. Finally there was Yom Kippur, the Day of Atonement, during which the people fasted and sought to make atonement for their sins.

Writer and date
See 'The Pentateuch'.

Most scholars acknowledge that chapters 17 to 26 contain very ancient material. Fifty-six times the book itself claims that the Lord gave its contents to Moses. Allowing for later editing, the ancient tradition of Mosaic authorship has yet to be disproved. Nevertheless many scholars give the book a post-exilic date.

Structure and contents
1. The sacrifices 1:1–7:38
   Burnt offering 1 and 6:8–13   Cereal offering 2 and 6:14–23   Peace offering 3 and 7:11–38   Sin offering 4:1–5:13 and 6:24–30   Guilt offering 5:14–6:7 and 7:1–10
2. The priests 8–10
   Consecration and ministry 8–9   Rules for the priests 10
3. Laws of uncleanness 11–15

THE OLD TESTAMENT CALENDAR

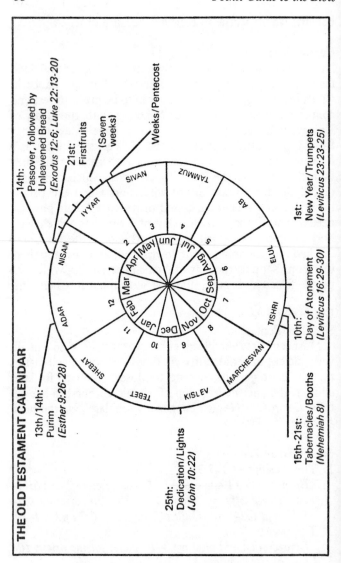

14th: Passover, followed by Unleavened Bread
(Exodus 12:6; Luke 22:13-20)

21st: Firstfruits

(Seven weeks)

Weeks/Pentecost

1st: New Year/Trumpets
(Leviticus 23:23-25)

10th: Day of Atonement
(Leviticus 16:29-30)

15th-21st: Tabernacles/Booths
(Nehemiah 8)

25th: Dedication/Lights
(John 10:22)

13th/14th: Purim
(Esther 9:26-28)

NISAN — IYYAR — SIVAN — TAMMUZ — AB — ELUL — TISHRI — MARCHESVAN — KISLEV — TEBET — SHEBAT — ADAR

Mar Apr May Jun Jul Aug Sep Oct Nov Dec Jan Feb

1 2 3 4 5 6 7 8 9 10 11 12

Study questions

1. Read Leviticus 4:1–6:7. What sort of sins could be forgiven under the old covenant? What was necessary before forgiveness could be granted? In 6:1–7 how was the offender to demonstrate this?

2. Leviticus 19:1 says, 'You shall be holy; for I the Lord your God am holy.' According to chs. 18–20, in what practical ways should God's people demonstrate this holiness?

3. From Leviticus 26 draw out the practical implications of God's covenant with Israel. In what ways does this chapter apply to Christians living under the new covenant?

4. Describe the ceremonies of the Day of Atonement (Lv. 16). Compare your notes with Hebrews 9 and write down the facts you learn about Christ.

5. In what ways is Christ's priesthood different from Aaron's (*cf.* Lv. 9; Gn. 14:17–20; Heb. 7:1–8:8)?

6. In a concordance look up some of the biblical references to 'offering' and 'sacrifice' in the prophets and in the New Testament. How does this add to the picture in Leviticus?

Reference books

R. K. Harrison, *Leviticus* (IVP, 1980)

J. R. Porter, *Leviticus* (Cambridge, 1976)

G. J. Wenham, *The Book of Leviticus* (Hodder, 1980; Eerdmans, 1979)

Numbers

This is the story of the trek of God's people from Sinai to Canaan, facing hardship, often discouraged, frequently rebellious. We see God's faithful care and watchfulness for them in spite of their disobedience, and his relationship with Moses, the man of God, sometimes impatient but always loyal to God and longsuffering with a fractious and exasperating people.

A month after erecting the tabernacle, and while the Israelites were still at Sinai, a census was taken of the fighting men and of the Levites responsible for the tabernacle ceremonies, and from that numbering this book takes its name. From this time the tribes were to be a military people, fighting their way to Canaan. Detailed precision was the order of the day.

It is just here, in the details of God's instructions, that we see his deep involvement with his people. They are a sign of God's presence with Israel; he is a holy God and therefore the people must live holy lives in his presence. He requires complete loyalty and consistent behaviour, and this comes out in both the narrative and the laws and regulations of the book of Numbers.

The continuing story of Israel's waywardness and disobedience only serves to emphasize again the amazing grace of our covenant-keeping God. The Lord has delivered them, is guiding and providing for them, and tells them just how to live right and pleasing lives. Their wilful dismissal of his instructions is always punished with a Father's love, but their disobedience will not thwart his purposes either for them or, through them, for the rest of mankind. So the people wander in the desert for 40 years, and the first generation of refugees dies there, but ultimately Israel reaches the 'promised land'. And in Canaan, when the other tribes forcibly resist the intrusion of the Israelites, God, the Lord of history, delivers his people and his plans are fulfilled.

The book of Numbers, then, is not just about facts and figures. It is about the unchanging God and the people he loves and disciplines.

Summary

Following a census of the fighting men and Levites, instructions are given for pitching camp and preparations are made for the march from Sinai to Canaan. The grumbling, the jealousy of Miriam and Aaron, and the refusal to enter the land bring progress to a halt (1–14).

The wanderings for the next forty years are a long and sad interlude, then once again Israel is on the march and the people journey from Kadesh to Moab east of Jordan and north of the Dead Sea. At the end of the trek, as at its beginning, there is a census of the soldiers and Levites. In the plains of Moab preparations are made for entering the land (15–36).

The census numbers

According to Numbers 2:32, the total number of men who could bear arms was 603,550; this would imply a total number of Israelites of between two and three million. Some people have doubted the credibility of such a high figure. How could so many people cross the Red Sea in one night, how could they be supported in the wilderness or be accommodated before Mount Sinai or in the land of Canaan? While some scholars are able to accept the figures at face value, most believe there is a problem. Various partial solutions have been proposed: the Hebrew word *'elep*, 'a thousand', could be translated 'family', 'tent group' or 'clan': its vowels could be changed to read *'allup*, meaning officer or trained warrior. This would make it possible to estimate a figure of 72,000 for the whole migration. It may be that the wilderness region was not as barren in the days of the exodus as now. Some believe that the census list in Numbers represents a later period of Israel's history. The problem is complicated and various mathematical solutions have been proposed. 'The apparently high figures are beyond absolute disproof, while no alternative interpretation has yet adequately accounted for all the data involved' (K. A. Kitchen, *IBD*, p. 1647).

Writer and date
See 'The Pentateuch'.

Little can be added to what is said about authorship of the Pentateuch. It is felt that various data, such as reference to Moses in the third person (1:1; 2:1, *etc.*), to his meekness (12:3), and that, apart from the list of stopping-places given in chapter 33, literary activity by Moses is not mentioned, indicate that the book is post-Mosaic. On the other hand, a Mosaic origin for the book is suggested by names afterwards forgotten (33:13), snatches of primitive song (21:14, 17, 27), laws which refer to situations which, in post-Mosaic times, had ceased to exist (19:3, 7, 9, 14), references to Egypt and its food (11:5) and the antiquarian remark about Hebron (13:22). We do not know when the book received its final form.

Structure and contents
  I. At Sinai 1:1–10:10
     1. Ordering the camp 1–4
     2. Laws 5–6
        Leprosy 5:1–4　Trespass 5:5–10　Marriage 5:11–31　Nazirite 6:1–21　The Aaronic blessing 6:22–27

Study questions

1. From Numbers 13–14, what can you learn about
a) faith, b) rebellion and its consequences, c) prayer,
d) forgiveness?

2. Compare Numbers 16 with 1 Corinthians 12:4–11. In
the light of the Corinthian passage, what did Korah, Dathan
and Abiram fail to understand? In what ways do you see
the same kind of failure operating in church life today?

3. Consider the teaching of the following New Testament
passages on the events of Numbers: Hebrews 3–4; Jude 5–
16; Revelation 2:14.

4. In a concordance look up the references to 'law' in the Psalms. How does the psalmist's attitude contrast with that of the children of Israel as we have seen it in the Pentateuch so far?

Reference books

I. L. Jensen, *Numbers, Journey to God's Rest-Land* (Moody, U.S.A., 1968)

A. Noordtzij, *Numbers* (Zondervan, 1983)

G. J. Wenham, *Numbers* (IVP, 1981)

Deuteronomy

The title 'Deuteronomy' is taken from the Greek translation of 17:18 and means 'repetition of the law'. Among the Jews it was known as 'these are the words', or, more briefly, 'words'.

This is the book our Lord Jesus Christ quoted during his temptation (8:3; 6:16; 6:13, *cf.* Mt. 4:1–11). It is quoted over eighty times in the New Testament and early Christians frequently referred to it.

The book is not merely a recapitulation of the laws given in Exodus, Leviticus and Numbers, but follows a specific treaty pattern for the people in covenant with their God (see section on 'Covenant' in Genesis). The covenant theme is very prominent. Moses, introducing the Ten Commandments in abbreviated form (ch. 5), says, 'The Lord our God made a covenant with us in Horeb'.

Some scholars believe that there is a close resemblance between the covenant theme and the kind of treaty-covenant made *c.* 2000 BC between Hittite kings and their vassals.

It is held that Deuteronomy seems to follow the recognized pattern. It outlines the parties involved and their relationship to each other to date, lists the responsibilities of each, contains a central document drawn up and looks at its future outworking in terms of blessing and curse. This much is standard. But the outstanding feature of Israel's 'treaty' is the fact that a holy God should choose to enter into an agreement with sinful people (see also the section on 'Covenant').

The Lord is unique in power and in love as well as in

his person, and these have been demonstrated to Israel supremely in the deliverance from Egypt. He will keep his covenant to bring them into Canaan. The covenant requires the people of Israel for their part to give unconditional loyalty to the Lord. Obedience to the covenant will result in blessing, and disobedience will bring a curse on every aspect of the nation's life.

Summary

The Israelites have at last reached journey's end and in the plains of Moab, east of the River Jordan where it enters the Dead Sea, preparations are made for crossing into Canaan.

In three addresses to the people, Moses reviews the wilderness wanderings (1:1–4:43), repeats the Ten Commandments, applies and extends them, gives instructions for settling in the land (4:44–28:68) and looks back in retrospect and forward in prospect (29–30). He appoints Joshua to succeed him, composes his song, gives his blessings to the tribes, dies and is buried in the land of Moab (31–34).

Major themes

1. *Grace* Moses emphasizes that it was not due to any superiority on their part that the Lord had chosen and delivered Israel. Indeed, they were a stubborn people and had repeatedly provoked the Lord (9:6, *etc.*). Not because of their own abilities (8:11–18) or their own righteousness (9:4–5) would they occupy the land. The sole reason for their privileged position was the Lord's unmerited favour towards them. He loved them simply because he loved them (7:6–8).

2. *Loyalty* The Lord had pledged himself to Israel in a solemn covenant: 'I am the Lord your God'. The corollary of this was: 'You shall have no other gods before me' (5:6–

7). Not only were they forbidden to make images themselves (5:8), they were commanded in the strongest terms to tear down the pagan images they would find in the land (7:4–5). But their loyalty to the Lord was to go beyond just avoiding pagan worship; they were positively to love the Lord their God with all their heart, and with all their soul, and with all their might (6:5). This personal devotion was also to be demonstrated in joint worship and ritual.

3. *Obedience* This loyalty was to be expressed in obedience to the Lord's commands, ceremonial, moral and social. 'Be careful to do them', Deuteronomy repeatedly insists, not because the Lord wanted to keep his people in grovelling subjection, but so that it might 'go well' with them in the land (5:33; 6:18, *etc.*). It was for their own good that they were to obey (6:24), as well as in order to reflect the holiness of the Lord whose people they were (7:6, 11). Obedience would result in blessing, but disobedience would bring a curse (ch. 28).

Writer and date
See 'The Pentateuch'.
   J. A. Thompson says in his commentary that current views about the date and authorship of Deuteronomy may be classified into four groups:
1. A substantial Mosaic date and authorship. There are several references to Moses speaking, and two to his writing (1:5, 9; 5:1; 27:1, 9; 29:2; 31:1, 30; 33:1; 31:9, 24).
2. Although the book contains a great deal of material contemporary with Moses, it was compiled in the days of Samuel (*c.* 1000 BC).
3. It was written in the Hezekiah-Josiah period (687–609 BC).
4. It is post-exilic (*c.* 400 BC).
   'One thing is clear. The book is based firmly on the historical figure of Moses and in some way or other en-

shrines words which he spoke to Israel in Moab' (Thompson, p. 68).

Structure and contents
1. First address: prologue to the covenant 1:1–4:43
    Preface 1:1–8   Horeb to Kadesh 1:9–46   Kadesh to Bethpeor   2–3   Importance   of   obedience   4:1–40 Historical note: cities of refuge 4:41–43
2. Second address: the covenant expounded 4:44–28:68
    Preface 4:44–49   Ten Commandments (abbreviated) 5:1–22   Comments, application and recollection 5:23– 11:32   Additional rules and laws 12–26   Writing the commandments 27:1–10   The curses and the blessings 27:11–28:14   The consequences of disobedience 28:15–68
3. Third address: the covenant recapitulated 29–30
    In the wilderness, in the land, in captivity 29:1–28 Secret things and revealed things 29:29   In the land again 30:1–10   Final appeal 30:11–20
4. Closing events of Moses' life: covenant renewal 31–34
    His successor 31   His song 32   His blessings 33   His death 34

Study questions
1. How do chs. 1–3 illustrate Moses' statement that Israel was 'a stubborn people' (9:6)? What resulted from each instance of disobedience?
2. Read 4:1–14; 6:1–9; 11:18–21. In two columns list a) all the things the Israelites are told to do with God's laws; b) the reasons why these things were to be done. What does this show about how important God's laws are to God's people?
3. How did the Lord promise to bless the people if they obeyed him (7:12–15; 8:6–9; 11:8–15; 28:1–14)? What were the dangers in all this (6:10–12; 8:10–20)? How might this apply to Christians today?
4. What principles of social justice can you find in chs. 15,

19 and **24**? How would you like to see them put into practice in your own society? As a beginning, how can you practise them in your own life?
5. With 6:13; 6:16 and 8:3 compare Matthew 4:1–11. How did these verses help the Lord Jesus Christ in his temptation?

Reference books

P. C. Craigie, *The Book of Deuteronomy* (Eerdmans, 1976)
J. Ridderbos, *Deuteronomy* (Zondervan, 1984)
S. J. Schultz, *Deuteronomy* (Moody, U.S.A., 1971)
J. A. Thompson, *Deuteronomy* (IVP, 1974)

Joshua

The Lord 'brought us out . . . that he might bring us in and give us the land', said Moses (Dt. 6:23). Here is the record of the Lord's faithfulness. He brought his people into the land he had promised them. Hence the book links the first five books of the Old Testament, Genesis to Deuteronomy, with all the rest.

The book is the story of Joshua. It begins with the Lord's commission to him to be strong and courageous and to study and obey the law of the Lord (1:6–8), and ends with his challenge to Israel to serve only the Lord now that they are settled in the land (24). The first half of the book tells of the conquest of the land under his leadership and the second half of his settling the tribes in their new inheritance.

Summary

Joshua succeeds Moses in leadership (c. 1240 BC), and is commanded to be courageous and to study and obey the book of the Law. He sends two men to spy out Jericho and they are helped by Rahab. The whole company crosses the river Jordan which is dammed by a blockage at Adam up river. The circumcision of a new generation marks the resumption of obedience to the covenant. Jericho falls but Achan disobeys the ban on looting and an attempt to capture Ai fails. After the punishment of Achan and his family, Ai is captured and the Law is read and the covenant renewed on Mount Ebal (1–8).

Gibeon and three other cities a few miles north of Jerusalem obtain a treaty with the Israelites by cunning and deception. This leads to war with five Amorite kings. Their city states, except Jerusalem, are destroyed and the whole of the south from Kadesh-barnea to Gibeon is now under Israelite control (9–10).

Attention turns to the north. Hazor, Galilee, and Canaanite cities on its borders are subjugated. A summary of Joshua's achievements and a list of the defeated Canaanite kings brings this section to a close (11–12).

Although the land is not wholly conquered and a significant number of the people of the land remained unsubdued (*e.g.* 15:63), it can now be divided among the tribes. Precedence is given to Reuben, Gad and half Manasseh who had been happy to settle on the east of Jordan and who had left their families there when they came with the other tribes to conquer the land. Then Caleb, who 'wholly followed the Lord', receives his inheritance. The remaining tribes can then receive their land. Special priestly cities are allotted to the Levites for they receive no tribal inheritance. Six cities, three on each side of the Jordan – north, central and south – are designated cities of refuge as a protection against the blood feud and for those who cause accidental death (13–21). Reuben, Gad and Manasseh, with their allotments on the east of the Jordan, go home and an altar of witness is set up as a perpetual reminder that they belong to the people of God. Joshua reminds the people of God's faithfulness and of the importance of loyalty, expressed in obedience to him. The covenant is confirmed and Joshua dies. The land was never wholly possessed (Jdg. 2:1–3). Joshua fulfilled his mission but with his death, the vision was lost (22–24).

Major themes

1. *Leadership* The book of Joshua is a record of success and failure. Success, because they conquered almost whenever they attacked. Failure, because they failed to obey the terms

of the covenant: '. . . you shall drive them out before you. You shall make no covenant with them or with their gods. They shall not dwell in your land, lest they make you sin against me' (Ex. 23:31–33).

Joshua's leadership was the secret of their success. God had prepared his leader. Born in Egypt, he was given the name which means 'the Lord saves', the Hebrew equivalent of Jesus. He belonged to the tribe of Ephraim which was the most influential of the tribes at this time, and his grandfather had led that tribe during the wanderings. His childhood and youth had been influenced by Egyptian civilization and culture. He quickly became Moses' lieutenant and was his companion at Sinai (Ex. 24:13). He was notable for having 'wholly followed the Lord' (Nu. 32:12) and had demonstrated military leadership at Rephidim. But immediately before his first confrontation with the Canaanites, he was very forcibly reminded that he was on God's side and not God on his. 'Are you for us, or for our adversaries?' he asked. 'No; but as commander of the army of the Lord I have now come', replied the mysterious visitor before the battle of Jericho (5:13–14). And that battle was no battle in the real sense of the word, for the strategy Joshua employed by divine command demonstrated that the Lord of hosts leads his people, and Joshua, like all other human leaders, is his subordinate (6:3–5, *cf.* Ps. 44:3). He was reminded, too, as he assumed the leadership, that success depended upon his knowing and obeying 'the book of the law' (1:8).

2. *God's faithfulness and human obedience* Three times in Joshua reference is made to renewing the covenant. (See section on 'Covenant' in Genesis.) Immediately after the Jordan is crossed, the people are circumcised because this part of the covenant had been neglected during the wanderings (5:5). After the capture of Jericho and Ai, the Law is read at Mount Ebal as Moses had commanded (8:34–35;

Dt. 11:29). Then before his death, Joshua again calls on the people to renew their covenant with the Lord (24:1–27). This emphasis on the covenant demonstrates that the Lord's faithfulness to his covenanted word was the reason for their inheriting the land. He had promised to give them this land (Gn. 15:7, 18–21; 26:2–5; 28:13–14) and he has kept his promises (11:23; 21:43–45; 23:14). By the same token, the Lord requires obedience from his people. God's covenant, which depends upon his faithfulness for its fulfilment, also requires the people's obedience and loyalty if they are to receive its benefits. 'The Lord our God we will serve, and his voice we will obey' (24:24).

3. *Faith* The theme of faith is closely linked with obedience. In the Bible faith is neither a leap in the dark nor a dependence on human reason. It is trust in what God has promised which shows itself in obedience to what he has commanded. At the crossing of the Jordan, the priests were required to dip their feet in the water before it stopped flowing (3:15). The strategy for conquering Jericho was based entirely on faith in a God who does what he says he will: 'You shall march round the city . . . and the wall of the city will fall down flat' (6:3–5). When the writer to the Hebrews cites this as an example of faith, he also goes on to explain that Rahab's hiding of the spies was an act of faith in the God of Israel (Heb. 11:30–31, *cf.* Jos. 2:6–21). At the end, Joshua urges the people to be faithful to the Lord. Then he adds, 'And if you be unwilling to serve the Lord, choose this day whom you will serve' (24:15). Faith in the Lord implies a deliberate and express decision to trust him.

Writer and date

Jewish tradition has consistently maintained Joshua as the author. Certainly some parts of the book suggest the work of an eyewitness (*e.g.* 5:6; 15:4). The frequent use of the phrase 'to this day' (*e.g.* 15:63; 16:10), references to 'Great Sidon' alongside 'Tyre' and to the Phoenicians as 'Sidonians' (11:8; 13:4–6), and the reference to Joshua writing chapter 24:1–25 (24:26) suggest an early date and support the contention that the material is very old. But references to Joshua's death and to events which occurred after his time indicate later editing at least (24:29–30; 14:13–14, *cf.* Jdg. 1:10, 20).

Traditional criticism has regarded Joshua as an extension of the Pentateuch and has maintained that the same basic sources J, E, D, P are found in Joshua (see 'The Pentateuch').

A more recent theory holds that Joshua, Judges, 1 and 2 Samuel and 1 and 2 Kings are one continuous work which dates in final form from the exile. It has been called the 'Deuteronomic history' because it is thought to express Deuteronomy's theological viewpoint. The author's intention was to show how Israel's sin took her from the triumphs of Joshua and David to the disaster of the exile.

Perhaps the wisest course is to suspend judgment until we know more and to accept that the writer is anonymous and the date of the book's final compilation unknown.

Structure and contents

I. Into the promised land 1–5
    1 Joshua assumes the leadership 1
    2. Spies into Jericho 2
    3. Crossing the Jordan 3–4
    4. Circumcision and the cessation of the manna 5

II. Conquering the promised land 5:13–12:24
    1. The centre:
        Jericho 5:13–6:27   The sin of Achan 7   Ai 8:1–29   The Law read at Mount Ebal 8:30–35   The deceiving Gibeonites 9
    2. The south: Amorites, and the north: Jabin of Hazor 10:1–11:15

Study questions

1. Draw out of the story of Rahab all the lessons you can about faith (ch. 2, *cf.* Heb. 11:31).

2. In crossing the Jordan what was God's part and what was required of the people (3:1–17, *cf.* Phil. 2:12–13)?

3. What lessons should Christian leaders in any sphere learn from 5:13–15?

4. 24:15c, *cf.* verse 11. What are the modern 'gods' which challenge our allegiance to the Lord Jesus Christ?

5. What mistakes comparable with those of the Israelites in 9:3–15 do we make today?

6. In a Bible atlas locate the sites of the campaigns in Joshua.

Reference books

J. Gray, *Joshua, Judges, Ruth* (Marshall Pickering, 1986; Eerdmans, 1986)

E. J. Hamlin, *Inheriting the Land* (Handsel, 1983; Eerdmans, 1983)

M. H. Woudstra, *The Book of Joshua* (Eerdmans, 1981)

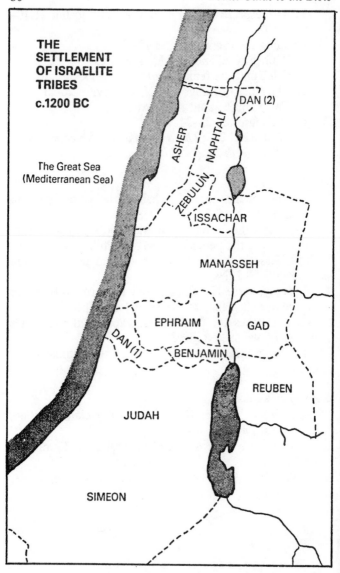

THE
SETTLEMENT
OF ISRAELITE
TRIBES
c.1200 BC

The Great Sea
(Mediterranean Sea)

ASHER

NAPHTALI

DAN (2)

ZEBULUN

ISSACHAR

MANASSEH

EPHRAIM

GAD

DAN (1)

BENJAMIN

REUBEN

JUDAH

SIMEON

Judges

The words with which the book closes, 'every man did what was right in his own eyes' (21:25), are an excellent summary of the contents. We may expect to meet unpleasantness in some of its pages. Several of its heroes are crude and violent. Samson's life, for example, is a story of lust, passion, anger, selfishness and greed. It is easy to wonder why such a record is included in the Bible. But its very distastefulness has important things to teach us.

The Bible is a realistic book and that is especially true of this part of it. It does not whitewash its heroes. It recognizes everyone, except Christ, as a sinner. Not even the greatest of God's people are sinless.

God is sovereign and God is unchanging both in his holiness and his love. Ultimately his purposes will be fulfilled. His plans cannot be destroyed, but he does allow us temporarily to frustrate them if we wish. He fulfils his plans either with or without our co-operation. We may choose which it shall be. Yet when his people stray from him, he does not let them go. He will pursue and chastise them until they return to him.

Judges shows the Israelites repeatedly turning their backs on God in favour of other, superficially more exciting and colourful, foreign deities such as Baal. On each occasion, they are thereby weakened and the Canaanites gain supremacy over them until God graciously brings a judge to lead them back to obedience and prosperity. But when the leader is gone their faith falters again.

Historically this book is the link between Joshua and the

prophet Samuel. It spans a period of something like 150 to 200 years (*c.* 1200–1050 BC). None of the judges can be dated with complete accuracy. Some of them may have overlapped. It should be noted that the period of the judges did not end with this book. The book of Ruth and the first twelve chapters of 1 Samuel should be included in any discussion of this period.

Summary

As an introduction, some aspects of the history of the con-quest of the land are recapitulated and the Lord's angel rebukes the people for disobeying the command to make a complete conquest. Following the death of Joshua, there is a moral and religious decline amounting to apostasy. The summary in 2:11–23 outlines a cycle which occurs six times in the next 150 years. 'The people of Israel did what was evil in the sight of the Lord. . . He sold them into the power of their enemies . . . Israel cried to the Lord . . . the Lord raised up a deliverer.'

Six of the judges (Shamgar, Tola, Jair, Ibzan, Elon and Abdon) are sometimes called minor judges because they receive only brief mention. The activities of the other six (Othniel, Ehud, Deborah, Gideon, Jephthah and Samson) are more extensively treated.

The Lord provides Othniel to save the nation from the king of Mesopotamia and Ehud to save them from Eglon of Moab. In the north a woman, Deborah, leads them to victory over Jabin, king of Canaan. Jael's destruction of Sisera, Jabin's commander-in-chief, after inviting him into her tent is a classic example of the ruthlessness of a deter-mined woman in war (3:7–5:31).

Gideon, visited by the Lord's angel, is terrified and learns that 'the Lord is peace'. He takes the courageous step of destroying his father's altar to Baal and gains a second name, Jerubbaal, 'let Baal contend'. Still uncertain about his call, he puts out a fleece asking God for a miraculous sign through it. The first time it is wet in the morning though the ground around is dry, and the second time it is wet on the ground but dry on the fleece. His defeat of the Midianites is notable for the reduction of his army from 32,000 to 300 wholly committed soldiers and for his unconventional strategy with trumpets, pitchers and torches and the battle cry of 'A sword for the Lord and for Gideon' (6:1–8:32).

Jephthah's devotion to the Lord is marred by a rash vow and the sacrifice of his own daughter. Human sacrifice was strictly forbidden to Israelites but Jephthah's antecedents were half Canaanite and he lived in days when 'the word of the Lord was rare'. He saved the country from the king of Ammon (10:6–12:7).

Samson is perhaps the best known of the judges. His great physical strength was a direct gift from the Spirit of God. His inability to exercise self-control, especially over his passions, reduced him to a powerless slave and almost brought about the defeat of his people. In the end his flickering faith stimulated his moral courage and in order to defeat the Philistines, he sacrificed his own life (13:1–16:31).

The appendix to the book consists of two unpleasant stories which illustrate the depths to which many parts of the country had sunk spiritually and morally.

The tribe of Dan had settled in a strip of land between Judah to the south and Ephraim to the north, with access to the Mediterranean Sea (*cf.* Jos. 19:40–48). They find their boundaries too limiting. Looking for new territory they encounter Micah, a man of Ephraim, who has acquired a household idol and an apostate Levite acting as his priest. They steal the idol and the priest and journey north to Laish near the headwaters of the Jordan. There they establish themselves and rename the city Dan after their tribal ancestor. Dan became the northernmost city of Israel (Jdg. 20:1) and the site of one of the golden calf idols of Jeroboam II (782–753 BC) (*cf.* 1 Ki. 12:9f.) (17–18).

In the second story, a dissolute Levite with his concubine lodges for the night in Benjaminite country at Gibeah. The Gibeonites attempt to use the Levite for homosexual purposes. Instead, they misuse the concubine so appallingly that she dies. The Levite dismembers her body and sends its parts as an avenging rally call throughout Israel. The other tribes make war on the Gibeonites and eventually defeat them. Since no other tribes will supply them now with wives they are permitted to seize girls dancing in the fields around Shiloh. This is the low point of Israelite history. The narrative itself says, 'such a thing has never happened or been since the people of Israel came up out of the land of Egypt' (19:30), and about 400 years later the prophet Hosea refers to corruption 'as in the days of Gibeah' (Ho. 9:9) (19–21).

Judge

The Hebrew word translated 'judges' is much wider in meaning than the English translation. *Shophetim* describes those whom God chose to 'judge' the nations who oppressed his people. Sometimes they may have acted as magistrates. But the Hebrew 'judge' was supremely a deliverer, a national hero called by God at a time of national, or at least tribal, crisis.

The land

'The land of Israel' at this time stretched from Mount Hermon in the north to Kadesh-barnea in the south, and from the Mediterranean to the territory on the east bank of the Jordan and Dead Sea where the tribes of Reuben, Gad and half Manasseh lived. The Israelites were surrounded by enemies: the Mesopotamians in the far north-east, the Moabites and Ammonites in the east, the Canaanites in the north-west, the Philistines in the west on the Mediterranean seaboard, the Amalekites in the Sinai peninsula and the Midianites in Arabia.

Moral problems

For the Christian the book raises moral problems. Few would wish to justify Ehud's cunning, Jael's ruthless treachery or Samson's profligacy. There are two general points worth remembering in this respect.

Firstly, the principle of progressive revelation is relevant. The revelation of God in the Old Testament was extended and completed with the incarnation of the Son of God. This is not the same as saying that the Old Testament revelation is wrong, but only that it is incomplete. The point is illustrated by the references to 'the Spirit of the Lord' in Judges. The phrase must not be entirely equated with New Testament references to the gift of the Holy Spirit. New Testament theology insists that holiness of life is closely associated with the gift of the Spirit. In Judges, however, the Lord's Spirit may come upon a man or woman to give leadership ability or physical strength without producing godly character. In other words, we must not look for the high standards of Christian living and witness in a pre-Christian culture.

Secondly, we must not assume that the Lord then, any more than now, always approves the methods used by those whom he has chosen to achieve his purposes: God may make a man a vehicle of his revelation or a channel of his power quite apart from the quality of the life of the individual concerned. In the Old Testament we find him employing the most unlikely agents.

For a satisfactory and fuller treatment of this subject see Cundall, pp. 41–45.

The opening phrase

The opening phrase of the book 'After the death of Joshua . . .' can create problems if it is taken to refer to the first chapter, since the events described in it took place in the lifetime of Joshua. If, however, the phrase is taken as the title of the whole book, then the first chapter will provide the background for events of the post-Joshua age. That this was the intention of the editor is indicated by his description of the death of Joshua in 2:6–10.

These dates (from Cundall, p. 32) may serve as a useful guide provided they are treated as approximate.

1230	Entry into Canaan	1100	Gideon
1200	Othniel	1080	Abimelech
1170	Ehud	1070	Jephthah
1150	Shamgar	1070	Samson
1125	Deborah		

Writer and date

Nothing is known about the author or the date of writing. Scholars discuss probabilities deduced from incidental evidence provided by the text. Much of the writing is very old, possibly even contemporary with the events described. The favourable references to the monarchy (19:1; 21:25) suggest a date in the reign of David or Solomon (*c.* 1000 BC), but the phrase 'until the day of the captivity of the land' (18:30) implies that the final completion of the book was after the fall of Samaria in 722 BC when Hezekiah was king of Judah. Some feel that the author's philosophy of history requires a date after Josiah's reformation (621 BC).

Like the other historians from Joshua to 2 Kings, the author adopts what is known as the 'Deuteronomic' philosophy of history. Obedience to God's will brings prosperity whereas disobedience brings disaster. When the tribes were loyal to the Lord and his covenant, they were united and strong. When they worshipped the Baals of Canaan, they were divided and powerless.

Structure and contents

   I. Introduction 1:1–3:6
      1. Israel's failure 1:1–36
         Conquest of South Canaan 1:1–21   *Capture of*

Study questions

1. Collect the teaching in Judges about the Holy Spirit. A concordance (see page 21) will help.

2. How does Judges illustrate the principle that God chooses to use the foolish, weak and base (*cf.* 1 Cor. 1:26–29)?

3. What spiritual principles can you see in the lives of a) Gideon, b) Jephthah, c) Samson, d) Deborah which might be of help to the Christian?

Reference books

A. E. Cundall and L. Morris, *Judges and Ruth* (IVP, 1968; IVP, 1971)

J. Gray, *Joshua, Judges, Ruth* (Marshall Pickering, 1986; Eerdmans, 1986)

Ruth

Ruth is one of the two Bible books named after a woman. Whilst clearly belonging to the times of the judges, its atmosphere contrasts with that of the book of Judges. Instead of corruption, treachery and debauchery, we find faithful dealing, loyalty and love.

The book shows that a Gentile, a Moabitess, figures in the genealogy of King David, and so of Christ himself. There was always the danger that the racial distinctiveness of Israel, so necessary at the time to prevent contamination with heathen religion and ways, might develop into an arrogant assurance that the Israelites were God's favourites. And indeed it did. Too often the Israelites remembered the first part of the Abrahamic covenant, 'I will bless you and make your name great', and forgot the purpose of it, 'in you shall all the families of the earth be blessed'. The book of Ruth is a corrective to that mistake. It shows that even in Old Testament times God welcomed into his people those from non-Israelite nations who trusted in him.

Summary

An Israelite family in time of famine emigrates to Moab where the two sons marry Moabite girls, Ruth and Orpah. These two sons and their father then die, and the bereaved wife and mother, Naomi, insists on returning to Israel. Ruth refuses to let her go alone (1:1–18).

When Ruth and Naomi arrive in Bethlehem, Ruth gleans in the fields of Boaz, a kinsman of Naomi (*cf.* Lv. 19:9–10). Taught by Naomi, Ruth claims an ancient kinsman's right to marry Boaz, and bears a child who is a forbear of King David (*cf*. Dt. 25:5–10) (2–4).

Writer and date

Some hold that Ruth is a work of fiction: Naomi, Ruth and Boaz, it is said, are too good to be true. We do not know when the book was written and dates differing as widely as the time of Samuel (*c*. 1075–1035 BC) to after the exile (537 BC) have been suggested. Most scholars hold a date between 450 and 250 BC). But there are arguments for a much earlier date. It is written in classic Hebrew which suggests an early date.

Traditionally, authorship has been ascribed to Samuel, and much of the evidence would seem to favour a date in the early days of the monarchy (*c*. 1000 BC).

Clearly the book has affinities with the book of Judges. It is placed with the Writings in the Hebrew Bible, but the Greek Old Testament and the Vulgate (the Latin Bible) placed it after Judges.

Structure and contents

1. Elimelech and family move to Moab 1:1–5
2. Naomi and Ruth leave Moab 1:6–18
3. They arrive in Bethlehem 1:19–22
4. Ruth gleans in the fields of Boaz 2
5. Ruth claims her rights of kinship 3
6. Boaz marries Ruth 4:1–12
7. Ruth is a great-grandmother of David 4:13–22

Study questions

1. What lessons about loyalty do you learn from this book?
2. What teaching about providence, guidance and the Lord's caring do you find?

Reference books

A. E. Cundall and L. Morris, *Judges and Ruth* (IVP, 1968;

IVP, 1971)

W. J. Fuerst, *Ruth, Esther, Ecclesiastes, Song of Songs, Lamentations* (Cambridge, 1975)

J. Gray, *Joshua, Judges, Ruth* (Marshall Pickering, 1986; Eerdmans, 1986)

R. E. Murphy, *Wisdom Literature: Job, Proverbs, Ruth, Canticles, Ecclesiastes, Esther* (Eerdmans, U.S.A., 1981)

1 and 2 Samuel

Samuel, the last of the judges, is a very different person from any of the others. In character, personality, moral integrity and devotion to the Lord, he towers over them all. He occupies a unique place in the history of Israel. He was chosen to guide Israel from theocracy (rule by God) to monarchy when the people demanded it, and he did not fail.

God chose Samuel to speak for him and stand firm when all around the Israelites were in disarray, weakening their convictions and losing their priorities. In particular, their loss of vision concerning the one true God led to their request for a leader they could see: 'a king to rule over us'.

God also chose these national leaders. Though Samuel, as God's spokesman, stood against Israel's desire to have a human ruler rather than the Lord alone, he pointed out God's chosen men. But the history recorded in the books of Samuel shows how inadequate and imperfect any human ruler must be.

Saul, the first king of Israel, came of a wealthy family and was tall and handsome. Yet he is a pathetic and tragic figure. Trials and temptations seemed to produce in him a spirit of rebellion, pride, envy and jealousy. His acts of disobedience – the offering of sacrifice, the making of a rash vow and the deliberate disobedience over the Amalekites (1 Sa. 13:9; 14:24; 15:9) reveal a proud spirit, determined to assert its own independence, and the Lord rejected him as king.

David was a born ruler. He consolidated the tribes into

a nation and secured undisputed possession of Canaan.
Passion, tenderness, generosity and fierceness went to make
up his character. A great man, he also had great lapses and
failures, but he was Israel's greatest king. His reign was the
golden age of the nation and the type of the more glorious
age which would one day crown the nation's history when
Christ, David's greater son, should reign.

Summary

The first book bearing Samuel's name links the days of the
judges and the establishment of the kingdom under Saul.
It records the birth, call and work of Samuel; the anointing,
and eventually the rejection, of Saul as king; the coming of
David, the shepherd, to the court, his wanderings as an
outlaw, and the death of Saul and Jonathan, his son. These
events span a period of forty years (*c.* 1050–1010 BC).

The second book records the kingship of David. His
reign over Judah begins in Hebron and soon extends to the
northern tribes of Israel. He captures Jerusalem and reigns
there as king of all Israel. Then it describes God's covenant
with David; his failure and sin over Bathsheba; the heart-
break of the rebellion of his son, Absalom, and his return
to end his years in peace in Jerusalem. The book covers a
period of forty years (*c.* 1010–970 BC).

Kingship

Although the books of 1 and 2 Samuel make it clear that
the Israelites' reasons for wanting a king were not ones that
God could approve of, the whole idea of kingship becomes
a central theme in the history of God's dealings with Israel,
and one which God uses quite wonderfully in preparing
them for the coming of the great king, Messiah.

Ancient near eastern countries were often ruled by kings,
and there was already, traditionally, a very close association
between the nation's king and the nation's god. The king's
authority was directly attributed to the god, and he was

regarded as being the representative or descendant of, or
even identified with, the god. In Israel, also, the king was
considered to rule with God's authority and to be anointed
with God's power, though he was in no sense thought to be
divine.

The king serves to unite the nation. The Israelites are
surrounded by alien, hostile nations who worship false
gods, and God's people are all too easily led astray or
discouraged. Under the king, the scattered tribes can be
united as the people of God. He brings solidarity and tremendous potential for building up the people's faith in the
Lord, their provider. The sense of being 'the nation' is
being grasped again.

The Israelites are exultant and have high ideals, vision
for the future and confidence. So the theme of kingship, as
it runs through these books, is a great and glorious one.
But that very focus becomes a teaching point for God with
his people. For their trust is still in man, the king, and so
it is ill-founded. Saul, with the makings of an ideal king,
degenerates into a weak, vindictive despot and is eventually
almost dismissed in the accounts because of his failings.
David, the real core of the kingship theme, a glorious ruler,
and 'a man after God's own heart', is yet shown to be
human and sinful. Thus God is bringing out through Israelite history and through the account preserved for us,
the inevitable imperfections of human rulers. The 'coming
one', the king Messiah, however, will be the perfect ruler.

Religion

Here again we see the souring of elements of Israel's life
that have so much potential for good. The priesthood begins
to abuse its God-given protection and provision (1 Sa. 2).
The people, seeing the corruption of the priests of God,
lose their confidence in God, too. Practices from surrounding nations, such as cultic prostitution, are introduced; the
sacrifices become a disgrace. And the ark, containing the

Law and symbolizing God's presence, is used superstitiously as a lucky charm against military defeat. With their trust thus misplaced, the people are in need of God's discipline. Defeat comes, and the ark is captured for a time.

Saul's failure as a leader for God's people is emphasized by the faithlessness he displays in consulting a medium (1 Sa. 28). Witchcraft was a fairly common feature of life, but the Israelites knew that God forbade it. Here their leader, the king they preferred to God alone, resorts to superstition.

Writer and date

In the Hebrew Bible these two are one book. They seem to have formed part of a larger historical work consisting of Joshua, Judges, Samuel and Kings (sometimes known as the 'Deuteronomic history' because it reflects the themes and emphases of the book of Deuteronomy). So its final edition must date from after the beginning of the exile in the sixth century BC, and must have been intended to teach the people about God's faithful relationship with them and his demands on them in those dark days.

Probably an earlier edition existed before the exile, however, and this, in turn, was clearly based on earlier sources. Some of these sources may have dated from the time of the events they record (see 2 Sa. 8:16–17).

We do not know who wrote the books or put them into their final form.

Structure and contents

1 SAMUEL
 I. Eli and Samuel 1–7
  1. Life at Shiloh 1–3
      Birth of Samuel 1:1–2:11   Eli, his sons, Samuel 2:12–26   Eli and the man of God 2:27–36   The call of Samuel 3

4. Absalom 13:1–19:7
    *His sister and Amnon 13:1–33   His flight and return
    13:34–14:33   His revolt and David's flight 15:1–
    16:14   His counsellors 16:15–17:23   His death and
    David's lament 17:24–19:7*
5. David's return to Jerusalem and Sheba's rebellion
    19:8–20:26
6. Appendix 21–24
    *Saul's descendants 21:1–14   Philistines 21:15–22
    A psalm of David 22   David's last words 23:1–7
    His mighty men 23:8–39   The census and plague 24*

Study questions

1. From 1 Samuel 8–10 and 16, what can you discover
about the way God calls and equips his servants?
2. Read 1 Samuel 17 and 24. What do these two incidents
reveal about the character of David, and particularly his
attitude towards the Lord?
3. What are the dangers of dabbling in the occult shown
in 1 Samuel 28 (*i.e.* how was Saul harmed)?
4. What does 2 Samuel 7 teach us about God's grace and
the appropriate response to it?
5. What may we learn from 2 Samuel 11 and 12 about
a) temptation; b) repentance; c) forgiveness?
6. In what way does Samuel display the marks of a true
prophet (see p. 158)?

Reference books
P. R. Ackroyd, *The First Book of Samuel* (Cambridge, 1971)
H. W. Hertzberg, *I and II Samuel* (SCM, 1979; Westminster,
    1965)

1 and 2 Kings

Kings continues the story of the 'decline and fall' of the nation of Israel. It covers vast tracts of history, taking in rulers, pretenders, rebellions, exposing corruption and impending judgment.

In Solomon the monarchy reaches its highest point in worldly terms, but begins the decline to its lowest in spiritual terms. He begins by asking for wisdom from God above all things, but the 'good business' of his political marriage alliances eventually turned him from the Lord to worship foreign idols.

Always God has his spokesmen, the prophets. The characters of these men of God tower over the petty squabbles, meanness and intrigue of the kings. Yet even they are not portrayed in an unrealistic, superhuman way. Their failures, as well as their triumphs, have lessons for us. And above all, the books of Kings continue to show us the God behind human history and how he deals in love and justice with a sinful and rebellious people.

These books, like all biblical history, are written from the religious and prophetic point of view, not from that of the secular historian. Their aim is religious and spiritual. The compiler is not concerned to write history as we conceive it today. Some kings and events important in secular history receive short shrift here, whilst others of little importance to the ordinary historian receive fuller treatment.

Historical background
It is necessary to grasp the importance of three critical

landmarks in Israelite history if these books are to be understood.

The first is the *division of the kingdom* after the death of Solomon (*c.* 930 BC), when the ten tribes in the north rebelled against the south. From then on we must get used to thinking in terms of the *northern kingdom of Israel*, with its capital first at Shechem and then at Samaria; and the *southern kingdom of Judah* (including Benjamin), where David's descendants continued to reign in Jerusalem.

The second is the *fall of Samaria* to the Assyrians in 721 BC when a representative proportion of the ten tribes was deported to various parts of the Assyrian Empire (2 Ki. 17). Other peoples were imported into northern Israel. They intermarried with the Israelites left there and became the despised 'Samaritans' of later days and of the Gospels.

The third is the *fall of Jerusalem* in 587 BC to the Babylonians, preceded ten years earlier by the deportation of the cream of the Jews to Babylon (2 Ki. 24–25).

Recording method

From *c.* 930 BC onwards when the kingdom divided, the compiler has to adopt some system for recording side by side the events of the two kingdoms. His method is simple. He records the line of the kings in the northern kingdom, Israel, until it overlaps with a change of king in the southern kingdom, Judah; then he switches to the line of Judah, and then back to Israel and so on. It is helpful, using two coloured pencils – one for Judah and one for Israel – to draw lines down the margin of the Bible so as to show at a glance in which kingdom the events took place. The outlines will help in this.

Summary

David is dying and there is an attempt by Adonijah, one of David's sons, to succeed to the throne in place of the chosen Solomon. David intervenes and Solomon is anointed king.

Solomon asks the Lord for wisdom rather than long life or riches. He builds the temple and consecrates it to the Lord with a great dedicatory prayer. But shortly after this he turns away from the Lord and descends to the level of an ostentatious eastern potentate. His heavy taxation of the people makes them ready for revolt, and when his son, Rehoboam, succeeds him, the ten northern tribes split away under Jeroboam I and form the northern kingdom (1 Ki. 1:1–12:24).

Whilst the succeeding kings of Judah (the southern kingdom) are a mixture of good and bad, all the kings of Israel (the northern kingdom) are consistently bad. The formula 'he walked in the way of Jeroboam who made Israel to sin' frequently occurs (1 Ki. 12:25–16:34).

During the reign of King Ahab, the prophet Elijah appears suddenly upon the scene. He confronts the idolatrous prophets of Baal on Mount Carmel and then, threatened by Ahab's heathen wife, Jezebel, flees for his life to the Sinai peninsula. There the Lord meets him and he returns to Israel with the command to anoint Jehu as king of Israel and Elisha as his own successor. He has another confrontation when Ahab, encouraged by Jezebel, attempts to confiscate Naboth's vineyard (1 Ki. 17:1–22:53).

Elijah continues his work into the reign of Ahaziah of Israel (*c.* 853–852 BC; not to be confused with Ahaziah of Judah, *c.* 841 BC) and, in a dramatic event, Elisha watches Elijah being taken directly from earth to the presence of God, and then succeeds him as prophet (2 Ki. 1:1–2:25).

In five miracles which show God's care for ordinary people, Elisha makes a widow's cruse of oil into enough to pay her debts, promises that a barren woman will have a son and restores him to her when later he dies, makes poisonous food edible and provides food for the hungry. He humbles Naaman, commander-in-chief of the Syrians, but heals him of leprosy. Later, in a war between Syria and Israel, Elisha develops a kind of supernatural power to know the Syrians' location and plans. Eventually the Syrians besiege Samaria but Elisha shows his young assistant that the Lord's invisible hosts are protecting them (2 Ki. 2:26–6:17).

Elijah and Elisha were prophets 800 years before Christ, yet their lives demonstrate a spirituality like that of the New Testament and the modern believer can learn much from them. Elijah's career has many parallels with the life of Moses and in many ways he forms a link between Moses and the later eighth-century prophets, providing continuity in the prophetic tradition.

The kings of Israel, all of them bad, led the kingdom to doom and in 721 BC Samaria fell to the Assyrians. The kingdom of Judah continued for another 135 years or so, and then Nebuchadnezzar of Babylon captured Jerusalem and deported much of the population to Babylon in 597 BC. Between the fall of Samaria and that of Jerusalem (587 BC) the good kings Hezekiah (716–687 BC) and Josiah (640–609 BC) and the bad kings Manasseh (687–642 BC) and Amon (642–640 BC) play their part in the fortunes of the southern kingdom (2 Ki. 6:18–21:26).

Under Josiah extensive reforms were carried out on the basis of a 'book of the law' found accidentally in the temple. In view of what 2 Kings 22–23 tells us about this book – its emphasis on obedience, the disastrous consequences of disobedience, the covenant and the central place of worship – it may have been the book of Deuteronomy. Josiah did away with the pagan shrines, renewed the nation's commitment to God's covenant and re-established the Passover (2 Ki. 22:1–23:30).

But the last four kings before the fall of Jerusalem all did evil, and there was no escaping the Lord's judgment on the land (2 Ki. 23:31–25:30).

Writer and date
It is clear that the writer of Kings had a particular per-

spective on his nation's history. Each king is assessed not in terms of his political exploits but in terms of how far he 'did evil' or 'did right' in the sight of God. Evil resulted in judgment; obedience resulted in blessing. The kings who receive the writer's approval are those who trust in the Lord and obey the commands of Moses.

The writer's language is often reminiscent of Deuteronomy, and his purpose in writing seems to be to show how the message of Deuteronomy worked out in practice in the nation's subsequent history. Deuteronomy records God's covenant with the nation, and the laws and commands which they were to keep as their part in the agreement. It lists the blessings which would result from obedience and the curses which would follow disobedience. It abhors pagan religion and emphasizes one place of worship for God's people. The books of Kings show how, so often, the covenant was neglected, the laws and commands were flouted, pagan religion was embraced, and many shrines were set up in the land. Consequently, 'the Lord was very angry with Israel, and removed them out of his sight' (2 Ki. 17:18), and destruction 'came upon Judah at the command of the Lord, to remove them out of his sight' (2 Ki. 24:3).

The two books are one in the Hebrew Bible. Often the author quotes his sources, including 'the acts of Solomon' (1 Ki. 11:41) and the 'Book of the Chronicles of the Kings of Israel' (1 Ki. 14:19, *etc.*). The release of King Jehoiachin from prison in Babylon (561 BC) is the last event recorded (2 Ki. 25:27). The book, in its final form, was completed after this date, possibly around 550 BC.

Structure and contents

1 KINGS
   I. David's closing days 1:1–2:11
      1. The contest for the succession 1
      2. David's dying charge 2:1–11

Study questions

1. What can you learn from Solomon in 1 Kings 3? Write a definition of 'wisdom' as exemplified in this chapter.

2. What does Solomon's prayer at the dedication of the temple teach us about the Lord's relationship with his people (1 Ki. 8:22–61)?

3. Draw out the two strands of Elijah's life as man of prayer and man of action. See 1 Kings 16:29–17:12; 17:8–10; 18:20–38; 21:1–19.

4. Read 1 Kings 19. How does the Lord help Elijah in his failure and depression? What can you learn from this about the best way to help a friend in a similar state?

5. What experiences did Naaman have to go through in order to receive healing, and what was his attitude afterwards (2 Ki. 5)? What principles does this illustrate for anyone seeking restoration from the Lord?

6. Read Deuteronomy 7:1–16; 8:19–20. How are these warnings and promises borne out in the downfall of the northern kingdom (2 Ki. 17)?

7. 'I have found the book' (2 Ki. 22:8). What was the result (chs. 22–23)? Similarly, what results follow when someone 'finds the book' today?

Reference books

F. F. Bruce, *Israel and the Nations* (Paternoster, 1963; Eerdmans, 1963), pp. 35-92

J. Ellul, *The Politics of God and the Politics of Man* (Eerdmans, U.S.A., 1972)

G. H. Jones, *1 and 2 Kings*, 2 vols. (Marshall Pickering, 1984; Eerdmans, 1984)

B. O. Long, *1 Kings* (Eerdmans, U.S.A., 1984)

D. F. Payne, *Kingdoms of the Lord* (Paternoster, 1981; Eerdmans, 1981)

A. W. Pink, *Gleanings from Elisha* (Moody, U.S.A., 1972)

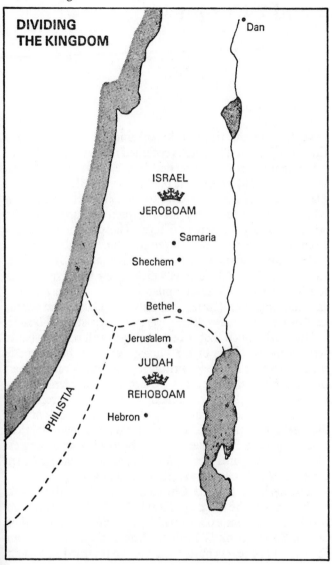

DIVIDING
THE KINGDOM

Dan

ISRAEL

JEROBOAM

Samaria

Shechem

Bethel

Jerusalem

JUDAH

REHOBOAM

Hebron

PHILISTIA

1 and 2 Chronicles

'The Lion of the tribe of Judah' might be the motif for
these two books. The events recorded are parallel with, and
often identical to, those related in the books of Kings. In
the Hebrew Old Testament the books are called 'Words of
Days', *i.e.* journals. The Greek Old Testament calls them
'Omissions' because they are regarded as supplementing
what is already written in Kings. The present title dates
from the time of Jerome, in the fourth century AD.

Though we start with a united kingdom under David,
the book recounts the events which follow the division into
north and south. The compiler has little interest in the
northern kingdom (Israel) but only in Judah in the south,
that of David, whereas there were five dynasties of Israel.

Obviously much that is recorded here will repeat what is
written in the books of the Kings, although the author is
much more deliberately writing ecclesiastical rather than
political history. Sometimes the accounts supplement and
complement each other. Sometimes there are discrepancies
particularly where figures are concerned. Some of the
Hebrew manuscripts are imperfect. Some of the numerical
discrepancies may be due to errors in copying manuscripts.
Transcribing figures is notoriously open to mistakes. Other
differences may be due to a difference of aim.

It seems likely that the 'Chronicler' compiled this account
of the times of the kings specifically for those Hebrews who
had returned from exile to build a new life in their land of
origin. So the book is aiming, through these stories from
the past, to be an encouragement to the returned exiles and

to provide guidelines for building a new worshipping community.

Summary
David establishes his capital at Hebron for seven years after the tragic death of Saul. But he knows the strategic importance of Jerusalem which had never been wrested from the Jebusites. With brilliant strategy he conquers it and eventually, with mishaps in the process, brings the ark of the covenant to the city. He plans to build a permanent replacement for the tabernacle and is encouraged by the prophet Nathan to make full preparations for the building, but is warned that the privilege of doing the work would be given to his son, a man of peace. The Lord promises that his dynasty shall last for ever (1 Ch.1:1–22:19).

The Chronicler gives lists of Levites, priests, gatekeepers, army divisions, *etc*. Movingly, David exhorts his son, Solomon, now named to be his successor, wholly to follow the Lord with all his powers, emotion, intellect and will, and calls upon the nation to do the same. With a magnificent prayer, still used today, the solemn proclamation of Solomon as king, the life of David, shepherd, courtier, king, sinner, man of God, comes to its earthly end (1 Ch.23:1–29:30).

Solomon begins his reign well with a prayer for wisdom rather than for wealth or honour. He builds the temple and offers it to the Lord with a great prayer of dedication. Tragically, from this point Solomon decreases in stature. The famous visit of the queen of Sheba shows that he has become a typical eastern potentate of the time, with love of wealth and power and ostentation (2 Ch. 1:1–9:31).

After his death, under his son Rehoboam, the kingdom tragically divides into north and south, caused partly by Rehoboam's arrogance but largely by Solomon's extravagance and consequent heavy taxation of the people. The Chronicler is now not interested in the kings of the northern kingdom but describes the succession of the southern kings, the kings of Judah, until the fall of Jerusalem to the Babylonians (*c.* 587 BC) and the return to Jerusalem by command of Cyrus, king of Persia (*c.* 538 BC) (2 Ch. 10:1–36:16).

Much of this is paralleled in 2 Kings but every now and then some fresh aspect or additional snippet of useful information is given by the Chronicler.

The line of David

Whilst the books of Kings also stress the theme of kingship in the Hebrews' unfolding history, 1 and 2 Chronicles are much more specific in their concentration on the Davidic dynasty. David's tribe, Judah, is seen as the true Israel, while the northern kingdom, as long as it continues to rebel, will be cut off from the purposes of God. The future of the nation under God depends on the continuation and faithfulness of the Davidic line. The extensive genealogies are included to show the sacred line through which 'Messiah' would come.

The temple

A great deal of the material which is new to the accounts in Chronicles concerns the temple. For the Chronicler, the links between the Davidic dynasty and the temple were so strong that he was encouraging the returned exiles to see their rebuilding of the temple as a step on the way to restoring the monarchy. David's arrangements for the original temple, therefore, occupy considerable space. The nation's leaders are seen as the founders of true, stable worship in God's temple, rather than military victors. The temple services, its priests, Levites, singers and all that has to do with worship are highlighted.

Writer and date

In the Hebrew Bible these books are one and are part of

the Writings. Probably they originally formed one work with Ezra and Nehemiah. Tradition assigns a common authorship to Chronicles and Ezra. It may have been written soon after the exile for its last reference records the end of that period (2 Ch. 36:22–23), but the list of Jehoiachin's descendants covers six generations after the exile, which might indicate a date *c.* 400 BC (1 Ch. 3:17–24). The Chronicler apparently used various sources, among others the books of Samuel and Kings (1 Ch. 9:1; 29:29; 2 Ch. 9:29; 12:15; 20:34; 24:27; 26:22; 32:32; 33:19).

Structure and contents

VII. Solomon proclaimed king and death of David 29:21–30

2 CHRONICLES
  I. King Solomon 1
       His wisdom 1:1–12   His wealth 1:13–17
 II. The temple 2–7
     1. King Hiram provides materials 2
     2. Measurements and furniture 3:1–5:1
     3. Dedication 5:2–6:11
          The ark 5:2–10   The glory 5:11–14   Solomon's address and prayer 6   The fire, offerings, Feast of Tabernacles 7:1–10   The Lord's message to Solomon 7:11–22
III. Solomon's other activities 8
 IV. The visit of the queen of Sheba 9:1–12
  V. Solomon's wealth, power and death 9:13–31
 VI. Kings of Judah after Solomon 10:1–36:16
     1. Rehoboam *c.* 931   10–12
     2. Abijam *c.* 913   13
     3. Asa *c.* 911   14–16
     4. Jehoshaphat *c.* 870   17:1–21:3
     5. Jehoram *c.* 848   21:4–20
     6. Ahaziah *c.* 841   22:1–9
     7. Athaliah *c.* 841   22:1–23:21
     8. Joash *c.* 835   24
     9. Amaziah *c.* 796   25
    10. Azariah (Uzziah) *c.* 767   26
    11. Jotham *c.* 740   27
    12. Ahaz *c.* 732   28
    13. Hezekiah *c.* 716   29–32
    14. Manasseh *c.* 687   33:1–20
    15. Amon *c.* 642   33:21–25
    16. Josiah *c.* 640   34–35
    17. Jehoahaz *c.* 609   36:1–14
    18. Jehoiakim (Eliakim) *c.* 609   36:5–8

Study questions

1. From 1 Chronicles 15–17, what can you learn about the character and expression of worship? How does this passage illustrate Romans 12:4–8 and 1 Corinthians 14:40?
2. What can you learn from 1 Chronicles 28–29 about the attitudes we should have in doing any work for the Lord?
3. How does 2 Chronicles 8–36 illustrate God's promises (positive and negative) in 7:11–22?
4. Read 2 Chronicles 20. What does this episode teach about prayer and faith in times of trouble?
5. There is a saying that 'the church must be always reforming itself'. What principles can you see in 2 Chronicles 29–31 to guide this reformation process?

Reference books

F. F. Bruce, *Israel and the Nations* (Paternoster, 1963; Eerdmans, 1963), pp. 28-96

D. F. Payne, *Kingdoms of the Lord* (Paternoster, 1981; Eerdmans, 1981)

M. Wilcock, *The Message of Chronicles* (IVP, 1987)

H. G. M. Williamson, *1 and 2 Chronicles* (Marshall Pickering, 1982; Eerdmans, 1982)

L. J. Wood, *Israel's United Monarchy* (Baker, U.S.A., 1980)

Ezra

This is one of the most exciting books in Jewish history. Here is recorded the wonderful day when the prophecy of Jeremiah (Je. 29:10) was fulfilled, and after their seventy years in captivity in Babylon Cyrus, king of Persia, issued the edict in 538 BC which set the Jews free to return to Jerusalem and their homeland.

The book records the edict of Cyrus allowing captive nations to return home, and tells how some of the Jews, first under the leadership of Sheshbazzar and then under Ezra, availed themselves of the opportunity. Many Jews, however, preferred to remain in Babylon.

For the Christian the book speaks of restoration and of the faithful fulfilment of God's purposes through even a sinful people. God has not forgotten his promises concerning the continuity of the line of King David (through whom the Saviour will come). When all is said and done, God is still in the midst of his people, claiming their worship, and so the temple must be rebuilt.

Through the centuries, the books of Ezra and Nehemiah have given inspiration and encouragement to the people of God when they have met opposition and had difficult tasks to do. The salutary warning, however, is that even then the people were forgetful, indolent and faithless.

Summary
Cyrus' decree sets in motion the return under Sheshbazzar, the arrival in Judah, the setting up of the altar in Jerusalem, the re-establishing of worship, and the laying of the temple

foundation. Due to opposition from the Samaritans, work on the temple and on the city walls is brought to a halt (1:1–4:24).

Sixteen years later the prophets Haggai and Zechariah give encouragement and stimulus for the new beginning of the work (520 BC), which is completed in four years on 3 Adar (10 March 516 BC). This second temple is dedicated and the Passover is restored (5–6).

Between chapters 6 and 7 there is a gap of sixty years.

Ezra the scribe leads the second return in 458 BC, seventy-nine years after the first. He is sent by the Persian king, Artaxerxes I (464–423 BC), with a commission to regulate religious and moral conditions. The main problem is that some of the Jews had married heathen women, thus endangering the purity of the nation's religious and moral life. The people repented and the reform was achieved (7–10).

Historical background
See 'Historical background to the exile' (pp. 155-57).

Since the backgrounds of Ezra and Nehemiah appear to be identical in many ways, we would expect much of the information they contain to overlap. Working out the precise order of events has proved notoriously difficult, however, and scholars continue to discuss why the facts and figures do not always seem to tally and whether the events of Nehemiah preceded or followed those in Ezra.

Writer and date
The book is a continuation of Chronicles (2 Ch. 36:22–23) and includes Ezra's own memoirs, narrative, registers, letters and proclamations. Ezra appears as the writer of chapter 9 and he may have been the compiler of the whole book. Many scholars ascribe the book, along with Chronicles and Nehemiah, to an unknown author, the Chronicler, who may have compiled his books, using earlier material (c. 400

BC). No-one can be certain. Chapters 4:8–6:18 are written in Aramaic.

Structure and contents

    I. The return under Sheshbazzar 1–4
1. Cyrus' decree, preparations for the return and the lists of those who returned 1–2
2. The altar set up, worship re-established and the temple foundation laid 3
3. Opposition. Rebuilding of temple and walls ceases 4

   II. Work on the temple resumed 5–6
1. Haggai and Zechariah 5:1–2
2. Opposition and letter to Darius from Tattenai 5:3–17
3. Darius confirms Cyrus' decree 6:1–15
4. Dedication of the temple and restoration of the Passover 6:16–22.

(Nearly sixty years elapse between chapters 6 and 7. Confucius, the Buddha, Herodotus, Thucydides and Socrates lived during these years.)

III. The return under Ezra 7–10
1. Ezra's return, his companions, and the arrival in Jerusalem 7–8
2. Report on intermarriage 9:1–5
3. Ezra's prayer 9:6–15
4. Mixed marriages abolished 10

Study questions

1. What principles for worship can we learn from ch. 3?
2. What three good principles for Bible study do you find in 7:10 and how can you apply them in your life?
3. What can be learnt about confession of sin from ch. 9?
4. Build up a character sketch of Ezra from his book.

Reference books

D. J. A. Clines, *Ezra, Nehemiah, Esther* (Marshall Pickering, 1984; Eerdmans, 1984)

F. C. Fensham, *The Books of Ezra and Nehemiah* (Eerdmans, U.S.A., 1982)

F. C. Holmgren, *Israel Alive Again* (Handsel, 1987; Eerdmans, 1987)

D. Kidner, *Ezra and Nehemiah* (IVP, 1979)

Nehemiah

Nehemiah is the outstanding example of that rare individual, the man of prayer and the man of action combined. For him there is no line between the secular and the spiritual.

God's work is invariably opposed by his enemies. Three dangers then arise. We become so occupied in resisting the opposition that we cannot get on with the work; or we pray hard and look for a miracle; or we work frantically to get the work done and do not pray. Nehemiah seems to have got the balance exactly right. The best way to resist the Lord's enemies is to get on with the Lord's work, but prayer and work are to go hand in hand: 'Take . . . the sword of the Spirit . . . Pray at all times' (Eph. 6:17–18).

The events narrated in the book take place at the time of the return of the Israelites from exile in Babylon (see historical background to Ezra).

Summary
Nehemiah, an important official of the court of Artaxerxes I in Persia, receives news of the desolate state of Jerusalem a dozen or so years after Ezra had returned there. Nervously, but with prayer, he approaches the king and obtains permission to go to Jerusalem. There he surveys the ruins and begins the rebuilding in 444 BC (1–3).

The builders meet fierce and varied opposition but Nehemiah, by prayer and action, steadfastly resists. He puts into effect various social reforms and the wall is finished (4–6).

A census is taken. The Law is publicly read by Ezra, the Feast of Tabernacles is celebrated, a fast of repentance is held and a covenant of obedience to the Law is signed (7–10).

Arrangements are made to people Jerusalem, the walls are dedicated and a service of great joy and thanksgiving takes place in the temple area (11–12).

Nehemiah returns to Artaxerxes in Persia (c. 433 BC) and then makes a second visit to Jerusalem. During his second term of office he carries out further reforms (13).

Writer and date
The book is made up of personal memoirs of Nehemiah in the first person singular, plus documents and chronicles. Ezra could have been the compiler of most of it. For further comments see the section on Ezra.

Structure and contents
1. The journey to Jerusalem 1–2
2. Building the wall, opposition and hindrances 3:1–6:19
3. Lists of those who returned 7:1–73a
4. Reading, explaining and obeying the Law 7:73b–8:18
5. Renewing the covenant 9–10
6. Lists of those who lived in Jerusalem 11:1–12:26
7. Dedication of the wall and arrangements for temple services 12:27–47
8. Nehemiah's second administration 13

Study questions
1. In what various ways was the building of the wall opposed and how did Nehemiah meet each case (4:3–6:15)?
2. Make a collection of the references in this book to a) prayer and b) action. What teaching, helpful for the Christian today, do you find in them?
3. In addition to prayer, list the other characteristics of great leadership which Nehemiah shows.

4. Read ch. 8 and 10:28–39 carefully. In what ways can you apply them to a) Bible reading today, b) public worship today and c) our response to God's Word today?
5. Trace on a map the route of Nehemiah's return.

Reference books

D. J. A. Clines, *Ezra, Nehemiah, Esther* (Marshall Pickering, 1984; Eerdmans, 1984)

F. C. Fensham, *The Books of Ezra and Nehemiah* (Eerdmans, U.S.A., 1982)

F. C. Holmgren, *Israel Alive Again* (Handsel, 1987; Eerdmans, 1987)

D. Kidner, *Ezra and Nehemiah* (IVP, 1979)

Esther

It is startling to realize that Esther, a book which speaks so eloquently of the providence of God, nowhere mentions his name. Indeed it is the overruling providence and sovereignty of God which is the central fact of the book. There is much which seems sordid to us today. It is altogether a sad tale of intrigue and corruption, and even Esther, the 'heroine', resorts to vengeance and bloodshed (9). But God is working out his ultimate universal purpose through even this, and his covenant love for his people does not fail.

The book records an attempted persecution of Jewish expatriates in Persia during the reign of Xerxes (Ahasuerus), king of Persia (486–465 BC). In the providence of God, the tables are turned and the Jews take revenge on their enemies.

The Jewish feast of Purim was inaugurated to commemorate the event, and the book of Esther is read annually in the synagogue at this feast, the congregation traditionally booing every time the wicked Haman is mentioned!

Historically, the book fits between chapters 6 and 7 of the book of Ezra.

Summary

Ahasuerus (Xerxes), king of Persia, deposes his queen, Vashti, for refusing to be put on show. Esther is chosen to replace her. Two chamberlains conspire against the king but Mordecai, Esther's cousin who had adopted her, discovers and reports the plot. Haman is made chief vizier and, enraged by Mordecai's lack of servility, issues a cruel decree to slaughter every Jew in the land (1–3).

Mordecai encourages Esther, from her privileged position, to take action and eventually, at the risk of her life, she goes to the king (4). The book makes its greatest impact at this point with these words: 'For if you keep silence at such a time as this, relief and deliverance will rise for the Jews from another quarter, but you and your father's house will perish. And who knows whether you have not come to the kingdom for such a time as this?' (4:14).

Haman plots to hang Mordecai but the tables are turned and Haman hangs instead (5–7). The Jews destroy their enemies and the Feast of Purim (lots) is established (8–9).

Special problems of Esther

Apart from the vengeful attitudes which we have mentioned earlier, the book constitutes a problem for the Christian reader because nowhere does it even mention the name of God. Esther's instructions are to fast before she approaches the king (4:16), and presumably this also involved prayer, but the text nowhere states it. Yet we have noted that the central fact of the book is God's sovereignty over the affairs of men, and perhaps even these peculiarities are intended as a silent testimony. The Septuagint (the second-century BC Greek translation of the Old Testament) contains extra passages which do not exist in the Hebrew. These 'additions' can be read in the Apocrypha. Perhaps they were added by the translator to make the work look more 'religious', since they emphasize God's activity in the affair.

Writer and date

Nothing is known either of the writer or of the date of writing. There is the possibility that the book comes from the official records of the Persian court, which would explain why God is nowhere mentioned.

Contents

Study question

Illustrate from the book of Esther the sovereign purpose and protection of God (*cf.* Rom. 8:28).

Reference books

D. J. A. Clines, *Ezra, Nehemiah, Esther* (Marshall Pickering, 1984; Eerdmans, 1984)

R. J. Cogins and S. P. Re'emi, *Israel Among the Nations* (Handsel, 1985; Eerdmans, 1985)

W. J. Fuerst, *Ruth, Esther, Ecclesiastes, Song of Songs, Lamentations* (Cambridge, 1975)

R. E. Murphy, *Wisdom Literature: Job, Proverbs, Ruth, Canticles, Ecclesiastes, Esther* (Eerdmans, U.S.A., 1981)

Job

The problem of suffering is the theme of the book of Job. It is cast in the form of a drama, and is a literary masterpiece quite apart from its religious significance. Tennyson called it 'the greatest poem of ancient or modern times'. But the Christian values it most for its inspired spiritual teaching. For Martin Luther it is 'magnificent and sublime as no other book of Scripture'.

The problems we have with suffering can probably be reduced to four questions, as David Clines has pointed out in *BCT*. The book gives no satisfactory answer to the question, 'Why does suffering happen?' That is not its purpose. Nor is it really concerned with 'Why has this happened to me?', although the subject is mentioned and Job's friends give partial answers. The book makes a significant contribution to the question, 'Is there such a thing as innocent suffering?' Both the author and God attest Job's innocence (1:1; 6:30; 9:15; 42:7f.).

But the author's real intention is to deal with the question, 'What am I to do when I suffer?' To this he gives two answers: recognize the greatness and the goodness of God and put your trust in him in spite of your suffering; and calmly accept God's will (1:21; 2:10). And when suffering presses so hard that acceptance is no longer possible, and bitterness, a sense of isolation and even of persecution by God become overwhelming, then the anger and frustration are not to be suppressed but brought to the Lord in prayer. Job does not merely protest, he protests in the right direction. Persistently he calls upon God and it is his painful and importunate prayer which brings an overwhelming sense of the Lord's greatness. It is in this personal encounter with the Lord that his tensions are resolved and his troubles ended (42:1–6).

Summary

The prologue opens with Satan obtaining the Lord's permission to touch all that belongs to Job except his own person. He loses first his wealth and then his children. Next Satan obtains permission to attack Job himself. When he is afflicted with repulsive sores and is urged by his wife to curse God and die, he maintains that man must be prepared to trust God for better or for worse. As his mental distress increases, he finds life bitter and wishes either that he had never been born or that he had died at birth (1–3).

The main portion of the book consists of three cycles of discussion between Job and his friends Eliphaz, Bildad and Zophar, who travel far to comfort him. Their intentions are good but they are hopelessly doctrinaire and are unable to relate their 'theology' to life. They maintain, with increasing vehemence, that Job is suffering because he is guilty, perhaps of some secret sin. He should turn in repentance to God. Job challenges them to prove that he has deserved such calamities and begs God to leave him alone (4–14). Sometimes his resentment towards the Lord breaks through and is forcefully expressed: 'I will not restrain my mouth; I will speak in the anguish of my spirit; I will complain in the bitterness of my soul' (7:11); 'though I am blameless, he would prove me perverse' (9:20); 'The earth is given into the hand of the wicked; he covers the faces of its judges – if it is not he, who then is it?' (9:24); 'And if I lift myself up, thou dost hunt me like a lion' (10:16).

In the second cycle, the 'friends' make no allowance for the stress he is under. His bitter resentment at his lot and his attempts to justify himself prove his guilt. Bildad and Zophar remind him of the fate of the wicked. Job complains that their so-called comfort is miserable and pleads with them to show him a little pity. He again affirms his innocence and insists that he will be vindicated at the end (15–21).

The third cycle is a rehash of the friends' previous arguments. Job will not abandon his claim to integrity. Man becomes wise through reverencing God and abandoning evil. Nostalgically he reviews happier times. He appeals to be heard and vindicated (22–31).

After the three cycles, Elihu, with the arrogance of youth, attempts his explanation. He has been called 'the original angry young man'. God answers man by dreams and by illness. God cannot do wrong, he renders exact retribution. Let Job confess his sin. God is almighty, all-wise and great (32–37).

As Elihu's tirade peters out, God himself speaks. Although he is so great, he is near the godly and he cares. As the Lord speaks, Job's conception of his greatness grows, he admits his own creatureliness and says, 'I had heard of thee . . . but now my eye sees thee; therefore I despise myself' (38:1–42:6).

The Lord severely rebukes Eliphaz and his two friends. Job prays for his friends and 'the Lord restored the fortunes of Job, when he had prayed for his friends' (42:7–17).

Wisdom literature
The books of Job, Proverbs and Ecclesiastes, along with short passages in other Old Testament books, are often described as 'wisdom literature' – a form of literature common in the ancient near east.

There were two basic types of wisdom literature: the 'proverbial' and the 'speculative'. Proverbial wisdom literature is characterized by short, pithy sayings concerned with everyday, homely matters and containing a practical guide to personal happiness. A good example in the Bible is the book of Proverbs. The speculative type of wisdom literature consists of lengthier explorations of the meaning of human existence and the problem of suffering. These often take the form of monologues (like Ecclesiastes) or dialogues (like Job). The discussion is always in concrete terms, however, and so we have human suffering presented in the life of the man Job.

The aim of wisdom literature was to provide practical guidance for everyday life. For 'wisdom' was not abstract and theoretical; it was concerned with down-to-earth realities. The word could almost be translated 'skill in living', and indeed it is used to describe people with technical and manual skill (such as Bezalel and his colleagues who built and furnished the tabernacle: see Ex. 31:1–11, where the word is translated 'ability' in the RSV).

Although wisdom literature existed throughout the ancient near east, the Old Testament adds a dimension not found elsewhere. It recognizes that it is 'the fear of the Lord' that is 'the beginning of knowledge' (Pr. 1:7, *etc.*). God himself is wise (Jb. 12:13ff., *etc.*); therefore wisdom on the human plane consists of reflecting God's ways. Pagan wisdom is futile (Is. 19:12ff., *etc.*).

Kings, because of their heavy responsibilities, particularly needed wisdom. Solomon, recognizing this, specifically prayed for wisdom from the Lord at the outset of his reign (1 Ki. 3:4–15). The account is immediately followed by an example of Solomon's wisdom in action, as he judges a difficult case (1 Ki. 3:16–28).

A special category of 'wise' people was associated with the royal palaces. They advised the king in governmental matters, and also taught and trained disciples. They were the guardians and promoters of traditional wisdom, and it seems that it was they who committed it to writing (*cf.* Pr. 25:1).

Satan

The word 'satan' means an adversary and sometimes it is

used in the Old Testament of a human adversary without any reference to a personal devil (*e.g.* 1 Sa. 29:4). Some commentators hold, therefore, that we are not meant to see any reference to the devil in the opening chapters of Job. The satan is one of God's servants with the role of an investigator. Some would go so far as to say that he is a kind of *agent provocateur*. In a book of 42 chapters he does not appear after the second chapter. He is not the subject or even a theme of the book, but almost seems to be used as a device for introducing the discussion about suffering.

Nevertheless, most commentators assume that he is to be identified with the devil here, even though the teaching given about him is less than that of a fully developed Christian theology. His activities are certainly harmful to Job. Other Old Testament passages express the same outlook (1 Ch. 21:1; Zc. 3:1f., *etc.*), and the New Testament writers base their teaching about the devil on these passages.

Satan is the personal 'prince of evil' and the Lord is the good and righteous God, but they are not equals. Sovereignty belongs to God alone. Satan may operate only with the permission of the Lord who, in his unsearchable wisdom and goodness and for man's ultimate good, postpones the day of Satan's destruction. Through the ages until that day Satan has access to God with the angelic sons of God (1:6–12, *cf.* Rev. 12:10); may touch a child of God only with the Father's permission (1:12, *cf.* Lk. 22:31–32); is responsible for some human suffering (2:7), and roams round looking for someone to devour (1 Pet. 5:8).

Motives for loving God
A theme related to suffering is also prominent in the book. Why do we love God? Few people love him with singleness of mind. Most of us, if we are discerning and honest, must admit to ulterior motives even in the best and highest that we do. Job, says Satan, loves God only because he has blessed Job with material prosperity (1:9–11). The Lord

taught Job to trust him even when Job had no visible evidence of God's care for him. Material prosperity was understood as God's blessing upon the righteous. Job's trial was allowed in order to prove, among other things, that Satan was wrong.

Faith under trial

The faith of one of God's people under trial is another subsidiary theme of this book. Job's faith remains firm when he loses property and children (1:21), but his faith is more severely tested when distressing illness attacks his body (3:3, 11, 20–21). It seems to be badly shaken when he speaks of God tearing him in his wrath and dashing him to pieces (16:9, 12), and reaches its nadir in chapter 19 (19:8–10). But then it seems boldly to revive as he expresses his confidence that the Lord will vindicate him at least after death if not on earth (19:25–27). With reviving faith, he begins to see that the doctrine that the good are blessed and the wicked suffer in this life is true only in a general sense but not always in particular circumstances (21:1–34). With a new understanding of the greatness of God, Job finds himself able to trust even where he cannot understand. At the end his faith is as strong as at the beginning but it is a faith that has been tested and made stronger by suffering.

Zophar's third speech

There is a section of Job's reply at the end of the third cycle of speeches where Job contradicts what he has previously said and appears to agree with the arguments of his friends (27:13–23). There is also a shorter-than-usual speech by Bildad and no speech by Zophar in this cycle. It may be that the roll has been broken at this point and part of it lost and that 27:13–23 is a fragment of Zophar's third speech.

Writer and date

The author and date of the book are unknown. It has the flavour of ancient times and the record of the argument between Job and his friends may date back to the days of the patriarchs. A high antiquity is also suggested by the reference to Job along with Noah and Daniel in Ezekiel 14: 14, 20. It is possible that the story of Job was told for many centuries before the composition of the book. There is some general consensus among scholars for a date between 600 and 400 BC, but some have suggested a time as early as Solomon (*c.* 950 BC) and others as late as 250 BC.

Structure and contents

I. The prologue 1–2
   1. Job, the upright, before his trials 1:1–5
   2. First assault 1:6–22 and second assault 2:1–10
   3. Job's friends 2:11–13
II. The speeches 3–31
   1. Job's lament 3:1–26
   2. First cycle of speeches
      Eliphaz 4–5   Job answers   6–7
      Bildad 8   Job answers 9–10
      Zophar 11   Job answers 12–14
   3. Second cycle of speeches 15–21
      Eliphaz 15   Job answers 16–17
      Bildad 18   Job answers 19
      Zophar 20   Job answers 21
   4. Third cycle of speeches 22–26
      Eliphaz 22   Job answers 23–24
      Bildad 25   Job answers 26
   5. Two more speeches by Job 27–31
III. Elihu's speeches 32–37
      First 32–33   second 34   third 35   fourth 36–37
IV. The Lord speaks and Job replies 38:1–42:6
   1. The Lord's first speech and Job's answer 38:1–40:5

Study questions
1. Read through the book and briefly summarize a) the friends' conclusions about the cause of Job's suffering and b) Job's own feelings on the matter. Why do you think God was more pleased with what Job had said than with the arguments of the three friends (42:7–8)?
2. What do you learn about suffering from 'the look behind the scenes' given in chs. 1–2?
3. Why can we with confidence trust ourselves to God (*e.g.* 38:4; 42:2; 42:10)?
4. Try to pick out the main points that this book makes about the problem of suffering. Does the full Christian revelation add to this picture?

Reference books
F. I. Andersen, *Job* (IVP, 1976)
N. C. Habel, *The Book of Job* (SCM, 1985; John Knox, 1981)
D. Kidner, *The Wisdom of Proverbs, Job and Ecclesiastes* (IVP, 1985)
R. E. Murphy, *Wisdom Literature: Job, Proverbs, Ruth, Canticles, Ecclesiastes, Esther* (Eerdmans, U.S.A., 1981)

Psalms

Imagine the awe and thrill we would feel if it were possible to touch a piece of a robe worn by Christ, or to handle a chair he had made, or even to see the remains of the house where he lived. Many people do not realize that we can hold in our hands, in translation, a copy of the hymn book he used, for his hymn book was the book of Psalms.

There are three reasons why the Psalms are still, by common consent, so prominent in the worship of Christians of all denominations. First, they transport us through 2,000 years of time and put us in touch with Christ. The words we recite are the words he recited. Secondly, there is no other form of prayer and praise which so exactly suits all kinds of people living at all kinds of time. Thirdly, the Psalms put us in touch with God's people and the way they worshipped their Lord centuries before Christ came.

Christ nourished his spiritual life on the Psalter. Satan brought Psalm 91 to his mind in the temptation. On the cross he quoted the opening verse of Psalm 22. Very probably the hymn he sang with his disciples at the end of the Lord's Supper (Mt. 26:30) was the Hallel, the great hymn of praise which consists of Psalms 113–118. His declaration of himself as the Good Shepherd is reminiscent of 'The Lord is my shepherd' (Ps. 23). Before the cross he quoted from Psalm 6:3. Two of the Beatitudes in the Sermon on the Mount find their inspiration in Psalms 37:11 and 24:4. It is not surprising, therefore, that the Christian church followed his example and incorporated the Psalms into its devotional life.

The book of Psalms is the hymn book and prayer book of Solomon's temple, with the addition of some later psalms. The majority of them were composed to be sung in worship and many are plainly tied to the temple rituals, the variety of offerings (see Leviticus), days of fasting and other national celebrations. The breadth of worship and of human experience which they bring to us makes them a rich inheritance for the Christian church.

The Psalms look back over the span of human history and they praise God for who he is and for what he has done. Sometimes they refer to God's generous deeds in creation and provision for all men (what we sometimes call 'common grace'). Sometimes they look back to particular events in the history of God's people and praise him for his might and his mercy. Often the psalm is ascribed to a particular individual or to a particular feast, and this context helps us understand the details of the psalm and why the people are praising God.

The Psalms are not all praise, though. There is confession, and there is even complaint (see section on the imprecatory psalms). God's people knew it was impossible to hide anything from him and so they bring everything to him in their worship. This is why the book of Psalms has been such a source of encouragement to convicted, troubled and discouraged Christians. They declare that, though everything around is in chaos, 'Yet will I praise him'.

There is another important distinction to remember when approaching the Psalms. They have been valued by God's people through the ages because so many speak for 'the ordinary person'. They are cries of joy, pain and repentance from the man of God. But there are also psalms which have a definite 'royal' strand to them. Often they refer to David, but sometimes to the future king who will follow in 'David's line', the Messiah. Looking out for the distinctive characteristics of this type of psalm will help us to understand what sometimes seem like strange details and obscure references.

The selection of psalms which has been preserved for us is actually a collection of collections. It contains a combination of songs for national, personal and public worship. Some psalms are very clearly linked with personal experiences recorded elsewhere (*e.g.* Ps. 51 with David's sin in 2 Sa. 11–12).

As the church separated from the synagogue, the Jewish tunes were lost to the Christian community. Efforts have been made ever since to produce music so that the Psalms could be sung as well as recited. Gregorian and Anglican chant are notable examples. But in spite of their beauty and the fervent protestations of the musically educated, ordinary people have never found them easy. The difficulties created by the lack of metre in Hebrew poetry have been surmounted by paraphrasing the Psalms into verse. Few people realize how many of our popular hymns are paraphrases of the Psalms. Psalm 23 in the metrical version has become one of the best-known 'songs' in the English-speaking world.

Summary

The psalms divide into 5 books, each section ending with a doxology (*e.g.* 41:13).

Book I: 1–41 is the oldest section and all the psalms are ascribed to David except 1 and 33.

Book II: 42–72 has an ecclesiastical outlook, and since the covenant name of God, 'Yahweh' (the Lord), is used much less frequently than the more general 'God', it would seem that this book was compiled at a time when the name was beginning to be regarded as too sacred to be spoken.

Book III: 73–89 includes a section of the psalms of Asaph (73–83), and four psalms attributed to the sons of Korah (84; 85; 87; 88).

Book IV: 90–106 begins with the psalm of Moses; 101

and 103 bear the name of David; and 95–100 were possibly used at the Feast of Tabernacles.

Book V: 107–150 is mostly anonymous, but it includes two notable sections. The Hallel, the great act of praise (113–118), was used at the feasts of Passover and Tabernacles; probably it was 'the hymn' sung by Christ and the apostles after the Last Supper (Mt. 26:30). The 'Songs of Ascents' (120–134) may have been used by pilgrims on their way up to Jerusalem for the feasts.

In recent years, 'form criticism' has identified a number of categories of psalms (hymns, laments, thanksgivings, prayers and pieces for royal occasions) that are found in the Psalter and elsewhere in the Old Testament. In this way scholars have been able to suggest a probable historical situation in which a particular psalm was used. Thus, whereas some scholars were beginning to claim that many psalms belonged to the time after the exile, a later trend has been to regard most psalms as belonging to the period of the monarchy.

The Psalter indicates the great spiritual wealth of the Old Testament congregation, a wealth which was inherited by the church of the new covenant.

Hebrew poetry

This subject will repay study, and the reader is referred to one of the books listed below. Briefly, Hebrew poetry involves not rhyme and metre but rhythm and choice of words, and especially what is called 'parallelism'.

In parallelism a statement is made and then repeated in different words, or extended. This means that there is more time for the thought to 'sink in' and more than one aspect of the matter can be presented. Sometimes the second line of the 'couplet' is almost a straight repetition of the first, sometimes it amplifies or develops the idea, sometimes it emphasizes by stating the negative 'side of the coin'. You will find many examples of each kind in the Psalms.

In understanding a verse of Hebrew poetry, therefore, we must interpret the verse as a whole and must not draw a distinction between the two parts of the verse. Thus, 'He made known his ways to Moses, his acts to the people of Israel' (Ps. 103:7). It does not say that God made known only his *ways* to Moses and only his *acts* to the people of Israel. It is the verse as a whole which tells us that God was seen actively to work by Moses and the people of Israel whom he led.

The best translations try to reproduce something of the Hebrew rhythm. When they are used regularly, one quickly begins to enjoy the rhythm both of words and thought.

The Hebrew verb

The many permutations to be found in translations of the Psalms can be very confusing until we realize that the Hebrew verb does not have tenses in the sense that modern languages do. The forms of the Hebrew verb express two main ideas, that of completion and that of continuation. It was important to a Hebrew to know whether an action was continuing or had been completed. Both a completed action and a continuing action might be past, present or future. This accounts for the great variety to be found in translations and paraphrases of the Psalms. If each action may be completed or continuous, and at the same time past, present or future, the possible variations in translation are considerable. None of them alters the basic meaning of the verses, but until one understands this, the Psalms can be confusing.

Examples can be found by comparing any two versions of the Psalter. In Psalm 42:3 the RSV translates with a past tense, 'tears have been my food', but the NEB with a present tense, 'tears are my food'. In Psalm 67:6–7 the NIV translates with future tenses, 'the land will yield its harvest', but the RSV with past tenses, 'the earth has yielded its increase'.

Generalized experience

The Psalms speak in terms of 'generalized experience'. They are seldom precise. This has a bearing in three ways.

Many of the positive statements in the Psalter are true in a broad and general sense. In the whole sweep of history, and in the ultimate purpose of God, the good man prospers whereas the wicked are blown away like the chaff (Ps. 1), but it is not always true in a precise, particular way in the short term. Indeed, the Psalms themselves admit this. One psalm (73) is given over to a meditation about it. The first psalm is not only idealistically right, it is also historically correct in the long term, in the language of generalized experience.

The characteristic of generalized experience will affect our approach to the Psalms, especially if we come to them for the first time. Because they are a distillation of the broad gamut of human experience – misery, joy, broken-heartedness, despair, triumph, hilarity, complaint and praise – on every page of the Psalter some verse or phrase will be relevant to my condition now while, as we have said, the rest may seem irrelevant. We should not be troubled when this happens. In time, especially in a lifetime, more and more verses in each psalm will come alive as they speak to our condition. The thing to remember is that however we feel, whether we are deep in the 'miry pit' or whether our 'little hills rejoice on every side', there is a psalm to fit our mood or state. This accounts for the enduring and universal appeal of the Psalms. There is a continuity both of human life and the experience of God from then to now.

Conversely, their generalized experience makes them serviceable as moulds into which we pour our personal or corporate praises or prayers of the moment. It is this principle which underlies their use in liturgical worship. The Psalms are not meant to be used in church so that when we sing or recite or read them every verse is literally meant by every member of the congregation. They are to be used as moulds into which each individual member of the congregation pours his or her spiritual emotions while the fellowship corporately sings or recites them.

The Psalms are quoted in the New Testament more than any other Old Testament book.

The imprecatory psalms

Christians, taught to pray for those who despitefully use them, will have a problem with calls for vengeance found in some psalms (*e.g.* 35:1—8; 55:15; 58:6; 59; 69; 109; 137:8—9).

There are three possible ways of dealing with the problem: to reject as unchristian all the imprecatory psalms; to accept them and justify them; or to steer a middle course such as the following.

To the question, 'Can a Christian use these calls for vengeance?', we must answer a categorical 'No'. Where they clearly call for personal vengeance, they are entirely unacceptable today. But in repudiating them we shall do well to remember two things.

Firstly, they belong to the old covenant and, as we have said elsewhere, although the old covenant is a true revelation of God, and is to be revered as such, it is partial and inferior to the new covenant. It is unfair to expect those under the old covenant to have the same understanding as those under the new. In particular, the future life and the grace of the gospel were but dimly apprehended. Where justice is guaranteed in a life beyond this, there is not the same urgency to cry for vindication now. Where a knowledge of God's amazing grace is known, there is a willingness to forgive as we have been forgiven ('forgiving one another, as God in Christ forgave you', Eph. 4:32).

Secondly, we should recognize that some of the imprecations are a spontaneous and involuntary outburst of the moment, the voicing of uncontrollable anguish. Derek Kidner speaks of 'the shocking immediacy of a scream'.

Sometimes, however, they are concerned not with personal reprisal, but with the Lord's honour. A holy anger when others are hurt or wrongly treated is characteristic of Christ, as is zeal for the Lord's house (Jn. 2:17).

These psalms recognize that there is a moral balance for the universe and a moral governor (God) whose responsibility it is to maintain that balance. Sin and evil upset the balance and challenge the governor's authority. They proclaim that 'the wages of sin is death', and that God 'has fixed a day on which he will judge the world' (Rom. 6:23; Acts 17:31).

These passages may be used by Christians if they draw the spiritual truths out of them. Let the imprecations be turned against our own deceitful actions and impure motives and against the hosts of evil spirits in the heavenlies, and they lose their vindictiveness and become a cry for the judge of all the earth to do right (Gen. 18:25).

Writer and date

Two thirds of the Psalter has titles bearing names, and since these titles appear in the Greek Old Testament they must be older than 150 BC, which means that the traditions are very long-standing. The name may indicate the author of the psalm, or it may refer to the experience of that person. When our Bible prints 'A Psalm of David', for instance, it may mean 'A Psalm to David', and may not have been written by him.

One is ascribed to Moses (Ps. 90), 73 to David, 2 to Solomon, 12 to Asaph, 11 to the sons of Korah, and one each to Heman and Ethan, the Ezrahites. The references to Asaph may be to earlier collections of psalms.

Study questions

1. Psalms were written mainly for corporate worship. What principles for this activity can you find, for example, in Psalms 24, 95, 115, 122, 133 and 149?

2. Compare Psalm 22 with the Gospel accounts of the crucifixion. In what specific ways was the psalm fulfilled in Christ's death?

3. Explain verse by verse what Psalm 23 means for practical Christian living today.

4. Make a list of commands to the believer found in Psalm 37:1–11.

5. What comfort from Psalm 103 would you offer to a Christian in trouble?

6. What can be learnt about prayer from Psalm 130?

7. What do you learn about God from Psalm 139?

8. Rewrite Psalm 150 in your own words.

Reference books

A. A. Anderson, *Psalms,* 2 vols. (Oliphants, 1972; Eerdmans, 1972)

B. W. Anderson, *Out of the Depths* (rev. ed. Westminster, 1983)

J. H. Eaton, *The Psalms Come Alive* (Mowbrays, 1984; IVP, 1986)

J. E. Goldingay, *Songs from a Strange Land* (Psalms 42-51) (IVP, 1978)

J. Hargreaves, *A Guide to the Psalms* (SPCK, U.S.A., 1973)

D. Kidner, *Psalms,* 2 vols. (IVP, 1973, 1975)

C. S. Lewis, *Reflections on the Psalms* (Fontana, 1960; Harcourt, Brace, 1964)

Proverbs

Practical, personal religion for the ordinary believer is the emphasis of the book of Proverbs. Much of the Bible rightly and necessarily consists of doctrinal teaching or of corporate instruction for the church, or of the application of the gospel to social life and its problems. Certainly in all this is to be found much advice, instruction and encouragement for the individual Christian. But nowhere, except in the book of Proverbs, and possibly the Psalms, will the Christian find gathered together in one place practical and experimental teaching for everyday living.

The detailed, proverbial nature of the book's material makes it impossible usefully to write fully about it without writing a commentary on each section. This has been done by Derek Kidner in his commentary on the book of Proverbs. His work is so outstanding that we recommend you obtain a copy and use it as you read Proverbs.

Because it has thirty-one chapters it is often used for daily Bible reading, one chapter a day each month. There is no better way of becoming acquainted with its down-to-earth wisdom.

The theme of this collection of wise sayings is to be found in 9:10 – 'The fear of the Lord is the beginning of wisdom', or paraphrased, 'A worshipping submission to the Lord is the continuing principle of wisdom' (Kidner, p. 59).

Summary
The book consists of seven collections of wisdom teaching. The first comprises thirteen lessons on wisdom given by a

sage to his disciple, the climax being the personification of Wisdom in chapter 8. There are two collections of Solomon's proverbs (10:1–22:16 and 25:1–29:27), and these support the picture of Solomon which we see elsewhere in Scripture (1 Ki. 3; 4:29–34; 10). They frequently use illustrations from nature (*cf.* 1 Ki. 4:33).

Sandwiched between these two collections are two others consisting of 'the sayings of the wise' (22:17–24:22 and 24:23–34). 'The wise' played a major part in education and in policy-making throughout the ancient near east (*cf.* Is. 19:11f.; Dn. 3:24, 27) including Israel (*cf.* 1 Ch. 27:32f.; Is. 3:3).

The sixth and seventh collections are 'the sayings of Agur' (30:1–33) and 'the sayings of Lemuel' – or, to be strictly accurate, the sayings of Lemuel's mother (31:1–9). We do not know who these men were. The book closes with an anonymous appendix on 'the perfect wife', written as an acrostic poem, verses beginning with successive letters of the Hebrew alphabet.

Writer and date
We have already seen that the book is a compilation of various collections and there is no reason to doubt the authenticity of these. We do not know when the book received its present form, but it may have passed through several stages as collections were added.

See also 'Wisdom literature', under Job.

Contents
1. Introduction: title, purpose and theme 1:1–7
2. Teaching about wisdom 1:8–9:18
3. The proverbs of Solomon 10:1–22:16
4. Thirty words of wise men 22:17–24:22
5. An excursus: more words of wise men 24:23–34
6. More proverbs of Solomon (Hezekiah's collection) 25:1–29:27

7. The words of Agur 30
8. The words of King Lemuel 31:1–9
9. An acrostic poem: in praise of a good wife 31:10–31

Study questions
1. As you read through the whole book, make six collections of proverbs under the following headings: discipline; hard work and laziness; money matters; honesty and dishonesty; friendship and neighbourliness; pride and humility.
2. List the characteristics of wisdom given in ch. 8. Which ones are found in Christ (*cf.* 1 Cor. 1:30)?
3. With a concordance study 'the fool'. What are his characteristics?
4. From this book give practical instructions to Christians on a) husband and wife, b) parents and children, c) old and young.
5. Paraphrase 31:10–31 to describe today's 'ideal wife'.

Reference books
D. Kidner, *The Wisdom of Proverbs, Job and Ecclesiastes* (IVP, 1985)

D. Kidner, *Proverbs* (IVP, 1964)

C. W. Turner, *Studies in Proverbs* (Baker, U.S.A., 1977)

Ecclesiastes

'Has life any meaning? Where is satisfaction to be found? How can the facts of injustice and death be met?' The writer might have been twentieth-century man. His problems are the problems which worry us today. The perplexities of the modern secular society are reflected in his thinking. Some have compared the book to Pascal's *Pensées*.

He calls himself 'Qoheleth', Ecclesiastes being the Greek equivalent. The name means 'one who convenes and addresses an assembly', the preacher. His exact identification is a problem for scholars. There seem to be clear references to Solomon, son of King David, and traditionally one of the wisest men of all time. Solomon lived 900 years before Christ and these read like 'extracts from his diary', published by some unknown editor at least 200 years before Christ.

Three phrases constantly recur in the book: 'man under the sun', 'a striving after wind' and 'vanity of vanities'. The first phrase gives the setting of the writer. He is viewing life on the human level, life with the supernatural omitted, the life of the thorough-going secularist.

These phrases raise the question of the message of the writer. What is he trying to say? Is he speaking as a secularist? The over-all tone of the book is pessimistic, and the references to God could be explained on the assumption that, like many a reasoning budding atheist, he occasionally turns to theism in the hope of finding a solution to the problems he meets. He could be the Old Testament counterpart of the nominal Christian, a man whose thinking is predominantly worldly-wise, but who occasionally gives a nod to God in an attempt to rationalize his problems and to provide a spiritual insurance policy for himself.

His chosen name, the preacher, however, seems to suggest that his aim is didactic. He intends to set out the philosophies of despair and pleasure and what today might be called the scheme of secular and humanistic thinking and the hedonistic refuge of the sceptic, only so that he may show how they come to disaster on the rocks of human experience. The passages expressing trust in God, even though his ways are inscrutable, are his solution for man's problems.

Summary

Is there any meaning to human existence? The preacher turns to various pursuits in a search for satisfaction but each ends in failure and eventually he gives up the struggle. All is vanity (1–2).

He is ruthlessly realistic and insists that both evil and death must be faced. Man's wistful intuition that somewhere there must be a solution to the riddle of existence is contradicted by injustice, unfairness and the fact of evil. Perhaps the answer is to be found in fatalism (3–6).

In a poem of exquisite but mournful beauty he sets out the philosophy of pessimism. The attempt of the anti-supernaturalist to ignore, forget or laugh at death is rigorously opposed. 'Death conquers all' must be the reasonable conclusion of those who choose to 'live under the sun' (7:1–9:18).

Is the theist any better off than the sceptic, the materialist and the secularist? 'Yes, he is', says the preacher. For the man who will fear God and keep his commandments, there is pleasure, friendship and contentment to be enjoyed in this life. He compiles hints for practical God-fearing living (10–12).

Ecclesiastes demonstrates the futility of life without God. It is left to the New Testament to expand the theism of Ecclesiastes and to present the Lord Jesus Christ as the Saviour for man's helplessness.

Writer and date

The language and diction indicate a time much later than Solomon. Young says, 'The author of the book was one who lived in the post-exilic period (after 537 BC), and who placed his words in the mouth of Solomon, thus employing a literary device for conveying his message.' It may be that the first verse is intended to suggest an ideal presentation of Solomon's outlook. There is no consensus of opinion about who the author was.

Structure and contents

1. Attempts to find meaning in life 1:1–2:26
   Life has no meaning 1:1–11   Philosophy 1:12–18 Pleasure 2:1–11   Death conquers all 2:12–23   Pleasing God 2:24–26
2. Life's discouragements 3–4
   Where's the pattern? 3:1–15   Injustice 3:16–17   Just an animal 3:18–22   Oppression and envy 4:1–4 Resentment and contentment 4:5–6   The miser 4:7–8 Friendship 4:9–12   Popularity 4:13–16
3. Life's dangers 5:1–6:9
   Worship 5:1–9   Wealth 5:10–17   Eat, drink and be merry 5:18–20   Wealth again 6:1–9
4. Fatalism and pessimism 6:10–7:29
5. Make the best of it 8–9
   Authority 8:1–9   Death again 8:10–9:6   Enjoy life 9:7– 10   Opportunity needed 9:11–17
6. Practical hints for living 10:1–11:8
7. Youth and age 11:9–12:8
8. Conclusion 12:9–14

Study questions

1. Which verses in Ecclesiastes do you find especially striking and why?

2. From this book counter the arguments of a) the secularist and b) the optimistic materialist.

3. Chapter 12 gives a poetic description of old age. Write down in your own words what each picture means.

4. Using 3:11 as your starting-point, map out the major themes and teaching of Ecclesiastes.

Reference books

M. A. Eaton, *Ecclesiastes, and Introduction and Commentary* (IVP, 1983)

W. J. Fuerst, *Ruth, Esther, Ecclesiastes, Song of Songs, Lamentations* (Cambridge, 1975)

D. Kidner, *The Wisdom of Proverbs, Job and Ecclesiastes* (IVP, 1985)

D. Kidner, *The Message of Ecclesiastes* (IVP, 1976)

Song of Solomon

If the church had listened to the message of this book, it would not bear the stigma today of being unrealistic about sex.

At first sight it is puzzling to find poems so blatantly sensual, glorying in the physical aspect of sex, in the Bible. But God made everything good, including the relationship between male and female.

Song of Solomon (also called Song of Songs and Canticles) crystallizes the Bible teaching that sex, physical sex, is good when it is enjoyed in the manner God intended. There are still very many people both inside and outside the churches who have an unscripturally negative attitude to sex. Their prudishness and inhibition is as unbiblical at one extreme as libertarianism is at the other. The beauty of the human form, male or female, and the delight of physical love-making within the bounds of marriage come from the Giver of all good gifts.

Only when this is fully appreciated and accepted is it right to use the book in another way. The New Testament calls the church 'the bride of Christ' (*e.g.* Eph. 5:23–33; Rev. 21:9). The Song can be used to illustrate this relationship between Christ and his church. This follows the pattern set by the Jews, who saw in it the relationship between Israel and the Lord. Some well-known hymns have been inspired by words in this book.

Summary
There are three main approaches to the structure of the

Song and so the content can be summarized in three different ways:

1. *Solomon and the Shulammite* On this view the book depicts the love that existed between Solomon and a Shulammite maiden whom he had brought to his palace. Chapters 1–2 record their praises of each other's beauty; chapter 3 is a soliloquy by the girl, and in chapter 4 Solomon praises her. In chapter 5 the girl describes a dream in which she cannot find her lover, but in chapters 6–8 they again rejoice in each other's love.

2. *The Shulammite, the shepherd and Solomon* Those who take this approach think that the real love-story was taking place between the Shulammite girl and her shepherd lover. She, however, has been captured and placed in Solomon's harem, where she daydreams about her true love and relates a recurrent dream about him to the other women (1:1–3:5). Solomon attempts to win her but her thoughts turn to her lover, and she recounts another dream about him (3:6–5:16). Again she refuses to be moved by Solomon's praises (6–7), and is finally reunited with her shepherd (8).

3. *Love-songs* Some see the book simply as a collection of love-songs or poems, perhaps to be used at a wedding. The *Good News Bible* divides the book into six songs.

There are difficulties in all these views and we do not really know how to work out the structure of the book. What is plain is the richness and beauty of the couple's love for each other, strikingly expressed in images drawn from both nature and fine architecture.

When reading the book for the first time, it is helpful to use the GNB or the NIV which provide sub-headings to distinguish between the words of the man and those of the woman.

Writer and date

The opening does not help in assigning authorship, for the first verse can mean that Solomon wrote it or that it was written for or about Solomon. Tradition assigns authorship to him and this is not impossible, but some scholars believe the book to be later than Solomon's time. The authorship is of little importance and certainty is impossible.

Study questions
1. Taking 2:7 as your starting-point, study the book's insights into personal relationships.
2. With the aid of a hymn book, and the scripture references at the heading of the hymns, make a list of hymns which find their inspiration in the Song of Songs.

Reference books

G. L. Carr, *The Song of Solomon* (IVP, 1984)

W. J. Fuerst, *Ruth, Esther, Ecclesiastes, Song of Songs, Lamentations* (Cambridge, 1975)

S. C. Glickman, *A Song for Lovers* (IVP, U.S.A., 1976)

J. H. Taylor, *Union and Communion* (Bethany House, U.S.A., 1971)

Historical Background to the Exile

From the middle of the ninth century BC, even before Amos, the earliest of the Old Testament prophets, the Assyrian Empire was dominant and harassing the countries of the middle east. Due to civil war, it had been weak during the reigns of Jeroboam II of Israel (782–753 BC) and of Uzziah of Judah (767–740 BC), but in 745 BC an Assyrian general named Pul seized the throne of Nineveh, assumed the title Tiglath-pileser III, and implemented a policy of aggression and expansion which continued for the next 150 years. It reached its climax when the Assyrians defeated the Egyptians and sacked the city of Thebes in 663 BC.

Damascus, Tyre and the northern kingdom of Israel became tributary to Assyria until King Pekah of Israel (740–732 BC and King Rezin of Damascus (750–732 BC) revolted and attacked Judah presumably in an effort to force her to join them in opposing Assyria (sometimes called the Syro-Ephraimite War; c. 735 BC). King Ahaz of Judah (732–716 BC; co-regent from 744 BC), against the advice of Isaiah, appealed to Tiglath-pileser of Assyria for help (Is. 7:3–9). Assyria reacted strongly. She first captured the Philistine cities to the south of Judah (743 BC) and then Damascus (732 BC). Israel yielded and lost Transjordan and Galilee, with deportations, and Judah became tributary to Assyria (2 Ki. 15:29; 16:9; 1 Ch. 5:6, 26).

With an increase in Egyptian power, Israel again revolted and Samaria fell to the Assyrians in 722 BC (2 Ki. 18:9–12).

Judah remained loyal to Assyria until Egyptian intrigues increasingly tempted King Hezekiah (716–687 BC) to rebel.

Hezekiah was one of the leaders in the west when most of
the empire rose in revolt upon the accession of Sennacherib
to the throne of Assyria (705–681 BC). The Egyptian army
collapsed in 701 BC and Hezekiah yielded to Assyria on
demanding terms (2 Ki. 18:13–16). The treacherous Sennacherib afterwards changed his mind and demanded the
surrender of Jerusalem, but Hezekiah, encouraged by Isaiah, refused to comply (Is. 36:1; 37:5–6, *cf.* Is. 33:1–12;
2 Ki. 19:5–7). Sennacherib wrote a threatening letter but
then suddenly abandoned the siege, perhaps because the
Assyrian army had been attacked by bubonic plague on the
Egyptian border (2 Ki. 19:8–9; Is. 37:9–37), and Hezekiah
was allowed to end his reign in peace.

Manasseh, Hezekiah's son (687–642 BC), remained loyal
to Assyria. King Josiah (640–609 BC) managed to strengthen
Judah's position but was killed when he foolishly tried to
intercept Pharaoh Neco of Egypt, who went to the help of
the Assyrians against the Babylonians in 609 BC (2 Ki.
23:29).

In fact, the Assyrian Empire had begun to crumble about
626 BC when Nabopolassar (626–605 BC), governor of southern Babylonia, took control of Babylon and destroyed Nineveh in 612 BC. His son, Nebuchadnezzar, as crown
prince, brought the Assyrian Empire to an end at the battle
of Carchemish (605 BC), when he also defeated the Egyptian
forces, threatened Jerusalem and took Daniel and his three
friends to Babylon (2 Ki. 24:1; Dn. 1:1). He became king
of Babylon in the same year (605–562 BC).

Until King Jehoiakim (609–597 BC) again linked Judah
with Egypt, Nebuchadnezzar kept him on the throne in
Jerusalem, but in 597 BC, infuriated by Jehoiakim's defec-
tion, he took Jerusalem. Since Jehoiakim had died, Nebuchadnezzar deported his son Jehoiachin to Babylon. The
prophet Ezekiel also went into exile at this time. Zedekiah
was placed on the throne. He, too, fell to the temptation to
ally himself with Egypt and the Babylonian forces sacked

Jerusalem (587 BC) and deported large numbers of Jews to Babylon. Thus there were three stages in the fall of Jerusalem, 605, 597 and 587 BC. At first the captives suffered great distress (Ps. 137) but eventually they settled down and lived quietly and in reasonable comfort. In 559 BC Cyrus II ascended the throne of Persia, defeated the Median army in 549 BC and united the kingdoms of Persia and Media. With the defeat of Croesus, king of Lydia, in 566 BC the empire of Cyrus absorbed the whole of Asia Minor. In 539 BC Cyrus took Babylon and issued the edict which allowed captive nations to return to their homelands (2 Ch. 36:22–23; Ezk. 1:1–4).

The Prophets

The word 'prophet' or 'seer' is applied to many individuals throughout the Old Testament. Abraham was the first to receive the name (Gn. 20:7, *cf.* Ps. 105:15) but Moses was regarded as the great example of prophetic character (see below; *cf.* Dt. 18:15–19; 34:10). But 'The Prophets' in our English Bibles usually refers to the books named after the cluster of individuals we call prophets who lived from the late eighth to mid fifth centuries BC, around the time of the exile.

Other religions had prophets who claimed to speak for their god, but most of these did so while in a state of trance or frenzied activity (see Elijah's contest with the prophets of Baal in 1 Kings 17). The rational, almost homely nature of many of the prophets of Yahweh stands out in sharp contrast to this (though Ezekiel in particular, and the Old Testament prophets generally, also have a strong element of the visionary).

The prophet was, first and foremost, one who was called by God, at his initiative, to know him. The different prophets came from many walks of life and had quite distinct personalities, but they all had this hallmark of a special, direct relationship with the Almighty God. And it was only because of this that they were able to speak God's words for the immediate circumstances and to look to what he was going to do in the future. They were 'seers' because they had God's perspective on the matters through their closeness to him; they were, as Alec Motyer has put it, 'in the know'.

We have seen how often and repeatedly the people of Israel 'forgot' the Lord their God who had called them his own, made them a nation and continued to preserve them. The prophets called the Israelites back to God and so they often appear at particular crisis-points in the nation's history. Too often the people took the lazy way out and hoped that the ritual and sacrifices which were meant to symbolize their penitence and their keeping of the covenant would serve as a substitute for them.

Each of the prophets brings a message to his contemporaries which, although varying with the circumstances, had certain basic themes. He reminded the Israelites that their God was still ruling in history, that he called his people to repentance, that morality and justice *did* matter and that therefore there would be both judgment and hope in the future (particularly through the 'Coming One' who would usher in a new age). And each had an uphill, discouraging and largely unrewarded ministry amongst a stubborn and self-centred people. They lived lives of sacrificial service to God and to his people, for they were called to be themselves a sign and a demonstration of what God was saying.

'The word of the Lord came to X' is the phrase that describes how God's message was revealed to the prophets. This is simple and direct, but ultimately mysterious. We do not know how God communicated with the prophets (though sometimes dreams and visions were involved), but we can recognize the conviction and authority with which they say 'Thus says the Lord'. How were the message and messenger authenticated? Scripture gives its own yardsticks: the words of a true prophet will always be fulfilled and his teaching will be orthodox; a false prophet's words will usually fail to be fulfilled (but see Dt. 13:1–2), and his teaching will be a perversion of established teaching.

The word of God through the prophets came in a variety of ways and is expressed variously, often with additional colour from the prophet's own background and personality; they were no mere 'typewriters'. Sometimes the prophecies came in the shape of parables or allegories (Is. 5:1–7; 2 Sa. 12:1–7; Ezk. 16; 23). Sometimes the prophet's role was a dramatic one, and he had to present an 'acted oracle' to the people (2 Ki. 13:14ff.; Je. 19; Ezk. 4). These dramatizations are more than a 'visual aid', however; they are an actual demonstration of the reality of the prophetic message.

In the form of the prophecy, as in every aspect of prophetic activity, the initiative lay with God. The prophet himself was always secondary; his message was more important than his person. Indeed it often exceeded the bounds of the immediate historical context and looked to 'Messiah' and the 'end times'. Its full meaning was sometimes beyond the appreciation of even the prophet himself; with Christian perspective we can see fulfilments of which the prophet of the old covenant was probably unaware. But through these men, called and faithful, God has spoken for all time.

Reference books

A. J. Heschel, *The Prophets* (Harper, 1962)

G. von Rad, *The Message of the Prophets* (Harper, U.S.A., 1972)

R. B. Y. Scott, *The Relevance of the Prophets* (Macmillan, U.S.A., 1944)

L. J. Wood, *The Prophets of Israel* (Baker, U.S.A., 1979)

Time Chart of the Prophets

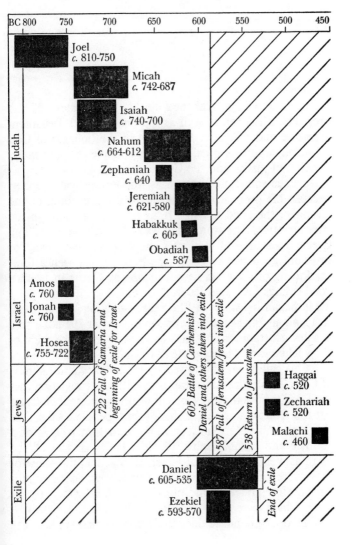

Isaiah

Isaiah is generally reckoned to be the greatest of the prophets. His book is seen as the peak of Old Testament literature and theology. His vision of the holiness of God (6) inspires him to reveal God to his people as, supremely, the God of justice and the God of love.

Isaiah is sometimes known as 'the evangelical prophet' because his prophecy lends itself to the preaching of the 'evangel', the good news of Jesus Christ, especially in the later chapters. The word itself was derived from him. The Greek translation of 40:9 uses the verb *euangelizomai*, 'to proclaim good news'. Christians have always seen a foreshadowing of the good news brought by Christ in Isaiah's good tidings for the exiles in Babylon.

He began his work in 'the year that King Uzziah died' (6:1), about 740 BC, and continued until after 701 BC. There is a Jewish tradition that he was sawn apart in the reign of the wicked king Manasseh (687-642 BC).

At his call he was overawed by the majesty and holiness of God. This stamped his ministry with the conviction that the Lord is both the awesome, altogether-different God and yet the God who is near to his faithful people. 'I dwell in the high and holy place, and also with him who is of a contrite and humble spirit' (57:15). He is God of all the earth as well as the God of Israel. In practice, this sense of the sovereignty of God made him unhappy about any reliance on foreign allies, and impatient with religious observances which were not coupled with social righteousness.

The background to his ministry was that Judah, the

southern kingdom, and Israel, the northern kingdom, were buffer states between the powerful Assyrian Empire in the north and Egypt in the south. Isaiah also foresaw the rising threat of Babylon when it replaced the Assyrian Empire.

It is helpful to consider the book in three parts. Chapters 1–39 contain history and prophecies related to Judah in Isaiah's own time (740–687 BC, *i.e.* over 100 years before the fall of Jerusalem in 587 BC). Chapters 40–55 relate to the days just before the exiles were allowed to return home by the edict of Cyrus, king of Persia, in 538 BC. This was 150 years after Isaiah's day. Chapters 56–66 are addressed to the returned exiles in Judea and Jerusalem after their return in 538 BC.

Summary

Judah's God is 'the Holy One of Israel' but, in contrast, the people are guilty – socially, morally and spiritually. One day Jerusalem will be God's city for all nations (2:2–4 is a prophecy shared with Isaiah's contemporary, Micah (Mi. 4:1–3)). For this reason the people's wickedness and pride must be eradicated, for there will be no evil in the city. The Jewish nation is God's vineyard. It produces only wild grapes, yet the Lord will not reject it for ever. Isaiah has a vision of God and is called to be his prophet to the people (1–6).

King Ahaz of Judah (732–716 BC) defies the Lord and is attacked by Syria and Israel (the Syro-Ephraimite war). Isaiah pleads with him to trust in the Lord but he turns to Assyria for help instead. The wickedness of the northern kingdom will end in its destruction by the Assyrians, though the conqueror, too, will be judged. The perfect king will come and set up the perfect kingdom and the earth will be God-centred (7–12).

The nations surrounding Judah and Israel are warned that judgment is also in store for them. Jerusalem will fall, its walls will be broken down, the temple will be destroyed and the people will panic. Indeed, God will judge the whole world but this, too, will ultimately lead to joy for the faithful (13–27).

Shortly before the fall of Samaria (722 BC), unwise negotiations with Egypt culminate in King Hezekiah of Judah's rebellion and the Assyrians' swift retribution in 701 BC. The religious and secular leaders mislead the people. Jerusalem will be besieged but not taken. Neither Egypt nor Assyria is to be trusted, but the Lord will save the people. Far in the future there will come a day of peace, justice and righteousness. There will be days before then when only those trusting God will survive (28–35).

Sennacherib, the king of Assyria, besieges Jerusalem (701 BC) but Hezekiah, encouraged by Isaiah, refuses to surrender. The Lord intervenes and Sennacherib withdraws (*cf.* 2 Ki. 18:13–19:37). Hezekiah is taken ill but through Isaiah the Lord promises him another fifteen years of life. He unwisely shows the treasures of his house to a Babylonian envoy and Isaiah foresees the exile to Babylon which was to happen more than 100 years later (36–39). (It may be that the last two sections (36–37 and 38–39) have been chronologically reversed. The first refers to the Assyrians and the second to the future rise of Babylon.)

There is a gap of over 100 years between the scenes of chapter 39 and those of chapter 40. For over fifty years the exiles had waited in Babylon and some began to believe that the Babylonian gods were stronger than the Lord, and that the exile would be permanent. (Most of this section is in poetry. The poems of Lamentations and some of these prophecies may have been used in worship during the last days in Babylon.)

So Isaiah brings to them a picture of God as the all-sovereign one. He exercises his will in the world of nature and through foreign kings. The prophecy looks forward to Israel being freed from Babylon (*c.* 550 BC), a remnant returning to their homeland. And the return will mean

more than freedom for God's people; it will mean the fulfilment of God's original plan to bless the world through
them (Gn. 22:18). The great deliverer is to be Cyrus, the
new king of Persia. With his encouragement, Jerusalem
and its temple will be rebuilt (40–48).

But the second theme in this great section is that, though
Israel is freed from foreign dominion, she is still ruled by
her own sin. Thus chapters 49–55 show how Israel can be
freed from that too, by the suffering servant of the Lord.
God has a glorious world-wide plan for his faithful servant
to perform (49–55).

The final section of the book contains prophecies relating
to Israel's return from exile. Some of the exiles, led by
Zerubbabel (see the book of Ezra), have returned to Jerusalem, although many preferred to stay in Babylon when
the time came. The people's sin has led to all kinds of
corruption, but God works in this far from perfect situation
to bring restoration to the faithful (56–59).

Both city and temple have yet to be rebuilt. Life for the
returned exiles is difficult but the Lord promises gladness
for those who mourn and success for those who are discouraged. The prophet resolves to pray constantly and the
Lord promises to work for those who wait for him. One
day from distant lands men will stream to Zion (60–66).

Major themes
1. *'The Holy One of Israel'* This description of Yahweh is
a particular characteristic of the book of Isaiah and is used
almost thirty times in its chapters. It expresses for Isaiah
the real tension which exists in God's relation to his people.
Because God is so holy his justice demands that he judge
Israel in her continuing sin. And yet because of his love he
does not break his covenant with her and will continue to
bless the faithful 'remnant'.

2. *'Remnant will return'* Herein lies another of Isaiah's

favourite expressions. He even gives one of his sons that name (Shear-jashub). It is in the idea of the remnant that Isaiah finds a reconciliation between his two apparently conflicting themes, the justice and the love of God.

Isaiah realized that merely to be 'Israel' by physical descent did not make a 'people of God'. There needed to be a resolution of the human problem of sin and guilt before that could be true. So he foresaw the removal of the inadequate nation and its kings; they would be cut down like trees and replaced (6:13; 11:1). With the remnant would come the king, the servant of God, who would triumph where others had failed. God's perfect plan was to be fulfilled even through the failure of Israel. This servant was the one who would accomplish all that Israel and her kings had so singularly failed to do. He would be, as H. L. Ellison puts it, 'the Remnant to whom the remnant had pointed'.

3. 'Servant of the Lord' Although this expression has been used before in the record of the people of Israel (of Moses and David, for instance), Isaiah brings a new, more particular definition to the term. Especially in the new section of the book beginning in chapter 40 there is developed a picture of one who is obedient, suffers to the point of death, and through whom the sin of the people can be removed.

Four poems are known as the 'Servant Songs'. In the first (42:1–9), the servant's mission is one of encouragement. In the second (49:1–13) he is sent not only to Israel but also to the whole world. In the third (50:4–9) he perseveres against opposition, and in the fourth (52:13–53:12) he suffers so that many may be forgiven.

Most Jewish and some Christian writers identify the servant with the whole nation of Israel or, at least, with a faithful remnant within it. Although there may be truth in this, there is a difference between the portrait of the servant in the songs and that of Israel in the main prophecy. Ideas that the servant is an Old Testament historical figure, perhaps Isaiah himself, are now less popular than they used to be.

The New Testament sees a portrait of the Lord Jesus Christ in the first poem (42:1-9, *cf.* Mt. 12:17-21) and in the fourth poem (52:13-53:12, *cf.* Mt. 8:17; Acts 8:32-34; 1 Pet. 2:21-24). Jesus himself applied 53:12 to himself (Lk. 22:37), and interpreted 61:1-2, a passage similar to the 'Servant Songs', as relating to himself (Lk. 4:17-19).

Thus *The Lion Handbook to the Bible* can say, 'The New Testament writers are in no doubt that the servant Isaiah foresaw – who would save men by suffering on their behalf – was Jesus Christ (Mt. 12:15-21). They have Christ's own authority for saying so (Lk. 4:16-21)' (p. 390).

Writer and date

The traditional Christian and Jewish view has been that Isaiah, the eighth-century BC prophet, is the author of the whole book, but this position has been maintained only by conservative scholars in the present century. The Hebrew scrolls support this (*cf.* Lk. 4:17). In the Dead Sea Scrolls, for example, the book covers two scrolls which divide the material in the middle, after chapter 33, not after 39 as most modern scholars do. Ecclesiasticus 48:22-25 (*c.* 200 BC) also attributes the whole book to Isaiah.

But the past century has seen much critical discussion of the stylistic and theological differences between chapters 1–39 and chapters 40-66. So, it has been argued, the book has been compiled from material not only from Isaiah but, later, from his 'school', which began with the disciples he undoubtedly had. Some arguments, it must be said, have been based as much on the presupposition that there is no such thing as predictive prophecy, as on any textual grounds. The Dead Sea Scrolls make no break between chapters 39 and 40, even though they begin chapter 40 on the bottom line of a page, where a gap could most conveniently have been left.

Most Old Testament scholars today, although disagreeing on many details, hold to the view that the first section (1–39) is substantially by Isaiah himself, that 40–55 is by a mysteriously anonymous and otherwise unknown sixth-century BC prophet in exile in Babylon ('Deutero-Isaiah'), and that 56–66 ('Trito-Isaiah') is by a school of Isaiah's followers in Jerusalem after the return from exile. Objectors point out that Isaiah presents a God 'declaring the end from the beginning and from ancient times things not yet done' (46:10), who challenges the pagan gods to try to do the same (41:23; 44:7). Prediction is a mark of God's sovereignty over history, his signature to his dramatic interventions in it. Not only does God foretell the Babylonian exile through Isaiah; beyond that he predicts the new covenant (59:21), the death and resurrection of Messiah (53:4–12), the worldwide spread of the gospel (66:18–21) and the life of the age to come (11:6–9; 65:17–25; 66:22–24).

Conservative scholars argue that if the possibility of predictive prophecy is allowed, there is no decisive argument against the view that the entire prophecy originated with Isaiah.

The book is very complicated and not at all uniform in its construction. The collection of visions and prophecies certainly belong to many different periods of Isaiah's life and prophetic task. The order is not entirely chronological, nor has it been organized consistently according to subject-matter. At the present time it is impossible to know just how the book was put together.

The major sections of the book have their own distinctive characteristics of thought and language, but there are also striking similarities which bind the book together as a unity.

Structure and contents

   I. The Lord's controversy with Judah and Israel 1–12
     1. The Lord and Jerusalem 1–5

Study questions

1. List the sins of Judah in ch. 1. Which of them can you
recognize in a) our society and b) our church today?
2. What aspects of his nature did God reveal to Isaiah in
ch. 6? How did Isaiah respond? Does your understanding
of, and response to, God need to be modified in the light
of this?
3. Chapters 7:10–17; 9:6–7 and 11:1–12:6 are often taken
as looking forward to Christ. With the aid of a commentary,
find out what these prophecies could have meant in Isaiah's
own day. In what ways are they supremely fulfilled in
Christ?
4. List all the characteristics of God mentioned in ch. 40.
In the light of them what would you say of the people's
reaction in 40:27? Are we ever like them?
5. In what ways does Christ fulfil the descriptions of the
servant in 42:1–4; 49:1–6 and 50:4–11?
6. Chapter 47 is about Babylon, an anti-God state, and 48
is about God's sinful people. What are the main features of
each? Can you see parallels today?
7. Read the account of Philip and the Ethiopian in Acts
8:26–38. The Ethiopian was puzzling over Isaiah's fourth

Servant Song (52:13–53:12). If you had been Philip, how would you have told the Ethiopian 'the good news of Jesus' from this scripture?

8. From the rest of ch. 58, answer the people's question in verse 3. What does this chapter teach you about the outward evidences of genuine religion (*cf.* Jas. 1:26–27; 2:14–17; 5:1–6)?

Reference books

R. E. Clements, *Isaiah 1-39* (Marshall Pickering, 1980; Eerdmans, 1980)

G. A. F. Knight, *Servant Theology* (Handsel, 1983; Eerdmans, 1983)

G. A. F. Knight, *The New Israel* (Handsel, 1985; Eerdmans, 1985)

H. C. Leupold, *Exposition of Isaiah* (Evangelical Press, 1977; Baker, 1977)

J. Ridderbos, *Isaiah* (Zondervan, U.S.A., 1985)

R. M. Whybray, *Isaiah 40-66* (Marshall Pickering, 1976; Eerdmans, 1976)

H. M. Wolf, *Interpreting Isaiah* (Zondervan, U.S.A., 1985)

E. J. Young, *The Book of Isaiah,* 3 vols. (Eerdmans, U.S.A., 1964, 1969, 1971)

Jeremiah

Jeremiah has been called the prophet of the broken heart. Some have even said that he is the nearest likeness to Christ to be found in the Old Testament. Indeed, in the days when Christ was on earth, some people thought he was a reincarnation of Jeremiah (Mt. 16:14).

A patriot, he was given the unenviable task of calling for surrender to one of the national enemies, Babylon, because he knew this to be God's purpose. It is little wonder that his sorrow and despair have come to be popularly misunderstood. 'A Jeremiah' brands a person today as a miserable pessimist. Of course, when he is compared with Christ, his deficiencies show. He pleaded to be spared when threatened with imprisonment and his resentment turned sometimes into vindictiveness.

Jeremiah came of a priestly family though we are never told that he himself practised as a priest. His home was at Anathoth, a town three or four miles north-east of Jerusalem, assigned to the Levites.

He was sensitive and tender in personality, a man of courage, who after forty years of opposition and sometimes persecution, remained unembittered by his experiences. He was commissioned not only to foretell Jerusalem's and the temple's destruction, but to urge and command that no resistance be given to the armies of Babylon.

The capture of Jerusalem and subsequent deportations for seventy years' exile were eventually inevitable because of the nation's political, religious and moral disobedience.

Jeremiah had first of all to contend with his own burden

of distress at what he saw happening and of having his diagnosis and remedy rejected by king and people (26:9–19; 36:22–25). Secondly, he had to discover and then to speak the Lord's will in a political crisis of frightening perplexity. Thirdly, although the political situation was frightening, he was convinced that Judah's spiritual apostasy was even more serious (1:13–16) – and that even in spite of Josiah's reforms.

He was the last prophet of the kingdom of Judah. His ministry lasted forty years from the last days of good King Josiah (640–609 BC), through the reigns of Jehoahaz (609 BC), Jehoiakim (609–597 BC), Jehoiachin (597 BC) and Zedekiah (597–587 BC), spanning the terrible events which led to the fall of Jerusalem in 587 BC, on through the short governorship of Gedaliah, drawing to a close in 585 BC after he had been forcibly taken to Egypt.

The book is a collection of prophecies from the mouth of Jeremiah together with stories from his life.

But the book is more than a collection of prophecies and narratives: it is foundational to the New Testament. He is the prophet of the new covenant, the covenant which effects a permanent change of heart and which Christ's death made possible. At the institution of the Lord's Supper our Lord used the words 'new covenant', from Jeremiah's book, to explain what he was doing (Je. 31:31, *cf.* Mt. 26:28).

Forty times Jeremiah is directly quoted in the New Testament, half of these quotations being in the book of Revelation.

Summary

The narratives and prophecies are not in chronological order, so it is not possible to give a consecutive summary. It is possible, however, to summarize the contents by using the historical background as a framework.

Jeremiah was a youth, perhaps under the age of twenty, when God gave him his unenviable task. The description of his call (1) is a classic to be compared only with those of Moses, Isaiah and Ezekiel.

At that time he had some idea of what was involved and would gladly have avoided the responsibility (1:6), but as he increasingly realized the nature of the task, his psychological and mental turmoil multiplied (15:10–11). The Lord appeared to be forsaking the nation and disaster was unavoidable (25:11; 29:10).

Political: Politically the end of the seventh century before Christ was one of the most fateful periods in the ancient history of the middle east. The Assyrian Empire was in decline and her domination of the surrounding countries was waning.

Both Egypt and Babylon were eager to be her successor. Judah was caught between the two mighty powers. The Babylonians asserted their strength in the north when they defeated the Egyptians at the battle of Carchemish in 605 BC, but this made the Egyptians more determined to keep a foot in Palestine.

It was a political crisis of major proportions for Judah and one which would have taxed the moral and spiritual resources of King David himself. But the five kings of Judah, Josiah, Jehoahaz (Shallum), Jehoiakim, Jehoiachin (Jeconiah, Coniah) and Zedekiah were all lesser men.

Josiah was loyal to the Lord and led a spiritual reformation, but he made an appalling error of judgment when he tried to intercept the Egyptians on their way to do battle with the Babylonians, and was killed (2 Ki. 23:29). After Josiah's death, Jeremiah suffered physical persecution (20:2). Jehoahaz, Josiah's son, reigned for only three months and was deported to Egypt.

The Egyptians placed his elder brother, Jehoiakim, on the throne. Jehoiakim was antagonistic towards Jeremiah and indecisive in his politics, intriguing first with Egypt and then with Babylon. In 597 BC Nebuchadnezzar marched on Palestine, but Jehoiakim died and Jehoiachin succeeded him before the Babylonians reached Jerusalem. They sacked the temple and deported Jehoiachin with some of the nation's leaders (2 Ki. 24:10, 14–15). Ezekiel was among the exiles at this time. Zedekiah, the youngest son of Josiah, and Jehoiachin's uncle, was placed on the throne. He was friendly to Jeremiah but unreliable and unable to control his advisers. Under their pressure he entered into negotiations with Egypt. The Babylonians took their revenge. For several months Jerusalem withstood a siege, although Jeremiah urged Zedekiah to surrender (21:3–10; 38:17–18). The city was destroyed, Zedekiah was blinded and, with many of the people, deported to Babylon (2 Ki. 25:5–7).

Jeremiah had tried before this to leave the city, but was imprisoned. He was treated well by Nebuchadnezzar (or Nebuchadrezzar) and supported Gedaliah, who was appointed by the Babylonians as governor (39:11–12). When Gedaliah was murdered, some of the Jews fled to Egypt and insisted on taking Jeremiah with them (43).

Spiritual: Jeremiah saw spiritual apostasy in the same terms as Hosea who had preceded him by a hundred years. Judah was guilty of spiritual adultery (9:2; 23:10).

In his temple address which stirred up so much antagonism, he vehemently denied that the holiness of the temple would prevent its desecration and the destruction of the city. The social injustice, the heathen practices, the breaking of the covenant and the formality of their religious practices would bring judgment. The land would become a ruin and a waste and for seventy years they would serve the king of Babylon (7:1–8:3).

The book has its message of consolation too. After the seventy years, the Lord would fulfil his promise and bring them back (25:12; 29:10).

By disobeying the Lord's commands, they had failed to

keep their part of the covenant. The day would come when
the Lord would introduce a new covenant, making it inter-
nal instead of external, because it would depend upon his
power to change their hearts (31:31–34).

The account of the writing, reading, burning and re-
writing of the scroll is a promise too of the indestructible
power of the Word of the Lord (36). Just before Jerusalem
fell, Jeremiah deliberately bought property to add strength
to his message that restoration would follow (32:1–15).

Writer and date
The authorship of the book is a disputed issue, yet Old
Testament scholar E. J. Young can say, 'There is no satisfactory reason for doubting that Jeremiah himself was the
author of the entire book.' The scribe Baruch appears to
have acted as amanuensis to Jeremiah (36:4). This may
explain why in some places Jeremiah is referred to in the
third person (*e.g.* ch. 26). The chapters do not seem to
form a chronological pattern. It may be that the disorderly
arrangement reflects the confusion and muddle of the time.
If so, this would imply that the book was in circulation
before *c.* 520 BC. Baruch was taken with Jeremiah to Egypt
(43:6). It may be that there he gathered and edited Jeremiah's prophecies.

Analysis
The book cannot be analysed section by section without
producing a rather complicated scheme. It is a collection of
prophecies by Jeremiah, some in prose and some in poetry,
along with narrative portions telling of the more outstanding experiences of his life.

Attempts have been made to divide it analytically: into
chronological sections; according to the five reigns through
which Jeremiah's ministry lasted; on the assumption that
the beginning and ending of the various 'scrolls' (36) can
be perceived. An attractive suggestion is that the compiler

followed a device known in antiquity whereby a long work was circulated in two halves. Hence *NBCR* divides the book between chapters 25 and 26. All attempts have to be qualified if artificiality is to be avoided.

The outline given in this book has followed a suggestion by H. L. Ellison that the first part of the book is mostly (though not all) in poetry and is also mostly (though not all) prophecy (1–25). The second section is mostly biographical stories about Jeremiah, and is mostly in prose (26–45). The third part, the prophecies to the nations, is mostly in poetry (46–51).

Structure and contents

*Zedekiah 22:1–9 Jehoahaz (Shallum) c. 609 BC
22:10–12 Jehoiakim 22:13–23 Jehoiachin (Jeconiah, Coniah) 22:24–30*

19. Leaders seen as wicked shepherds with the sheep *c.* 605–595 BC 23:1–8
20. Godless prophets and priests *c.* 605–595 BC 23:9–40
21. Parable of the two baskets of figs *c.* 605–595 BC 24
22. Seventy years' captivity prophesied *c.* 605–595 BC 25:1–14
23. Summary of prophecies against foreign nations 25:15–38

II. Biography – mostly in prose 26–45
    1. The temple sermon sequel *c.* 608 BC Jehoiakim 26
    2. The acted parable of the ox yoke *c.* 597–595 BC Jehoiakim 27
    3. The prophet Hananiah contradicts Jeremiah *c.* 597–595 BC Zedekiah 28
    4. The letter to the Jews in Babylon *c.* 597–595 BC 29
    5. The 'book' of consolation *c.* 595–587 BC 30–33
       Promises 30:1–31:30 New covenant 31:31–34 Immutable promise 31:35–37 Rebuilding Jerusalem 31:38–40 Jeremiah buys a field 32:1–15 Prayer and answer 32:16–44 God's message of restoration to Jeremiah in prison 33
    6. Zedekiah tries to free the slaves in response to God's message, but is thwarted 34
    7. The Rechabites *c.* 606–604 BC Jehoiakim 35
    8. The scroll – read, destroyed, replaced *c.* 606–604 BC Jehoiakim 36
    9. Jeremiah's arrest and imprisonment *c.* 587–586 BC Zedekiah 37:1–38:13
    10. Zedekiah again asks Jeremiah's advice *c.* 587–586 BC 38:14–28
    11. The fall of Jerusalem 587 BC 39
    12. Gedaliah aims to govern well but is assassinated

Study questions

1. Compare the call of Jeremiah (1:4–19) with that of Moses (Ex. 3:1–4:16), Isaiah (Is. 6) and Ezekiel (Ezk. 1:1–3:21). In what ways is Jeremiah's call a) similar to, b) dissimilar from theirs?

2. Read chs. 2–6 and list all the descriptions of Judah's sin. Based on this, write a paragraph on the nature of sin and the ways in which it finds expression.

3. From chs. 9–15 and 20 describe Jeremiah's relationship with the Lord.

4. Read Exodus 24, Jeremiah 11 and 31 and Luke 22:1–20. How was the old covenant broken? What was the crucial difference between the old and the new (*cf.* Ex. 24:12 with Je. 31:33)? List the features of the new covenant.

5. 'Faith is being sure of what we hope for and certain of what we do not see' (Heb. 11:1 NIV). What can you learn about faith from Jeremiah's example in ch. 32?

6. In chs. 42–44, trace the stages in the army officers' disobedience to the Lord. How did the Lord deal with them at each stage?

Reference books

C. L. Feinberg, *Jeremiah* (Marshall Pickering, 1982; Zondervan, 1982)

R. K. Harrison, *Jeremiah and Lamentations* (IVP, 1973)

I. L. Jensen, *Jeremiah and Lamentations* (Moody, U.S.A., 1966)

D. Kidner, *The Message of Jeremiah* (IVP, 1987)

J. A. Thompson, *The Book of Jeremiah* (IVP, 1987)

Lamentations

'There are perhaps few portions of the Old Testament which appear to have done the work they were meant to do more effectually than this' (A. W. Streane, 1892). For both Jews and Christians it has been a source-book for words to express confession, repentance and grief. Unlike other Bible books, it has never been connected with the theological disputes of the ages.

The Saviour's suffering has been crystallized and expressed for Christians in the words, 'Is it nothing to you, all you who pass by? Look and see if there is any sorrow like my sorrow . . .' (1:12). Although the book as a whole is not well known to most Christians, these words, along with 'The steadfast love of the Lord never ceases, his mercies never come to an end; they are new every morning; great is thy faithfulness' (3:22–23), are some of the best known in the whole Bible.

The book is made up of five poems, each of them is a heart-rending cry of desolation at the havoc and distress caused by the fall of Jerusalem in 587 BC. The first four are written in the *qinah* metre which suited the Hebrew funeral lament so well, and are acrostic (a different letter of the alphabet begins each verse or stanza).

Along with the despair, each poem includes prayers of confession and repentance, and they are not without intimations of hope and faith and prayer for restoration.

In the Hebrew Bible they are part of the Writings and are placed between Ruth and Ecclesiastes. The Jews recite the five poems at the Wailing Wall in Jerusalem and in the synagogues annually on 9th Ab (July), the anniversary of the destruction of the temple by Nebuchadnezzar.

Writer and date
Traditionally, at least since the Greek Old Testament came into use (*c.* 200 BC), the authorship has been ascribed to Jeremiah. Certainly the poems bear the marks of an eyewitness. It is possible that Baruch, Jeremiah's scribe, may have written some of them. There can be no certainty either about author or precise date, though it is highly probable they were written in the early years of the Baby-lonian exile.

Structure and contents
1. First dirge 1
    The lonely city 1:1–7   Jerusalem sinned grievously 1:8–11   Is it nothing to you? 1:12–22
2. Second dirge 2
    No vision from the Lord 2:1–9   Where is bread and wine? 2:10–13   Your prophets told lies 2:14–17   Look O Lord! 2:18–22
3. Third dirge 3
    My soul is bereft of peace 3:1–21   The steadfast love of the Lord never ceases 3:22–39   Let us return to the Lord 3:40–42   We live in danger and fear 3:43–54   You came near when I called 3:55–66
4. Fourth dirge 4
    Happier the victims of the sword 4:1–12   The sins of her prophets 4:13–20   Disaster for laughing Edom too 4:21–22
5. Fifth dirge 5
    Lord have mercy 5:1–10   Personal tragedies in national destruction 5:11–18   You O Lord are King for ever 5:19–22

Study questions

1. What was life like for the people of Jerusalem immediately after 587 BC (ch. 1)?

2. According to ch. 2, what characterized the Lord's judgment on the city? What good had come of it (verses 10, 18)?

3. How do you explain 3:22–39 following so closely on 3:1–21?

4. Read Jeremiah 14:13–16; 23:9–32; 27:12–14. How had Jeremiah's words been vindicated, according to Lamentations 4:12–20? What lessons can you learn from this?

Reference books

W. J. Fuerst, *Ruth, Esther, Ecclesiastes, Song of Songs, Lamentations* (Cambridge, 1975)

R. K. Harrison, *Jeremiah and Lamentations* (IVP, 1973)

R. Martin-Achard and S. P. Re'emi, *God's People in Crisis* (Handsel, 1983; Eerdmans, 1983)

Ezekiel

Ezekiel is in more than one sense a 'fantastic' book. The story it tells is fast-moving and full of drama. Ezekiel, like Jeremiah, uses himself to act out God's message, and the effect on his audience must have been startling. But along-side the earthiness of these 'acted parables' are spectacular visions full of weird symbols which are as difficult to understand as parts of Revelation and Daniel. The combination, though colourful, can seem all too much for the ordinary Christian reader and many are tempted to give up, thinking they cannot understand. With just a little help in understanding the background, however, the book can speak God's word as powerfully to the beginner as to the expert. The precise meaning of the symbols may not always be clear, but the message is plain enough.

Ezekiel was a priest, captured in one of Nebuchadnez-zar's early raids on the city in 597 BC, and taken to Babylon before the fall of Jerusalem in 587 BC. He began to prophesy about four or five years after being captured, in 592 BC, and continued until at least 570 BC. He lived near the river Chebar, possibly a canal, and was called by God to be the first prophet of the exile. He lived at the same time as Jeremiah though they were separated by hundreds of miles. Ezekiel lived and prophesied in Babylon, Jeremiah in Jerusalem.

The Lord suits the messenger to the message he gives. Ezekiel was a priest by training and thought in terms of ritual and symbolism. It is, therefore, not surprising that God revealed himself to him in symbols. The character of the vision which preceded his call influenced his ministry. Ezekiel himself used symbolism, role-play and bizarre illustration. You could almost say that he was a predecessor of those who teach with audio-visual aids and drama today. His colourful imagery lent itself to New Testament writers (*e.g.* the apostle John in the Revelation) when they wrote of the end of time (*e.g.* 1:5, 10, *cf.* Rev. 4:6–7; 2:1–3, *cf.* Acts 26:16f.; 9:6, *cf.* 1 Pet. 4:17; 27:28–36, *cf.* Rev. 18:11–19, *etc.*).

Summary

Ezekiel, like Isaiah, has a vision of God before he is commissioned to work for God. The Lord appears gloriously to him upon his strange and mystic chariot throne (1). He addressed him as 'son of man' as though to emphasize his humanity and fallibility in contrast to the Lord for whom he is the messenger. (2:3). The nations to whom he will speak are rebellious and, although they will not listen, he must insist on speaking (2:3–7). He is then sent back by the Spirit to his own house as an indication that, as watchman over their souls, he is called to speak to the exiles (2:9–3:3; 3:22–27). (Probably between five and six years later, just before he is brought the news that Jerusalem has fallen (33:21), he is re-commissioned in similar terms to prepare him for the second phase of his work (33:1–20).)

Ezekiel tries to prepare the Jews for the destruction of the temple and the fall of Jerusalem. They could not contemplate the thought that the Lord might leave his temple. He subjects himself publicly to the sort of deprivation and desolation that will come upon the people with the fall of Jerusalem (4–5). He enacts the life of an exile (12). He tells a vivid, extended tale of Jerusalem, the unfaithful wife (16). So the picture of sin and coming destruction is built up. Ezekiel heaps image upon image: the two sisters who are prostitutes (Samaria and Jerusalem) (23), the rusty cooking pot fit only for burning (24). Judgment is inevitable. The fall of Jerusalem vindicates Ezekiel's warnings in the eyes of the previously sceptical exiles. Nor do the surrounding nations escape. Chapters 25–32 list a series of prophecies of judgment upon Israel's neighbours, upon Tyre and Sidon and upon Egypt.

After the fall of Jerusalem in 587 BC (33:21), his message becomes one of encouragement and hope. Like a shepherd, God will rescue his lost sheep (34); the nation will be restored in its own land (36); the dry bones will live (37); and the Gentile forces who rise up against the restored nation will be gloriously conquered (38–39).

His detailed plans for a new temple in Jerusalem seem sometimes to suggest a literal interpretation, as though he were designing the new temple for use after the return from exile, and sometimes the impression is given that he is speaking prophetically and figuratively in terms which the apostle John afterwards used to describe heaven. Consequently there is much discussion among Bible students over these chapters (40–48). But for all the apparent tedium of the details, these chapters bring us back to our starting point and build up to the book's climax. For, as always, the temple symbolizes God's presence with his people, and the book ends with a glorious vision of God returning to the new temple, this time never again to leave it.

Symbols and visions

How to understand the flamboyant pictures in Ezekiel has been a perennial problem to the Christian church. The prophecy has many of the 'apocalyptic' characteristics of Daniel and Revelation. Quite obviously, to insist on a literal interpretation of the picture-language is to ignore its very nature. We would do well to remember that more obscure parts of Scripture are always to be understood in the light of clear teaching elsewhere in the Bible and it is helpful, as with biblical parables, to look for the main point and not be distracted by too much attention to details. Certainly the

Israelites, returning from exile, assumed that many of the details about the temple in chapters 40–48 referred to the 'end times' and they did not feel it necessary to put them into practice in their own age.

Major themes
1. *The awesomeness of God* Ezekiel is a prophet of the transcendent God (beyond our world), although he also recognizes his immanence (his presence in our world), for he experiences it (2). In his attempt to convey in earthly terms something of God's majesty, the prophet struggles with phrases like 'seated above the likeness of a throne was a likeness as it were of a human form' and 'it was like the appearance of brightness . . . ' (1:26; 8:2). The holiness of God is central in his thinking, as it was for Isaiah. Isaiah saw the Lord 'high and lifted up'; Ezekiel saw 'the appearance of the likeness of the glory' on the chariot throne (Is. 6; Ezk. 1). Originally holiness meant 'separateness'. The word comes to have moral content because the God who is holy is the good God. The otherness of God in his greatness, wisdom, goodness, omnipotence, omniscience and glory is Ezekiel's supreme theme, and it links together his other subservient themes.

2. *Individual responsibility* 'The fathers have eaten sour grapes, and the children's teeth are set on edge' must have been a parable in common use for Jeremiah also quotes it (Je. 31:29; Ezk. 18:2). Ezekiel asserts that this will no longer be so; he insists on the individual's own responsibility before God. He also speaks of corporate responsibility; his messages teach that it is the nation's accumulated wrongdoing which will bring about the exile. But Ezekiel declares that individual responsibility must balance corporate accountability. Citizens were avoiding their own guilt for the nation's present sins and then blaming the Lord for injustice (18:25). Fatalism and irresponsibility must be the

result of such imbalance. It is against this imbalance that Ezekiel protests and insists that each man, not his father or neighbour, is responsible for his own sins. If the individual is held responsible and yet fails, it follows that some provision is needed for personal failure: 'If a wicked man turns away from all his sins . . . he shall surely live' (18:21).

3. *The sins of the nation*   Four passages are especially relevant. Israel is the foundling rescued by the Lord, but rejecting him when she becomes adult (16:1–63). Her people did not cast away their 'detestable things' (pagan idols). They did not keep the ordinances. They rebelled against the Lord. For the sake of his honour in the world, punishment must follow (20:1–31). Like the harlot sisters (23:1–4), Israel has an uncontrollable passion for disloyalty to the Lord. Ezekiel sees idolatry, animal worship, nature worship and sun worship proceeding within the temple itself. For him this insult to the Lord's holy name is the worst sin of all and judgment is not only predicted but is imminent (8–10).

4. *Restoration for the nation*   After the fall of Jerusalem in 587 BC, Ezekiel's message turns to one of hope and promise. At the restoration, the Lord will give the nation a new heart, will sprinkle them with water indicating forgiveness and cleansing, and will put his Spirit within them to give them strength (36:24–28). In the vision of the valley of dry bones, the nation which is dead, very dead, will yet come alive as the Lord rebuilds it and puts his life into it. 'My servant David shall be king' (37:24). He will rule as a shepherd, caring for the weak and crippled among the flock (34:16, 23). Out of the sanctuary in Jerusalem will flow the symbolical water of life (47:1–12).

Writer and date
The unity of the book and its authorship by Ezekiel are

accepted by most scholars. They are reluctant to give any precise date for its compilation. 'How long or short an interval separated Ezekiel's visions and oracles from their being recorded in their present form is uncertain, but it was probably not more than a generation' (F. F. Bruce, *BCT*). It seems probable that Ezekiel knew at least some of the prophecies of Jeremiah (*e.g.* Ezk. 18:2, *cf.* Je. 31:29; Ezk. 34, *cf.* Je. 25:34–38; Ezk. 16:59–63, *cf.* Je. 31–34, *etc.*).

Structure and contents

Study questions

1. How did Ezekiel respond to the vision and call of God (1–3)? When God calls us to undertake difficult tasks for him, what can we learn from Ezekiel's experiences here?

2. What sins were people committing in the very temple itself (8)? Why did they think they could get away with it? What do you think are our modern equivalents of idol worship? From this chapter, what is God's attitude to idolatry?

3. What lessons can those who teach and minister to God's people learn from chs. 13 and 34?

4. Chapter 16 is a vivid picture of the story of the relationship between God and Israel. Try to 'translate' the passage from picture-language into everyday terms. Can you see any parallels with your own life?

5. Chapter 36: What blessings are promised to Israel (8–15)? Why did they go into exile (16–19)? Why were they brought back (20–24)? What would change (25–31)? How does this pattern of events apply to your own life?

6. From ch. 37 describe Israel's condition in exile. How would God restore the nation? Why? What would life be like afterwards? How do you think this passage applies to us?

Reference book
J. B. Taylor, *Ezekiel* (IVP, 1969)

Daniel

It is not generally realized that when Daniel was put in the lions' den he must have been an old man of between eighty and ninety. He was taken to Babylon along with his three companions, Shadrach, Meshach and Abednego (to give them their Babylonian names), when Nebuchadnezzar raided Jerusalem in 605 BC, and he must then have been a young man of nineteen or twenty.

Daniel, therefore, had seen the people of God oppressed and downtrodden for many years. It was hard to see the hand of God in their present circumstances and to believe in his sovereign, overruling power. His book is designed to be an encouragement to believers in succeeding generations to stand fast on God's Word and to trust in that part of his revealed purposes which speaks of protection for his people.

The book divides into a historical section (1–6) and a prophetical section (7–12). Chronologically some of the prophetical sections overlap with the history. The section 2:4–7:28 is written in Aramaic, whereas the rest is in Hebrew.

Daniel records the happenings of his exile for the encouragement of believers in time of opposition and persecution, and predicts the rise and fall of the great empires until the Messiah comes.

Summary
In exile in Babylon, Daniel and his three friends are selected for training prior to entering King Nebuchadnezzar's service. Although they refuse the lavish diet provided for them

(it would have infringed Jewish food laws), they outshine the other trainees (1). Daniel's wisdom is seen in his ability to explain (twice), and even recall (once), dreams sent by God to Nebuchadnezzar (2, 4).

His three friends, unwilling to bow to the great idol erected by Nebuchadnezzar, are thrown into the furnace only to come through it, in the company of 'one like a son of the gods', unharmed (3).

Belshazzar's famous feast is in progress and Daniel interprets the writing on the wall on the very night that Babylon falls to Darius the Mede (5).

Daniel continues to hold high office under the Persians and eventually his enemies are successful in a plot to frame him and he is hurled into the lions' den, but is found unharmed by the harassed king the next day (6).

The second section (7–12) is prophetic and apocalyptic and, like parts of Ezekiel, is used in the New Testament to describe, in highly symbolic language, the rise of persecution both in the first century AD and in the 'end times'.

The visions are in chronological order. The vision of the four beasts 556 BC (7) is usually taken to represent the empires of Babylon (lion), Medo-Persia (bear), Greece (leopard) and Rome (terrifying beast). The last is destroyed as 'one like a son of man' is given universal authority by the Ancient of Days (7). (But see under 'Writer and date'.)

The ram and goat vision (8) received its fulfilment when Alexander the Great defeated Persia in 330 BC, only to have his kingdom divided into four at his death. Eventually he was followed by the notorious Antiochus Epiphanes, ruler of Syria (175–164 BC), who persecuted the Jewish people so brutally that there arose a resistance movement called the 'Maccabean revolt', after its leader, Judas Maccabaeus. Because the archangel Gabriel refers to 'the end time', it may be that Antiochus foreshadows the antichrist (2 Thes. 2:8–10).

By this time the people have been in exile for seventy

years, but Daniel has not given up his constant prayers
for release (9). His identification with the sin of the people
and his urgent pleading for deliverance are about to be
answered. In the penultimate vision Daniel discovers that
behind the world events which can be seen, there lies an
unseen struggle involving the armies of heaven (10).

There is a selective forecast of 400 years of history in
chapter 11 focusing particularly on Antiochus. It should be
studied with the help of a good commentary.

The last chapter deals with 'the time of the end', and a
clear promise to Daniel of his resurrection when that time
comes (12).

Apocalyptic

The second half of the book of Daniel is often described as
'apocalyptic' literature. The word means 'unfolding', 'revealing' (Greek *apokalyptō*), and in Daniel it is the hidden
plans of God for the future and, in particular, his ultimate
triumph over evil powers, which are revealed. There are
apocalyptic elements in other Old Testament prophetic
books (*cf.* Is. 24–27; 56–66; Joel; Zc. 9–14). The 'end time'
is the central subject and there are references to angels and
to resurrection.

As this type of literature became more popular it developed distinct literary characteristics. This literary form is
anticipated in the bizarre symbols and cataclysmic visions
of Ezekiel and Zechariah (1–6). After the cessation of
prophecy, apocalyptic took over many Old Testament
prophetic elements and became a flourishing literature. It
was very popular in the dark days of the second century
BC. Many of the 'apocalypses' written then have the common themes of opposition between light and darkness, good
and evil, God and Satan, with God the final victor. They
also have the common features of visions and symbolic
numbers.

Writer and date

The majority of scholars today place the book in the time of the Maccabean revolt (*c.* 165 BC). It is argued that a writer long after the days of Daniel wrote up Daniel's story adding fictional material (some think it is all fiction and even that Daniel was a fictional character). According to this theory, the prophecies were written after the events they are supposed to have prophesied. The argument is based on the fact that the material relating to the second century is historically very accurate, while that concerning the earlier time of exile seems to be less so. This appears at first acquaintance to be persuasive, but some of the main planks of the original theory have been shown to be weaker than was supposed at first (see *IBD*). There is a significant minority of scholars who support the historicity of the book and a date in the sixth century BC.

Those who give the book a second century BC date cannot see the Roman Empire as the fourth (terrifying) beast in the visions of chapter 7, and so they divide Medo-Persia, making the four empires Media, Persia, Babylon and Greece; but although there were Median kings there never was a dominant Median Empire.

Structure and contents
I. Narrative 1–6
   1. Daniel raised to power in Babylon 605 BC 1
   2. Nebuchadnezzar's dream of the great image *c.* 603 BC 2
   3. Shadrach, Meshach and Abednego in the furnace of fire 3
   4. Nebuchadnezzar's dream of the tall tree 4
   5. Belshazzar's feast and the fall of Babylon 539 BC 5
   6. Daniel and the lions' den 6
II. Prophecy 7–12
   1. Vision of the four beasts *c.* 556 BC 7
   2. Vision of the ram and the goat *c.* 554 BC 8

3. Daniel's prayer and announcement of the seventy sevens *c.* 538 BC 9
4. Vision of the conflict in the heavens *c.* 536 BC 10:1–11:1
5. Prophecy to 163 BC – Greece, Egypt, Syria 11:2–12:3
6. The time of the end 12:4–13

Study questions

1. Read chs. 1, 3 and 6. a) Describe the environment in which Daniel and his friends found themselves. b) What was their attitude in that environment? c) How did the Lord vindicate them? d) Draw out the lessons for God's people today in our own ungodly society.
2. What effects did contact with followers of the God of Israel have on a) Nebuchadnezzar and b) Belshazzar (4–5)? Compare the responses of the two kings. What can you learn from this about the way God uses his people in an alien environment?
3. Jesus often referred to himself as the 'Son of man', a title drawn from Daniel 7. From that chapter, summarize what Jesus was saying about himself by his use of the term.
4. What does Daniel's example teach you about prayer (9:4–19)?
5. 'The Most High God is sovereign over the kingdoms of men' (5:21, NIV). How do chs. 2 and 7–12 illustrate this truth?

Reference books

R. A. Anderson, *Signs and Wonders* (Handsel, 1984; Eerdmans, 1984)

J. G. Baldwin, *Daniel* (IVP, 1978)

G. C. Luck, *Daniel* (Moody, U.S.A., 1969)

R. S. Wallace, *The Message of Daniel* (IVP, 1979)

E. J. Young, *Daniel* (Banner of Truth, 1973); *The Prophecy of Daniel* (Eerdmans, 1949)

Hosea

Hosea is the tender prophet of the Old Testament. His prophecies revolve round the word *hesed*, used 247 times in the Old Testament. The word is very difficult to translate into English: steadfast love, mercy, kindness, loving kindness are all attempts to do justice to the Hebrew word. It signifies the very special kind of love that the Lord has for his own people and that he desires from them. More poignantly than anyone else, Hosea demonstrates the faithful love of God who has pledged himself in covenant with his people.

The idolatry of the northern kingdom, Israel, around the years 755–722 BC deeply troubled Hosea. He regarded it as spiritual adultery, and saw a comparison between the agony of his own disrupted home life because of the unfaithfulness of his wife, Gomer, and the Lord's anguish over unfaithful Israel. Further, just as his own wife needed firmness, even severity, along with a determination never to give her up, so the Lord must deal with Israel in judgment but would never finally disown her, and would eventually restore her at great personal cost to himself.

The statement in 1:2 that the Lord told Hosea to marry 'a wife of harlotry' can be a problem to some. Certainly, if Gomer was already known to be a prostitute, Hosea's marriage to her must be seen as a specific command of God necessary for the continuing discipline of his people. It may be, however, that Hosea looked back on his marriage to a woman who proved to be unfaithful, and saw God's deliberate leading even in his personal tragedy.

Hosea's ministry lasted for thirty years or more, from the reign of Jeroboam II of Israel (782–753 BC) to that of Hezekiah of Judah (716–687 BC) (1:1).

Summary

Chapters 1–3 are an introduction to all that follows. Gomer, Hosea's wife, is unfaithful. As her three children are born, they are given names to emphasize his message at that time – 'Jezreel' because, at Jezreel, Jehu assassinated the royal family; 'Not pitied' because Israel must learn what it means not to be the beloved of the Lord; 'Not my people' because for a time the Lord will disown them. But restoration will follow and again they will be called 'sons of the living God'. As Hosea tries to retrieve his unfaithful wife from prostitution, so will the Lord redeem Israel (1–3).

Israel, the prostitute, indulges in social corruption, pagan and idol worship, repentance (sincere or insincere?), deception, murder, assassination, arrogance (4–8). Judah is included in the denunciations (5:8–15).

Israel has played the harlot and the people will become slaves to Assyria as once they were to Egypt. They have consecrated themselves to Baal and the Lord will cast them off. What this will mean is illustrated by the vine, the chip of wood and the heifer. The more they prosper like a luxuriant vine, the more their idolatry increases and so the idol at Bethel shall be carried to Assyria. The king of Samaria shall perish like a chip of wood on the water. Ephraim has had an easy time, like a heifer performing the congenial work of threshing, but now she must bear the yoke of seeking the Lord in repentance (9–10). Yet the Lord's love will not be withdrawn (11). Affluence does not excuse guilt (12). The Lord is both Saviour and judge (13). Hosea suggests the appropriate prayer for true repentance and the Lord promises restoration (14).

Major themes

1. *Grace and redemption* It seems that, after the birth of Hosea's three children, his wife, Gomer, fell back into prostitution and into slavery, for in 3:2 we see Hosea buying her back. Similarly, God promises restoration to unfaithful Israel. His wrath and judgment indicated love, not final rejection: 'How can I give you up, O Ephraim!', 'I will heal their faithlessness; I will love them freely' (11:8; 14:4). Hosea often refers to the grace and redemption demonstrated in the exodus from Egypt, and grace and redemption are Israel's only hope now. So they must repent (14:1–3).

2. *Knowledge of God* The root of Israel's sin was that there was 'no knowledge of God in the land' (4:1). 'Knowledge' in the biblical sense implies not intellectual learning but an intimate relationship (*cf.* Gn. 4:1). Israel had broken her relationship with the Lord and committed spiritual adultery (5:4). So when Hosea suggests words of repentance for the nation, he includes the exhortation, 'Let us know, let us press on to know the Lord' (6:3). And the climax of God's promise of restoration is, ' . . . and you shall know the Lord' (2:20).

Writer and date
Hosea gives us the date in 1:1. Since his prophecies must be before the fall of Samaria in 722 BC, the dates are between 755 and 722 BC.

Structure and contents
  I. Hosea and his wife 1–3
    1. Hosea, Gomer and their children 1:1–9
    2. Promise of Israel's restoration 1:10–2:1
    3. Unfaithful Gomer – unfaithful Israel 2:2–23
    4. Hosea faithful to Gomer – the Lord to Israel 3
 II. The Lord and Israel 4–14
    1. The Lord's accusation:

Study questions

1. What help, advice and encouragement would you give from Hosea 14 to someone who was conscious of being unfaithful to the Lord?

2. Try to explain the nuances of the word *hesed* as it is used in 2:19; 4:1; 6:4, 6; 10:12; 12:6.

3. Find all the verses you can in Hosea which proclaim 'God is love'. How do you reconcile this with God as judge, as seen in Hosea?

Reference books

D. Kidner, *The Message of Hosea* (IVP, 1981)

G. Campbell Morgan, *Hosea: The Heart and Holiness of God* (Baker, U.S.A., 1974)

Joel

A devastating plague of locusts which left Jerusalem stripped and bare was the occasion for this prophecy. Joel uses the locust plague to introduce his teaching about the day of the Lord and the outpouring of the Holy Spirit.

Summary
Like an invading army the plague of locusts ravages the city and the country, and Joel, seeing it as a warning of judgment, calls for a national day of prayer. For the day of the Lord, a day of judgment, is coming. If the people repent, God promises full restoration (1:1–2:27).

Looking to the future both God's Spirit and God's judgment will come on Israel and on all nations. At last the restored Israel will share God's blessing (2:28–3:21).

The day of the Lord
The manifest unfairness of life led the Hebrews to look for God to intervene in human history. They called this intervention 'the day of the Lord' but in the Old Testament it is not always clear whether the reference is to the final great judgment or to a lesser event which foreshadows it. Ellison's words on the subject are helpful: 'Since any and every major divine intervention, especially when it involved judgment, not merely foreshadowed the final intervention and judgment, but also for all that man could tell, might be its inauguration, the Day of the Lord is not used exclusively for the final intervention. This ambiguity has three main reasons, linguistic pecularities in Hebrew, the real link be-

tween the foreshadowing and the fulfilment, and the revelation to the prophet of the nature of the Day of the Lord but not of its date in time' (*Men Spake from God*, 1966, p. 21).

The prophecy in 2:28–32 is used by the apostle Peter (Acts 2:16–21) to explain the startling events of the day of Pentecost and as the text for his sermon on that occasion. But verses 30–32 go beyond the day of Pentecost and foretell the events leading up to the final great judgment (Mt. 24:29–31). This is, therefore, a good example of 'the telescoping of history' which is often a feature of prophecy.

Writer and date

Apart from the fact that his father's name was Pethuel, and. that he spoke to the southern kingdom (Judah), we know very little about Joel. He may have been connected with the temple, perhaps as a priest, since he mentions various aspects of temple worship. His name is shared by thirteen others in the Old Testament. The absence of any reference to Assyria or Babylon has led to the conviction that Joel prophesied either before their rise or after their decline. The date scholars assign to the book therefore varies as much as between 800 and 200 BC. There is some general agreement that Joel prophesied about 400 BC for a variety of reasons (*e.g.* Israel as the old northern kingdom does not appear and the life of the community centres around the worship of the temple as in the days after the return). He may be contemporary with Malachi, or with Jonah, Amos and Hosea. Dogmatism is impossible and unnecessary.

Contents

6. Judgment on the nations 3:1–15
7. Blessings on Israel 3:16–21

Study questions
1. Make a list of the things Joel prophesies in 2:28–32 and write short explanations of what you think they mean. Reference to Acts 2:16–21 and Mt. 24:29–31 may help.
2. Using 2:12–17 define what is meant by repentance.
3. Collect the references in Joel to 'the day', add to them any others in the Old Testament or New Testament with the help of a concordance, and build up a picture of its meaning.

Reference books
L. C. Allen, *The Books of Joel, Obadiah, Jonah and Micah* (Eerdmans, U.S.A., 1978)

G. Ogden and R. R. Deutsch, *A Promise of Hope—A Call to Obedience* (Handsel, 1987; Eerdmans, 1987)

J. D. W. Watts, *Joel, Obadiah, Jonah, Micah, Nahum, Habakkuk, Zephaniah* (Cambridge, 1975)

Amos

Although Jonah, Hosea and possibly Joel were his contemporaries, Amos (*c.* 760–750 BC) is the first of the prophets sent to Israel and Judah in the eighth century before Christ. Jeroboam II (782–753 BC; 2 Ki. 14:23–29) was on the throne of the northern kingdom (Israel), and Uzziah (767–740 BC) reigned in the southern kingdom (Judah). Amos preached about forty years before the fall of Samaria, the capital of the northern kingdom, because of the Lord's judgment on their sin.

He is also notable because, although he lived in the southern kingdom, he preached to the north. His home was at Tekoa, twelve miles south of Jerusalem to the east of the north-south road and not far from the main road to the west, hence his knowledge of world affairs. It is one of the most inhospitable regions of the world. He was a man of the desert and knew little about life's luxuries. As a shepherd he probably travelled to the fairs in the cities in the north to sell his wool, and this brought him into contact with the northern religion with its corrupt Canaanite fertility rites, its idolatry with the calf images set up in Bethel and Dan, and its neglect of the temple in Jerusalem.

But it was not only the idolatry which distressed Amos, he also castigated the people of Israel for the social ills which oppressed the poor in a time of affluence, often with violence, the partiality of the courts and the sharp practices in business. In a corrupt agricultural society, great riches could be obtained only by great wrong, hence his attack on the rich and especially on the wealthy indolent women.

Ignorance of God is the reason for Israel's moral condition, and Judah shares this with its hollow worship and its rejection of prophet and Nazirite. Amos insists that spiritual privilege brings spiritual responsibility. The children of the Lord's covenant are not immune from the Lord's judgment. On the contrary 'You only have I known of all the families of the earth; therefore I will punish you for all your iniquities' (3:2).

He is unique among the prophets of Israel because he insisted that he was essentially a layman and not a professional prophet. He did not have a prophetic training (7:14).

Nevertheless, he was a skilful public speaker. The oracles in the first two main sections demonstrate this (1:3–2:16; 3–6).

The classic poetical structures in which he conveys his message indicate also that he was educated. Some have, therefore, conjectured that he was more than a simple shepherd; perhaps he was a master shepherd with employees of his own. The word *noqed* in the first verse can have this meaning.

Summary

He begins by lambasting Israel's neighbours for their crimes, gross cruelty, immorality, inhumanity, fraud, all of them violations of the decencies of life (1:3–2:3).

We can imagine the delight of the men of Israel when they heard the attacks on their neighbours and their even greater delight when Amos includes his own country Judah in his denunciations (2:4–5). Then when they are fervently applauding, he turns his attention to their own crimes, the crimes of Israel (2:6 ff.)

In dramatic word-pictures, he shows that the law of cause and effect means that when a man of God prophesies it must be because the Lord has moved him to do so. The social disorders, the failure to learn from the Lord's merciful judgments, the injustice, the false spirituality, the false security, the luxury and the pride are carrying Israel along to judgment.

Amos made his base in Bethel, where idol worship had started again, for here was the heart of the problem: Israel had abandoned the true God for false gods who could be worshipped through temple prostitutes. The old festivals were empty shows; the sacrifices were meaningless and therefore useless; dishonesty in religion produced injustice in social life; the rich got richer and the poor got poorer and more oppressed. With deliberately crude language, Amos castigates the wealthy women of Samaria for their lack of compassion, their ruthlessness and the unceasing demands they make on their husbands for money so that they may continue in idleness and luxury and drunkenness (3–6).

The first two of five symbolic pictures of judgment are averted by the intercession of Amos. Between the third and fourth he is verbally attacked by Amaziah, the priest of Bethel, who reports him to King Jeroboam II (7:1–9:7).

But there is joy and hope at the end. After Israel has been shaken among the nations, the Lord will 'restore the fortunes of my people Israel' (9:8–15).

Writer and date
It does not seem improbable that Amos himself was the writer. He lived in a literate age and was a well-read man. He believed he was speaking God's words (3:7–8). It seems likely therefore that he would have committed them to writing. Some scholars believe there are later insertions. His references to God the Creator are held to be ahead of his time (*e.g.* 3:7–8); his allusions to Judah, when he was a prophet to Israel (*e.g.* 2:4), and the note of hope in a prophecy of judgment (*e.g.* 9:13–15), have been given as examples, though these difficulties are not insuperable. The text itself presents few problems. 'The text is one of the best preserved among the prophetic books' (E. Hammershaimb).

Structure and contents

1. Introduction 1:1–2
2. The crimes of Israel and her neighbours 1:3–2:16
   Damascus 1:3–5   Gaza 1:6–8   Tyre 1:9–10   Edom 1:11–12   Ammon 1:13–15   Moab 2:1–3   Judah 2:4–5   Israel 2:6–16
3. Judgment specified 3–6
   Cause and effect 3:1–8   Social disorder 3:9–15   Women of Samaria 4:1–3   Israel's failure to learn 4:4–13   Call to repentance 5:1–9   The dangers of: injustice 5:10–17; false spirituality 5:18–27; false security 6:1–3; luxury 6:4–7; pride 6:8–14
4. Visions of judgment 7:1–9
   Locusts 7:1–3   Fire 7:4–6   Plumbline 7:7–9
5. The altercation with Amaziah the priest 7:10–17
6. Two more visions of judgment 8:1–9:10
   Fruit 8:1–14   Altar 9:1–10
7. Promise of future blessing 9:11–15

Study questions

1. From 2:6 to the end of the book, list in two columns a) the expressions of false religion and b) the characteristics of true religion. See how the two descriptions compare with your own life and your own society.
2. Read through the book making a list of points concerning the social implications of being God's people.

Reference books

J. Marsh, *Amos and Micah* (SCM, J.K., 1965)
R. Martin-Achard and S. P. Re'emi, *God's People in Crisis* (Handsel, 1983; Eerdmans, 1983)
J. A. Motyer, *The Message of Amos* (IVP, 1974)
B. Thorogood, *A Guide to the Book of Amos* (SPCK, U.K., 1971)

Obadiah

Bitterness, hatred and revenge are the words we associate with this book, but also the principle of retribution.

The long rivalry between Isaac's two sons, Jacob and Esau, reaches its climax here. The antagonism following Jacob's supplanting of Esau (Gn. 27) passed to their children's children and there was continual friction between their descendants, the nations of Judah and Edom. Sometimes it was smouldering resentment and sometimes it burst into open war and horrifying acts of revenge. The fault does not always seem to have been one-sided (Nu. 20:14–21; 2 Ch. 25:11f.).

The culmination came when, at the fall of Jerusalem (587 BC), Edom (SE of the Dead Sea) not only gloated over its plight, but looted the city and even helped the invader.

The predictions of Obadiah were subsequently fulfilled when the Edomites were driven out of their territory by the Arabs during the fifth century BC. They fled to Judah and eventually were absorbed by the Jews.

It is perhaps significant that Herod the Great, an Edomite, was the bitter antagonist of Christ at his birth, and one of his sons, Herod Antipas, was described by Jesus as 'that fox' (Lk. 13:31f.). He was involved in the crucifixion and Christ 'made no answer' (Lk. 23:9).

Summary
Edom's pride, complacency and neutrality when kith and kin were in desperate trouble, and even worse her gloating, aggression and ferocity, were bitterly resented (1–14). If

God be just, Edom must one day suffer the same fate (15–16). When that day comes Israel will be saved and triumphant and on the day of the Lord the world-wide exiles of both northern and southern kingdoms of Israel will return to the land and the Lord will reign as King (17–21).

Writer and date

We know nothing about Obadiah. His name means 'the Lord's servant', and occurs a number of times in the Old Testament, but there is no reason to connect this prophet with any of the others who bear his name. The nearest we can get to the date is some time after the fall of Jerusalem in 587 BC.

A comparison of Obadiah 1–9 with Jeremiah 49:7–22 will indicate that there is some connection. Very likely Obadiah knew Jeremiah's prophecy (c. 627–585 BC) and so quoted it. Some think that both Jeremiah and Obadiah are quoting an older prophecy. Other scriptures which speak of Edom's treachery are: Ezekiel 25:12–14; 35:15; Psalm 137:7 and Lamentations 4:21f.

Contents

1. Obadiah's bitterness because of Edom's treachery 1–14
2. Edom's punishment on the day of the Lord 15–16
3. Israel's triumph on the day of the Lord 17–21

Study question

'As you have done, it shall be done to you' (verse 15). What had Edom done, and what form would the Lord's retribution take?

Reference books

L. C. Allen, *The Books of Joel, Obadiah, Jonah and Micah* (Eerdmans, U.S.A., 1978)

J. D. W. Watts, *Joel, Obadiah, Jonah, Micah, Nahum, Habakkuk, Zephaniah* (Cambridge, 1975)

Jonah

'For the love of God is broader than the measures of man's mind; and the heart of the Eternal is most wonderfully kind.' So runs one of our most popular hymns, and one of the scriptural justifications for the hymn-writer's words is to be found in the book of Jonah.

There is good evidence that Jonah was a real person. The son of Amittai, he prophesied during or shortly before the reign of Jeroboam II (c. 782–753 BC) at Gath-hepher in Zebulun and was a prophet of the northern kingdom, Israel.

It is a pity that controversy about the great fish and Jonah's historicity has deflected attention away from the book's exciting teaching. The God of Israel is the Saviour of the world and is concerned for all the peoples of the earth. That is the point. Jonah is the Scriptures' corrective for any who feel oppressed by the prophets' emphasis on judgment. Jonah himself says that he disobeyed God's call because he knew the loving character and merciful kindness of the Lord, and feared that he might cancel his plans for destruction after Jonah had announced them (4:2).

The book has created considerable controversy between those who hold that it records history and those who say it must be seen as a parable. Some of the argument has centred on Christ's references to Jonah (cf. Mt. 12:40; Lk. 11:30). Those who believe that the evidence justifies treating Jonah as historical must not so emphasize this that they forget the message of the book. 'Its subject is not a whale but foreign missions' (W. G. Scroggie).

Summary

The Lord calls Jonah to preach to the wicked capital city of the Assyrians, Nineveh. He takes a ship instead to Tarshish (Spain) to hide from the Lord. The ship runs into a storm and the superstitious sailors throw Jonah into the sea. A large fish swallows him (1). Inside the fish he prays and is thrown up on the beach (2). God's call comes a second time. Nineveh repents at his preaching and judgment is averted (3). Jonah is angry and depressed because the Lord changed his plans, and the Lord uses the withering of a plant (perhaps the *qiqayon*, a kind of castor-oil plant) to show how important are the souls in Nineveh (4).

Nineveh

The size of Nineveh has been a problem. Excavations suggest that the city had a circuit of seven miles. Yet it took Jonah three days to walk through it (3:4). The problem is resolved if we compare it with the city of London and Greater London. Perhaps the name refers to the whole administrative district, including Hatra, Nimrud and Khorsabad. This would be a circuit of about sixty miles.

Writer and date

There are inconclusive indications in the book that it is post-exilic and thus is written *about* Jonah rather than *by* him; *e.g.* 3:3 may indicate a time after the fall of Nineveh in 612 BC. But whether an early date, eighth century BC, or late, fifth century BC, is claimed for it, little can be said with certainty.

Contents

1. Jonah's disobedience, flight and disaster 1
2. His prayer from the depths 2
3. His second chance and Nineveh's repentance 3
4. Jonah's anger and the Lord's lesson 4

Study questions

1. Using Jonah as your source book, what would you say are the hindrances to, and the importance of, evangelism?
2. What basic teaching about prayer can you find in ch. 2?
3. What lessons for Christian living do you learn from Jonah's disobedience?

Reference books

L. C. Allen, *The Books of Joel, Obadiah, Jonah and Micah* (Eerdmans, U.S.A., 1978)

W. L. Banks, *Jonah, the Reluctant Prophet* (Moody, U.S.A., 1968)

S. B. Ferguson, *Man Overboard! The Story of Jonah* (Tyndale, U.S.A., 1982)

R. T. Kendall, *Jonah* (Hodder, U.K., 1978)

J. D. W. Watts, *Joel, Obadiah, Jonah, Micah, Nahum, Habakkuk, Zephaniah* (Cambridge, 1975)

Micah

Micah is best known for the foretelling of the birthplace of Christ in 5:2–4, familiar from its regular use at Christmas time. This and what has been called the 'vision glorious' in 4:1–4 are the highlights of what many find to be a difficult book.

The difficulties arise from two factors. The marked changes of thought in the book create a discontinuity which makes it difficult to find any logical sequence between the sections. Probably we are not meant to. Micah says in his introduction that his prophecies were spread over three reigns, so that it is consistent to find in the book a collection of prophecies given at different times over something like thirty to forty years.

The second factor is the strong Hebrew idiom and vivid pictorial language used. The outstanding example of this is the longest play on words to be found in the Old Testament (1:10–16), almost impossible to reproduce in translation (e.g. Beth-le-aphrah means 'House of dust', thus 'in Beth-le-aphrah roll yourselves in the dust'). It is helpful to read this passage in the NIV whose footnotes enable the reader to understand the puns.

Isaiah and Micah were contemporaries. But whereas Isaiah is the courtier-prophet, familiar with court and city, Micah is the country-prophet. He is especially concerned for the poor and under-privileged. But he is troubled also by the deluded attitude which believes that ceremonial, nominal religion and the presence of the living God would protect Samaria and Jerusalem irrespective of the people's conduct.

In several passages (*e.g.* 2:12–13) there is at least a reflection of Isaiah's doctrine of the remnant. The 'vision glorious' in 4:1–4 is an exact parallel with Isaiah 2:2–4. Either one borrowed from the other, or both reproduced an earlier prophecy.

Summary

Prophesying the fall of Samaria (722 BC), Micah sees the Assyrian army sweeping along the coastal plain towards Egypt overwhelming one town after another up the valleys to the gate of Jerusalem (1).

Rich upstarts in the city covet country estates and Micah champions the rights of the poor. After exile the Lord will make a new start with 'the remnant' (*cf.* Is. 7:3; 10:20) (2).

Unjust rulers, corrupt prophets and avaricious priests who believe that the Lord's presence will protect them, are deluded and invite judgment (3).

In days to come, all nations will come to Jerusalem to learn God's ways and there will be universal peace. Before then the exiles will return from Babylon, and Jerusalem, though besieged, will be triumphant. At Bethlehem the great ruler will be born and will reunite the people. The remnant will then be a company of faith (4–5).

The Lord invites his people to plead their case with him. He wants holy lives not costly sacrifices. Commercial sharp practices must cease (6).

Micah mourns Israel's situation, but realizes that when the Lord's judgment has been expended, she will be restored and her enemies vanquished. Thus the Lord will prove faithful to his covenant (7).

Writer and date

Micah came from the south and was a native of Moresheth Gath in south-western Judea on the borders of Philistia. He spoke to both kingdoms, the south and the north. His ministry covered three reigns: those of Jotham, Ahaz and

Hezekiah of Judah (*c.* 751–687 BC), and those of Pekah and Hoshea of Israel. His work in the days of King Hezekiah is favourably commented on in Jeremiah 26:18f.

Contents
1. The enemy approaches Jerusalem 1:1–16
2. Judgment on Israel's evil land-grabbers and the remnant restored 2
3. Judgment on rulers, priests and prophets 3
4. Jerusalem's future – the glorious vision 4:1–7
5. Jerusalem's present: snapshots during the siege 4:9–5:1
6. The ruler to come 5:2–6
7. The remnant to come 5:7–15
8. The Lord's requirements 6
    Plead your case 6:1–5   What does he want? 6:6–8 Stop sharp practices 6:9–16
9. After judgment, restoration 7

Study questions
1. Mark the references to 'the remnant' (or comparable phrases). What teaching can you gather from them?
2. List the social, religious and national sins of Samaria and Jerusalem castigated in Micah. Which of them do you find in national and church life today? How would the Lord judge them?
3. What will the ruler to come be like (5:2–4)? How far has this prophecy been fulfilled and what awaits fulfilment?
4. Study ch. 7. a) What was Israel's situation (1–6)? What sort of attitude might you expect this to lead to? b) What attitude does Micah in fact portray and why (7–13)? c) What can you learn about God, and about faith in him, from the prayer in verses 14–20?

Reference books
L. C. Allen, *The Books of Joel, Obadiah, Jonah and Micah* (Eerdmans, U.S.A., 1978)

J. L. Mays, *Micah: A Commentary* (SCM, 1976; Westminster, 1976)

J. D. W. Watts, *Joel, Obadiah, Jonah, Micah, Nahum, Habakkuk, Zephaniah* (Cambridge, 1975)

Nahum

'The measure you give will be the measure you get back.'
These words of Christ might be a sub-title for this book.
Its central message is that although God is love, if that love
is rejected and man remains unrepentant, judgment must
follow. Cruelty was common in ancient times but the Assyrians excelled in it and loved it. It is right to rejoice when
excessive cruelty and the power which perpetrates it are
destroyed.

For over 200 years the might of the Assyrian Empire had
terrified smaller nations. In 722 BC they had sacked Samaria, brought the northern kingdom of Israel to its end
and deported many of its people. Now just retribution is
about to fall on the Assyrian 'lion'. Nahum uses vivid
language and his imagery matches the events he describes.

Summary
God is good, therefore he must be 'indignant' with the
wicked, and therefore Nineveh must fall (1–2).

The rhythm of Nahum's words now begins the staccato
beat of the horses' hooves; Nineveh will receive a harlot's
punishment. Her fate will compare with that of Thebes,
once the capital of Egypt, which fell to the Assyrians amid
fire and slaughter in 663 BC. No attempt to withstand the
siege will save her. An elegy of death is pronounced on
king and commanders (3).

Writer and date
Little is known about Nahum. He was a native of Elkosh

but its location cannot be identified with certainty. His prophecy must fall between 663 BC when Thebes fell to the Assyrians (3:8) and 612 BC when Nineveh itself fell to the Babylonians. Probably Nahum's prophecy is closer to the latter date than to the former.

Contents

Study question
What facets of God's character are described in Nahum?

Reference books
R. J. Coggins and S. P. Re'emi, *Israel Among the Nations* (Handsel, 1985; Eerdmans, 1985)
J. D. W. Watts, *Joel, Obadiah, Jonah, Micah, Nahum, Habakkuk, Zephaniah* (Cambridge, 1975)

Habakkuk

The Christian thinker who is troubled by the paradoxes and contradictions of a world where it seems that 'might is right', but refuses either to let go of his faith or to turn his back on the world's problems, will find help in Habakkuk.

Summary
Habakkuk is a believer with a problem. He questions with his feet planted firmly on the rock of faith. He believes in the Lord God who is 'of purer eyes than to behold evil and canst not look on wrong'. Why, then, are bad men in Judah not punished? God answers that he is about to punish, using the Babylonians as his instrument (1).

This creates a second problem. Why use the Babylonians for they are worse than the bad men? The answer comes with a command to write it down very plainly (and, in essence, it is brief – nine words in Hebrew). In the midst of turmoil it is the individual's destiny that matters to God, 'Behold, he whose soul is not upright in him shall fail, but the righteous shall live by his faith' (2:4). The answer is spelt out in greater detail in a song taunting Babylon. She will fall and the Lord will be vindicated (2).

The third prayer asks God to show again his power as in the days of the exodus, and his mighty acts are recalled in a magnificent psalm. Habakkuk's faith is now such that though all material resources are withdrawn from him, he will find his happiness, strength and achievement in the Lord (3).

Three times Habakkuk recognizes the need for the thinking believer to be patient and quiet in the presence of God (2:1; 2:20; 3:16b).

Justification by faith

The words 'the righteous shall live by his faith' (2:4) are quoted by the apostle Paul in Romans 1:17 and Galatians 3:11 to support his teaching about justification by faith. The RSV rendering of these two New Testament quotations is 'He who through faith is righteous shall live'. Some readers feel that Paul has twisted Habakkuk's meaning from 'living by faith' to 'being righteous (or justified) by faith'. While the Greek phrase in Romans and Galatians can bear the RSV interpretation, it is better to translate it in line with Habakkuk 2:4, as the NIV does.

A second difficulty arises from the RSV marginal translation of *'emuna* in Habakkuk 2:4 as 'faithfulness' rather than 'faith'. If 'the righteous shall live by his faithfulness', doesn't that imply justification by works, rather than by faith? Was Paul wrong in his use of the verse?

The problem here springs from our inadequate understanding of the biblical meaning of faith. We are in the habit of thinking of it as just (intellectual) belief or just trusting God. But the Bible sees faith as a whole lifestyle, embracing intellect, attitude and action. We could almost paraphrase it as 'sticking with God' – in what we believe, in our confidence in him, and in the way we live in obedience to him. It is our humble response to God's sovereignty and grace.

So it doesn't really matter whether we translate Habakkuk 2:4 as 'faith (in God)' or 'faithfulness (to God)'. Both phrases suggest the trustful, obedient allegiance of the vassal to his overlord (see 'Covenant', p. 42). Both mean an end of confidence in oneself, and full confidence in God. From this it is clear that Paul was quite right to quote this verse in support of 'justification by faith' – justification by obedient trust in God, our only Saviour.

Writer and date

Nothing is known about Habakkuk apart from the book itself. Even the meaning of his name and its derivation are uncertain. Some derive it from a word meaning 'to embrace' because he brought his intellectual problems to God and got to grips with him.

It is also difficult to date Habakkuk with precision, but the reference to the Babylonians (Chaldeans) in 1:6 puts it at the end of the seventh century BC shortly after the battle of Carchemish (605 BC) when the Babylonians defeated Egypt and marched on King Jehoiakim. Whether we regard the passages 1:5–17 as predictive or descriptive of the Babylonians, and 2:6–19 as referring to Babylon or to the social ills in Judah under Jehoiakim (609–598 BC), or to Assyrian power at its height (669–626 BC), will influence any more precise reckoning.

Structure and contents

I. First prayer 1:1–11
 1. Why are bad men unpunished? 1:1–4
 2. God's answer 1:5–11

II. Second prayer 1:12–2:20
 1. Why use the Babylonians? 1:12–17
 2. First time of quiet waiting 2:1
 3. God's answer 2:2–19
  Brief and plain 2:2–5 Expanded 2:6–19 (Woes against Babylon for: greedy plundering; selfish security; ruthless empire-building; cruel humiliation; idol worship)
 4. Second time of quiet waiting 2:20

III. Third prayer 3:1–19
 1. The Lord's mighty acts 3:1–16a
 2. Third time of quiet waiting 3:16b
 3. Stronger faith 3:17–19

Study questions
1. What kinds of people might be described today by the woes of 2:6–19?
2. Summarize the teaching about faith in this book.

Reference books

D. M. Lloyd-Jones, *From Fear to Faith* (Baker, U.S.A., 1982)

M. E. Szeles, *Wrath and Mercy* (Handsel, 1987; Eerdmans, 1987)

J. D. W. Watts, *Joel, Obadiah, Jonah, Micah, Nahum, Habakkuk, Zephaniah* (Cambridge, 1975)

Zephaniah

In much Old Testament prophecy there is an oscillation between the Lord's severity and his gentleness. Zephaniah highlights this (*cf.* 1:4–18; 3:14–20).

The 'day of the Lord' is his theme. It is a day of judgment and chaos, of distress and wrath. He tells us that he spoke in the days of King Josiah of Judah (640–609 BC). It was in good King Josiah's reign that the 'book of the law' was found in the temple (2 Ki. 22:8). He led a reformation but its effects were short-lived. Some think that Zephaniah prophesied before the reformation and helped to bring it about. Others believe that it was because he saw it was a shallow and outward thing which did not touch the heart of the nation that he spoke of the coming 'day of the Lord'.

Sometimes he seems to point forward to the final great day at the end of time (*e.g.* 1:17–18) when God will judge all nations and all men.

The last section (3:14–18) would be remarkable for its cheerful promise of blessing in any Bible book, but coming at the end of the foretelling of so dire and calamitous a doom, it emphasizes its remarkable gentleness all the more.

Summary
Judah's idolatry, violence, fraud and indifference will lead to the day of wrath (1), a day which the Gentile nations as well as Judah need to fear (2). But it will leave a holy and humble people on whom the Lord will lavish his kindness: 'He will rejoice over you with gladness, he will renew you in his love' (3:17).

Writer and date

The superscription (1:1) places the book in the reign of King Josiah of Judah (640–609 BC). Local colour in the book suggests that Zephaniah lived in Jerusalem and the relatively long genealogy in the first verse indicates that he was a person of importance. His great, great grandfather may have been the Hezekiah who was king in Isaiah's day about seventy years earlier, and who, like Josiah, was faithful to the Lord. If this is so, Zephaniah must have been a young man when this prophecy was delivered.

Structure and contents

1. The day of the Lord and the sins of Judah 1
   Syncretistic worship 1–6   Foreign culture 7–8   Deceit and violence 9   Carelessness and complacency 10–13   Distress and wrath 14–18

2. The day of the Lord and the chaos of the nations 2
   Judah 1–3   Philistia 4–7   Moab and Ammon 8–11   Ethiopia 12   Assyria 13–15

3. The day of the Lord and a paradox 3
   The moral and spiritual breakdown of Jerusalem 1–7   A paradox: judgment and conversion 8–10   A humble remnant 11–13   Restoration – a song of joy 14–20

Study questions

1. What modern counterparts can you think of to the behaviour described in ch. 1, both in society and in the church?

2. From ch. 3 contrast the sins of Jerusalem with the righteousness of the 'remnant'. How would the Lord deal with each group of people?

Reference books

J. D. W. Watts, *Joel, Obadiah, Jonah, Micah, Nahum, Habakkuk, Zephaniah* (Cambridge, 1975)

Haggai

'A Christian is a proximate pessimist and an ultimate optimist.' If the first part of Bishop Gore's useful epigram is sometimes true, the second part always is. For the Christian it can always be said 'The best is yet to come'. Haggai gives the justification for this attitude. 'The latter splendour of this house shall be greater than the former' (2:9).

The book of Ezra provides the historical background for Haggai. Cyrus, king of Persia, issued his edict permitting the Jews to return to Jerusalem (539 BC). A party returned under Zerubbabel and the temple foundation was laid, but fierce opposition from the Samaritans brought the work to a standstill.

The discouraged, repatriated exiles turned their attention to settling down and to making themselves comfortable (1:2–4). Fifteen or sixteen years after the work had ceased (520 BC), Haggai and Zechariah encouraged the Jews to start again, and Haggai's book records his exhortations to them. Four years later in 516 BC the second temple was completed.

Haggai speaks to us, then, of our constant need to keep God's plan before us. The people had begun with good intentions but had not persevered. They had lost their God-given priorities and allowed other things, material concerns in particular, to crowd their lives, their thoughts, their hopes. The Lord had to bring them back to their senses, through the basic dissatisfaction which besets those who have lost their vision, and through the stern words of Haggai.

Summary

Haggai's four addresses are precisely dated:

29th August 520 BC: They were caring for their own houses rather than building the temple (1).

17th October 520 BC: There is no need to look back to 'the good old days'. The glory of the second temple will be greater than that of the first (2:1–9).

18th December 520 BC: Two questions addressed to the priest and their answers show that sin is contagious. As long as the temple is unbuilt, everything is tainted (2:10–19).

18th December 520 BC: The fourth address is shorter. Zerubbabel is promised that the sentence pronounced upon his grandfather Jehoiachin (Je. 22:24) is revoked and he is God's personal representative (2:20–23).

Writer and date

Nothing is known about Haggai apart from his book and the book of Ezra. He dates his addresses with precision. Recently it has been possible to synchronize the old lunar calendar with the Julian calendar, giving very accurate results. Nothing is known of him after 18th December 520 BC.

Contents

1. First address: inertia reproved 1:1–15
2. Second address: discouragement combated 2:1–9
3. Third address: blessing promised 2:10–19
4. Fourth address: Zerubbabel favoured 2:20–23

Study questions

1. It is often difficult for the Christian to balance his priorities – church, home, work, social life. What principles can you draw from 1:1–11?
2. What advice can you extract from 2:1–9 for Christians who constantly look for 'the good old days'?

3. In 1:5–6; 1:7; 2:15 and 2:18 he tells them to 'consider'
What points does he make when he uses the word?

Reference books

J. G. Baldwin, *Haggai, Zechariah, Malachi* (IVP, 1972)
D. L. Petersen, *Haggai and Zechariah 1-8* (SCM, U.K., 1985)
P. A. Verhoef, *The Books of Haggai and Malachi* (Paternoster, 1986; Eerdmans, 1986)

Zechariah

Zechariah and Haggai were contemporaries. While Haggai, in 520 BC, was prodding the repatriated exiles into starting again to build the second temple, Zechariah was providing the stimulus to lift them from the lethargy of discouragement and depression.

The book is in two parts. The first section (1–8) is contemporary with Haggai (c. 520 BC) and complements his book. It is an example of apocalyptic literature (see on Daniel, p. 193).

The style and content of the second section (9–14) are markedly different from those of the first. Gone is the apocalyptic symbolism; the circumstances are different, the visions have ceased, and the chapters look into the future when the king shall come.

Summary

'Return to me, says the Lord of hosts, and I will return to you' (1:3) summarizes his message.

On the night of 15 February 519 BC (it can now be dated precisely: see Baldwin, p. 29), eight visions were given to Zechariah:

1. Four horsemen demonstrate that the Lord's anger is aroused because there is no stirring among the nations to fulfil his purposes for Israel (1:7–17).
2. Four horns and workmen show that those who scattered Jerusalem shall be destroyed (1:18–21).
3. The city is being measured up for rebuilding but the Lord will be Jerusalem's protective wall (2).

4. Joshua, the high priest, as representative of a sinful people, is acquitted, indicating that with the coming of Messiah there will be a removal of guilt (3).

5. The lamp and olive trees are an illustration of divine resources available for the religious and national leaders (4).

6. The flying scroll proclaims that the word of God shall consume dishonesty (5:1–4).

7. The barrel and the woman foretell the removal of evil from the land (5:5–11).

8. Four chariots declare the Lord's sovereignty over all the earth (6:1–8).

Joshua is crowned, for he represents Messiah not only as priest but also as king (6:9–15).

The people of Bethel ask whether the fasts commemorating the fall of Jerusalem and the murdered governor, Gedaliah, need continue now that the temple is being rebuilt. The Lord's reply reminds them of the standards they refused to keep before the exile. In the future Jerusalem will be glorious and conditions will contrast sharply with those existing after the return, for Jerusalem will be the religious centre of the world (7–8).

The first of two oracles proclaims the arrival of Messiah, condemns careless leaders of the Lord's people, and foretells that the covenant will be broken and the nation divided (9–11).

The second oracle sees the Lord strengthening his people for a great battle and refining them. After the last battle, life-giving water flows from Jerusalem (12–14).

The New Testament quotes verses from these last chapters with reference to Christ. He is Zion's king and the smitten shepherd.

Writer and date

The prophet gives few details about himself, but there is some reason to believe that he may have been a priest. His ancestor Iddo was head of a priestly family (Ezra 5:1; 6:14).

He was familiar with the pre-exilic prophets and their language is on his lips.

There is controversy over the authorship and date of the last six chapters (9–14). Generally speaking the literary style is different, and Zechariah is not mentioned by name. There are no historical references. Matthew 27:9–10 quotes Zechariah 11:12–13 and ascribes these verses to Jeremiah.

The various views may be condensed into four possibilities:

1. The whole book is by Zechariah. Traditionally these chapters have been attributed to him. A fragment of a Greek manuscript from Qumran shows no gap between chapters 8 and 9.

2. The second part is later than Zechariah. A wide variety of dates is suggested.

3. 9:1–11:17, 12:1–14:21 and Malachi 1:1–4:6 are three anonymous prophecies, each beginning 'The burden of the word of the Lord . . .', which were added to the end of the Minor Prophets.

4. The chapters were written in the Greek period between 330 and 100 BC.

There are cogent arguments for the unity of the whole book. Definite thematic and stylistic links draw the book together (*e.g.* repentance and cleansing, the centrality of Jerusalem, the return of God's people and the subjection and conversion of their enemies). The change in atmosphere from the first eight chapters may show that the last part of the book belongs to Zechariah's later life, when the initial hope of the returning exiles had been replaced by disillusion with the nation's bad leadership. In every manuscript we possess, the fourteen chapters appear as one book.

Structure and contents
Part One: 1–8
  I. Introduction: call to repentance 1:1–6
  II. Eight visions 1:7–6:8
    1. The four horsemen – peaceful apathy 1:7–17

Study questions

1. Collect into one whole message the teaching of each of the visions in 1:1–6:8.

2. How do these passages in Zechariah point forward to the Messiah: ch. 3 and 6:9–15; 9:9–13 (*cf.* Mt. 21:5; Jn. 12:15); 12:10–13:1 (*cf.* Jn. 19:37); 13:7–9 (*cf.* Mt. 26:31); ch. 14 (*cf.* Acts 1:11)?

Reference books

J. G. Baldwin, *Haggai, Zechariah, Malachi* (IVP, 1972)

D. L. Petersen, *Haggai and Zechariah 1-8* (SCM, U.K., 1985)

Malachi

Malachi is concerned about nominal religion, and so his book is relevant whenever the Lord's people display a form of religion but deny its power.

He speaks to God's people, the chosen people, and is rewarded for his efforts when some at least listen to what he has to say (3:16). His prophecies display the following pattern: a statement by the Lord; a question by the people, with an air of injured innocence; and an elaboration of the original statement. This occurs seven times (1:2, 6, 7; 2:17; 3:7, 8, 13).

Summary
God's choice of them is proof of his love for them, but sacrifices without devotion to the Lord, and inferior sacrifices too, prove that they despise his name (1).

The priests neglect their duty of teaching the Law and the people are faithless to one another. This is especially obvious in divorcing their wives and marrying with heathen women. In the Lord's eyes this is apostasy (2:1–16).

Sorcery, adultery, perjury, oppression of the deprived, rejection of travellers, and withholding the tithe make them incapable of standing in the day of the Lord's coming (2:17–3:12).

They believe that it is vain to serve the Lord. But he takes note of those who are loyal and in the coming holocaust they will be preserved (3:13–4:3).

Finally the nation is encouraged to take a look back to the giving of the covenant and a look forward to the day of the Lord (4:4–6).

'I have loved Jacob'

The words 'I have loved Jacob but I have hated Esau' (1:2–3) can be a problem until we understand that Hebrew thinking uses opposites where we would use comparatives ('I have loved Jacob more than Esau'). The point here is that the Lord has a special love for his own, chosen people. 'A study of the verb "hate" in the Old and New Testament will show that "hate" may be used in the sense of a lesser love' (F. F. Bruce, *Answers to Questions*, Paternoster, 1972, p. 87).

Elijah the prophet

Elijah the prophet is named as the messenger who is to come (3:1; 4:5). It is there made clear that Malachi was not referring to a reincarnation of Elijah but to the herald who was to come in the spirit and power of Elijah. Although Malachi clearly saw himself as 'the messenger', it is equally clear that he is pointing beyond himself to the time when his words would be perfectly fulfilled. The New Testament shows that this in fact happened in the coming of John the Baptist, who prepared the way for Jesus (Lk. 1:17).

Writer and date

For several reasons many commentators regard Malachi as a title rather than a name. It means 'my messenger' (3:1). Joyce Baldwin, however, argues strongly that it is the name of a prophet who is unknown apart from this book.

Because he is concerned with evils which also troubled Nehemiah (*e.g.* Mal. 3:8, *cf.* Ne. 10:32–38, *etc.*) and because the temple is standing, he is usually placed just before or just after Nehemiah's first period as governor of Jerusalem. A date *c.* 460 BC is not improbable.

Contents

Study questions

1. How would you apply 1:6–2:14 to Christian ministry and worship? What principles can be deduced from it?
2. What principles for Christian giving can you draw from 3:6–12? What needs modification?
3. Pick out the three covenants about which Malachi writes. How does the Lord regard faithlessness to these covenants? What has he done and will he do about it?

Reference books

J. G. Baldwin, *Haggai, Zechariah, Malachi* (IVP, 1972)

G. Ogden and R. R. Deutsch, *A Promise of Hope—A Call to Obedience* (Handsel, 1987; Eerdmans, 1987)

P. A. Verhoef, *The Books of Haggai and Malachi* (Paternoster, 1986; Eerdmans, 1986)

The Apocrypha

The word Apocrypha means 'hidden (things)', and was applied to writings which were regarded as so important that they were hidden away from lesser mortals, but traditionally it is used in the reverse sense: a collection of writings originally not in the Hebrew Bible and so hidden away because they were inferior. This collection of Jewish literature, legends, poetry and history, appeared between 300 BC and AD 100 and is useful to give information about the intertestamental period.

These writings were included in the Greek version of the Old Testament and were familiar to the early church, but they are never quoted authoritatively in the New Testament.

The Roman Catholics at the Council of Trent (1545-64) asserted the full canonical status of most of the Apocrypha, but there is today a tendency for Roman Catholics to treat them as 'deutero-canonical'. The Anglicans and Lutherans continued to use them for their ethical value, and the Reformed churches gave them only the status of religious writings.

The sixth 'article' of the Church of England says of them: 'The other Books (as Hierome (Jerome) saith) the Church doth read for example of life and instruction of manners; but yet doth it not apply them to establish any doctrine.'

1 Esdras is a variant Greek version of Chronicles-Ezra-Nehemiah.

2 Esdras puts a prophecy into the mouth of the biblical Ezra which rejects the Jews in favour of the Christian church. It was composed in Hebrew *c.* AD 100.

Tobit was written *c.* 200 BC either in Hebrew or Aramaic and shows the influence of Persian beliefs and practices with an emphasis on angels. Tobit is deported by the Assyrians at the fall of Samaria in 722 BC. He has a guardian angel, Raphael, who helps him to drive away an evil spirit named Asmodaeus.

Judith is a work of fiction containing historical blunders. Judith, an attractive young Jewish widow, uses her charms to destroy a pagan general named Holofernes and so delivers the city and its people from destruction.

The rest of the chapters of **Esther** expand her story so as to correct the 'omission' of any references to God in the canonical book.

The Wisdom of Solomon was written in Alexandria *c.* AD 40 and contains an attack on idolatry similar to that of the apostle Paul in Romans 1:18–32.

Ecclesiasticus, or the Wisdom of Jesus ben Sira, was written in Palestine *c.* 200 BC in Hebrew. Its most famous section is often used at memorial services, 'Let us now praise famous men'. For a long time the Hebrew original was lost, but half of it was pieced together after discoveries in the Cairo genizah (a room attached to a synagogue for housing discarded religious books) in 1896.

Baruch purports to be the work of Jeremiah's scribe and belongs to a date just before the Christian era. It contains a confession of sin and a sermon on wisdom.

The Song of the Three Children is the *Benedicite Omnia Opera*, plus a prayer of Azariah, and was inserted between verses 23 and 24 of Daniel 3. The Benedicite is occasionally used at Morning Service in the Church of England.

Susanna tells how Daniel defended the good name of a beautiful Jewish lady against the accusations of two wicked men.

Bel and the Dragon attacks idolatry.

(The Song, Bel and Susanna are all additions to Daniel

probably composed originally in Hebrew or Aramaic.)

The Prayer of Manasseh is a confession of sin put into the mouth of King Manasseh. It first appeared in the *Didascalia Apostolorum*, in the third century AD, but may have been composed in the second century BC.

1 Maccabees records the historical conflict between Antiochus Epiphanes (175 BC) who set up the abomination of desolation in the temple, and the priest, Judas ben Mattathias (Greek form *Makkabaios*), and his sons, continuing the story down to 134 BC. It was probably written *c.* 100 BC.

2 Maccabbees is an abridgement of a longer work, is historically inferior to the first book and partly covers the same period. It emphasizes observance of the sabbath and the resurrection of the martyrs.

Intertestamental History

Prophecy among the Jews came to an end with Malachi (c. 450 BC). The first book of Maccabees mentions this several times: 'Thus there was great distress in Israel, such as had not been since the time that prophets ceased to appear among them' (1 Macc. 9:27). There is, therefore, no biblical book between Malachi and the New Testament. But the history of this 450 years is important for the understanding of the New Testament.

Under Persian supremacy 539–331 BC

For just over 200 years the Jews lived under Persian rule and their religion was influenced by Persian thinking. Zoroastrianism was the official religion of Persia at this time. It believed in a struggle between good and evil, but it tended to regard the two as equally powerful, and this is known as 'dualism'. The good spirit and his attendants were rivalled by the evil spirit and his supporters. The providence of God used this belief to expand Bible teaching about good and evil and about angels and evil spirits, but without the false dualism. It is important to recognize that 'Zoroastrian influences affected the fringes of Jewish faith and not its essence'.

Because the representative of the king, the civil governor, would usually not be a Jew, the prestige and authority of the high priest increased. Religiously, Judaism became more legalistic, a tendency which can be seen at the end of the book of Nehemiah. Probably synagogue worship as an institution began and grew during this time. The Diaspora,

Jews scattered throughout the empire and thus separated from Jerusalem and the temple, met together to read and expound the Law.

Aramaic replaced Hebrew as the *lingua franca* and in time, since the Law continued to be read in Hebrew, it was necessary to add an explanation in a language which the people could understand. This began orally but eventually was written down and so the *targums* were composed.

The Hebrew script was written with letters having angular shapes. It was now adapted to the Aramaic script and the square characters came into use and have continued ever since.

Under Greek supremacy 331–323 BC

A number of Greek settlements in Asia Minor, previously under Croesus of Lydia, but now part of the Persian Empire, revolted and were supported by some of the Greek states on the mainland. Thus began a struggle between Persia and Greece which ended with the total subjugation of the Persian Empire, Alexander the Great (336–323 BC) defeating Darius III at the Battle of Gaugamela in the Plain of Arbela east of the Tigris in 331 BC. In the course of this struggle, Alexander marched south to Egypt and, on the way, received the homage of the Jewish high priest, Jaddua, in Jerusalem in 332 BC.

But, generally speaking, the Jews in Judea were not involved in the actual hostilities. The reforms of Ezra and Nehemiah bore fruit in the orderly development of Jewish tradition and life, and the Jews made progress economically and politically in comparative peace and obscurity. Two specially important features of Greek culture were introduced throughout the vast empire (from Macedonia to Afghanistan and from Egypt to Thrace), the Greek city and the Greek language.

New cities rose, modelled on the Greek pattern, and the process known as 'hellenization' was set in motion. Alexander's soldiers, drawn from the whole Greek-speaking world, began to eradicate their variety of dialects and developed a common speech which, in time, became the *koinē* Greek in which the New Testament was written.

Alexander died in 323 BC before his son and heir was born. A muddled and confusing struggle ensued between his six generals who administered the empire as regents. Ptolemy, who ruled Egypt, and Seleucus, who administered Asia, are important for Jewish history. The Ptolemaic dynasty in Egypt lasted till 31 BC and the Seleucid dynasty in Asia until *c.* 65 BC. There was frequent hostility between them and Judea found herself back in the old situation of the buffer state between the kings of the north, the Seleucids, and the kings of the south, the Ptolemies, as the book of Daniel calls them.

Under Greek Ptolemaic-Egyptian supremacy 320–198 BC
In 320 BC Ptolemy I entered Jerusalem on the pretext that he wanted to offer sacrifice, but proceeded to annex Judea. It remained under Ptolemaic-Egyptian control for more than a century till 198 BC.

The new city of Alexandria in Egypt was attractive and many Jews settled there. They played an important part in commerce and prospered materially and intellectually, eventually replacing their Hebrew/Aramaic with Greek. One of the five wards of Alexandria was completely Jewish with its own special privileges and constitution. These hellenic Jews were to exercise a great influence on the development of Judaism and the preparation for the New Testament.

For their benefit, a translation into Greek of the Hebrew Pentateuch (Genesis to Deuteronomy) was begun in the third century BC and probably was given official approval by the Jewish leaders. This was the beginning of what is known today as the Septuagint (LXX), the Greek translation of the Hebrew Bible. A legend in the 'Letter of Aristeas' says that it was so called because seventy-two selected scholars made the translation on the island of Pharos in seventy-two days. Today, the name Septuagint refers to the Greek translation of the whole Old Testament, for the remaining books were also translated from Hebrew into Greek and added to the Pentateuch in the next 150 years or so.

The hellenizing process which had made rapid progress among the Jews in Egypt reached Judea. Among the upper classes Greek names and manners were adopted. This led to a gradual dissolution of the religious and moral bonds of Judaism, and at about the same time the Jews in Palestine became an object of contention between the Egyptian Ptolemies and the Syrian Seleucids.

Antiochus III (the Great) defeated the infant Ptolemy V's General Scopas at Panion, near the source of the Jordan, in 200 BC and Jerusalem recognized the Seleucid king as overlord in 198 BC.

Under Greek Seleucid-Syrian supremacy 198–142 BC

The measure of self-government which the Jews in Judea had acquired under both the Ptolemies and now the Seleucids meant that the high priest was recognized as the civil ruler, and the hereditary office became a matter of dispute and competition. Antiochus IV, called Epiphanes ('he who has appeared'), but sometimes nicknamed Epimanes ('madman') (175–163 BC), was asked to intervene. He entered Jerusalem and plundered the temple in 169 BC. The outburst of resentment which this sacrilege aroused among all sections of the Jews led to an outburst of savage fury by Antiochus against them. He sent armed forces into the country, which plundered and butchered indiscriminately. The practice of Judaism was forbidden under pain of death. The Jews were compelled to worship idols and an altar dedicated to the Olympian Zeus was placed upon the altar in the temple and unclean animals sacrificed upon it. This was the abomination of desolation spoken of in Daniel 11:31.

The inroads which Syro-Hellenic culture had made among the upper classes left Judaism ill-prepared to withstand this unexpected and fierce onslaught. Many faithful Jews were martyred.

In 167 BC Mattathias, the Hasmonean, who lived in Modin near Jerusalem, led a rebellion. After his death, his son Judas, named Maccabeus, perhaps meaning the Hammer, became leader of the insurrection in 166 BC. Brave, devout, sensible and resourceful, he defeated the Syrian army with a band of guerrilla fighters, entered Jerusalem and rededicated the temple in 164 BC. The feast of Hanukkah, Feast of Lights, is celebrated to this day in memory of the event. Judas entered into an alliance with Rome but was killed while fighting in 160 BC. Jonathan, his brother (160–143 BC), carried on the fight ably but with varying success and was eventually succeeded by his brother, Simon, the last surviving son of Mattathias.

Under the Hasmoneans 142–63 BC

Simon (143–135 BC) won independence for Judea and was made high priest and recognized as civil and military leader as well.

Simon's son, John Hyrcanus I (135–104 BC), was a successful ruler and enlarged the frontiers of Judea and raised it to a high degree of prosperity. He destroyed the Samaritans' duplicate temple on Mount Gerizim, and got entangled with the religious parties of Pharisees and Sadducees who had become rivals.

The Sadducees were a group in the national senate, the Sanhedrin, who retained control of it for fifty years and supported the Hasmoneans. They were never numerous but were wealthy and influential. In some ways, they were the materialists, secularists and rationalists of their time. They rejected belief in an after-life, in angels and demons and in the resurrection. Their origin and the origin of their name is shrouded with mystery.

The Pharisees arose probably towards the end of the second century BC and emerged as an opposition group to the Hasmonean dynasty during the reign of John Hyrcanus. Their aspirations became hard and dogmatic, their patriotism became partisan and they verged on the fanatical. They believed in angels, rewards and retribution, and in the resurrection. For them, oral tradition was of equal authority with the Law.

The son of John Hyrcanus I, Aristobulus I, reigned for about a year (104 BC). His mother and brother Antigonus were murdered.

He was succeeded by Alexander Jannaeus (103–76 BC), another son of John Hyrcanus I. Alexander engaged in a number of foreign enterprises and extended the boundaries of Judea. On his death, his wife Salome Alexandra assumed sovereignty by his bequest and ruled well for nine years, appointing one of her sons John Hyrcanus II to the high priesthood. She entrusted her younger son Aristobulus II to a military command. When she died in 67 BC, he seized his opportunity not only to assume the civil power but also to make himself high priest. Between them they brought the country to ruin and eventually ended the Hasmonean dynasty.

Under Roman supremacy 63 BC–
Both the brothers appealed to Rome. The famous Roman general Pompey marched on Jerusalem and took the defended temple by storm. It is said that, entering the Holy of Holies, he was struck with wonder and awe at the entire absence of any visible representation of the deity. The Jews, however, never excused his sacrilege. He left the temple treasures untouched and reinstated Hyrcanus as high priest and ruler of Judea (67–40 BC). Hyrcanus II was a weak and easy-going man, but he was supported by a wily and scheming Edomite, Antipater, who held the reins of government. Eventually, Hyrcanus was removed and the Roman Senate

appointed Antipater's son, Herod the Great, as king of Judea (40–4 BC). His reign was full of murders and outrages. He killed several of his wives and children and some members of the Sanhedrin. The Emperor Augustus is said to have remarked that it was better to be this man's swine than his son. He built a number of Grecian cities in honour of the emperors and introduced un-Jewish customs. To flatter his vanity, he rebuilt the temple in Jerusalem on a magnificent scale. At the end of his reign, the Lord Jesus Christ was born in Bethlehem.

Reference books

NCBR

F. F. Bruce, *Israel and the Nations* (Paternoster, 1963; Eerdmans, 1963)

H. L. Ellison, *From Babylon to Bethlehem: The People of God from the Exile to the Messiah* (Paternoster, 1976; Baker, 1984)

The Purpose of the New Testament

On any reckoning the Bible is unique. It contains national history and biography, law and poetry, proverbs and parables, letters and sermons, and any of these may be compared with such in other books. Yet to millions of people in all parts of the world this book is 'The Book' (the Greek word *biblos* from which 'Bible' comes simply means 'book'). For centuries it has been God's Book to millions. Its first section, the Old Testament, nearly 4000 times links what it says to such statements as 'The word of the Lord came to ———', 'Thus says the Lord', 'The Lord said'. Prophets claimed to be God's messengers, psalmists to speak by inspiration (see 2 Sa. 23:2). History is told as the acts of God explained by his servants who understood what he was doing. So Jewish and Christian people have turned to these Scriptures which we call the Old Testament to find in them God's word to enlighten and direct their lives, to lead them and keep them in the ways of God.

The Old Testament, however, is constantly pointing forward. It speaks of One who is to come and of things that God will do in the future. The central claim of the New Testament is that the day of the fulfilment of the Old has come. In the person of Jesus of Nazareth the expected Messiah has arrived. Previously men had had the spoken word of God through his messengers and the written word of Scripture, but now the living Word has come, the very Son of God made Man (Jn. 1:1–18 and Heb. 1:1–2).

This New Testament is a library, not a book. We have

twenty-seven writings from at least ten different authors. They are very different from each other. Four of them are records of the earthly life of Jesus Christ; one is the story of the spread of the good news of Jesus in the first generation of the church; others are letters to individuals, letters to churches, general letters that we might almost call sermons; at the end we have a book that tells of the 'last things', of God's final breaking into our human history in Jesus Christ who is shown to be King of kings and Lord of lords.

But although they are different in kind and in their particular purposes, they have their unity in that Jesus Christ is the central figure in each one. They tell us who he is, how he lived, how and why he died, and the fact that he rose again from the dead. What they record is presented as good news of salvation; how men are set free from sin, brought back to God, and given new life by the Holy Spirit in the fellowship of the church, and how that new life should be lived in a world often hostile to Christians. That earliest Christian creed, 'Jesus is Lord' (see 1 Cor. 12:3), is the unifying subject of all the New Testament.

Reference books

A. M. Hunter, *The Unity of the New Testament* (SCM, 1944); *The Message of the New Testament* (Westminster, 1944)

Joachim Jeremias, *The Central Message of the New Testament* (rev. ed. SCM, 1981; Fortress, 1981)

C. F. D. Moule, *The Birth of the New Testament* (3rd ed. Black, 1981; rev. ed. Harper & Row, 1981)

The Four Gospels

The New Testament begins with four books which we call 'Gospels', though whenever we use the word in this way we should remember that before the 'Gospels' came the 'gospel', that is, the good news concerning Jesus. Jesus himself preached good news when he began his work (Mk. 1:15). Then from the day of Pentecost the church took up the good news and preached it far and wide (see Acts 8:25; 14:7, 21). All four books alike tell the story of the life and death and resurrection of our Lord Jesus Christ. At some points the four Gospels are very similar. Two of them, or three of them, may give us an account of something that Jesus said or did in almost exactly the same words (see Mt. 8:1–4; Mk. 1:40–44 and Lk. 5:12–14; Mt. 23:37–39 and Lk. 13:34–35). At other times they give us rather different accounts of the same events, one Gospel giving details that the other does not (see Mk. 6:30–44 and Jn. 6:1–15). Each of the four Gospels tells us some things that none of the others tell us. The four were written by different people, at different times and in different places. The particular purposes of each of the four were different. Our knowledge of Jesus, who he is, and what he has done, is richer and deeper because we have four Gospels and not just one. As far as we can tell, all the Gospels were written in the second half of the 1st Century (perhaps all of them between 60 and 90 AD). It is important to note how Luke 1:1–4 tells us that there were other written records before he came to write his Gospel. It is even more important to realize that all four

Gospels were written while people who knew Jesus and had been with him in the time of his ministry on earth were still alive.

When these Gospels were written the good news of Jesus Christ was being preached in many lands and the Christian church was growing. Although, as we have seen, there were some written records, much Christian preaching and teaching was handed on by word of mouth from the apostles. So, for a number of reasons, there was need for reliable records that Christians could use, telling of the life and teaching, the death and resurrection of Jesus. It may help us in our understanding of the situation, and of the Gospels, if we think in four ways of that need for written records.

1.   Although the spoken word of preaching is very powerful (and it meant more 1900 years ago when there were very few books of any kind), yet it was realized how valuable it might be to put down in writing the great facts of the good news of Jesus so that those who had not come to believe in him might read and be challenged to faith. John (20:31) tells us that the purpose of the writing of his Gospel was that those who read it might 'believe that Jesus is the Christ, the Son of God, and that believing you may have life in his name'. Mark (1:1) says that he wrote that people might know how the good news of Jesus all began. We might speak of this as the evangelistic purpose of the Gospels, remembering that 'evangelistic' comes from a Greek word *euangelion* which means 'the good news'.

2.   It was realized that, through such writings, reasons might be given for believing in Christ and misunderstandings that hindered people from believing might be overcome. Luke addresses his Gospel to one who is called 'most excellent Theophilus', perhaps an important Roman governor or official. He wants him to have 'an orderly account' that he might 'know the truth' concerning the things of which he had been informed (Lk. 1:3–4). We might speak of this as the apologetic purpose of the Gospels, remembering that 'apologetic' comes from a

Greek word *apologia* which means 'defence'.

3. There was also a great need to give people further instruction in the faith when they had become Christians (Acts 2:42). They needed to know more of the life of Jesus, more of the things that he taught, so that they might see how they should live the Christian life. In the case of Matthew's Gospel, five large sections, nine chapters in all, are given to the teaching of Jesus. We can thus, especially in relation to this Gospel, speak of a catechetical purpose behind the writing, the word 'catechetical' coming from a Greek word *katachesis* which means 'teaching'.

4. There was probably also the desire and the need to have written records that could be read at times when Christians met for worship. We know that the Old Testament was read when Christians met in fellowship. In some cases there were writings of apostles that could be read also (see Col. 4:16). It would mean a great deal to Christians, when they met, to be able to read also of the life and teaching of Jesus, and especially the details of his death and resurrection which were the heart of the gospel that had been preached to them. Thus we may be right to add a liturgical purpose to the other purposes behind the writing of these four documents; and here in using the word 'liturgical' we are using a word that comes from the Greek *leitourgia* which means 'service' or 'worship'.

The first three Gospels, Matthew, Mark and Luke, are more like each other than any of them is like John's Gospel. The three are often called the 'Synoptic' Gospels from a Greek word which means that they see the ministry of Jesus from the same point of view, while John sees it from a different viewpoint and has a quite different arrangement in what he has written. It is not difficult to arrange the contents of the first three Gospels in parallel columns, putting side by side similar narratives from Matthew, Mark and Luke (we call such an arrangement in parallel columns a 'Synopsis' of the Gospels). John, on the other hand, chooses some of the most important incidents in the life of Jesus and uses them as 'signs' which show us who Jesus is and the purpose of his coming. And with most of the signs the teaching of Jesus is given at greater lengths than we have it in the other Gospels.

Reference books

NBCR

IBD Supplementary Volume, "Gospels"

D. Guthrie, *New Testament Introduction: The Gospels and Acts,* ch. 1 (IVP, 1970)

E. F. Harrison, *Introduction to the New Testament,* ch. 5 (Eerdmans, 1977)

R. P. Martin, *New Testament Foundations: A Guide for Christian Students,* Vol. 1 (rev. ed. Paternoster, 1985; Eerdmans, 1975)

W. Graham Scroggie, *A Guide to the Gospels* (Revell, 1975), *Matthew and Mark* and *Luke and John* (Ark Publishing, 1981)

Mark

When the Bible is being translated and printed in any language for the very first time, the first part of it to be done is usually Mark's Gospel. This is a regular policy of such organizations as the Bible Societies and Wycliffe Bible Translators. In many ways Mark is the simplest of the Gospels, presenting to us clearly and plainly the main facts about Jesus Christ and what he has done for us.

The purpose of the Gospel

The first words that we read as we open Mark are, 'The beginning of the gospel of Jesus Christ, the Son of God'. When we read these words we should forget for a moment that the four books, Matthew, Mark, Luke and John, are what we call Gospels. As we have said already, that was a later use of the word 'gospel'. In the first place the 'gospel' was the good news about Jesus Christ; so when Mark heads his little book with the words, 'The beginning of the gospel . . . ' he is meaning that he wants to tell how the good news all began. In the first century, when the Christians were preaching this good news from one country to another, people were asking, 'How did it all begin?' This book tells us. Mark, as we shall see, was a person well able to answer the question. We know (from Acts 12:12) that Mark's home was in Jerusalem in the days of the life of Jesus on earth. It is interesting also that a second century Christian writer, Irenaeus, said that, after the apostle

Peter died, Mark set down in writing what Peter had preached. His testimony, therefore, is that Mark's Gospel is concerned with the good news; and with showing us how there came to be such good news to preach.

In several important ways Mark tells us of 'the beginning of the gospel of Jesus Christ, the Son of God'.

1.   Mark tells us, even as these words of the title show, who the Person at the centre of the gospel message is.

(a) He is Jesus. This is his human name, the name that he was given when he was born. It also tells us the purpose of all that he came to do, because, as Matthew (1:21) shows us, Jesus is the Greek form of the Hebrew name that means 'Saviour' or 'God saves'.

(b) He is Christ. That is the Greek form of the Hebrew word, Messiah. Both words mean 'anointed king'. In other words he is the One whom the Jews looked forward to, because so many of the Old Testament prophets spoke of the Messiah whom God would send to his people. The name 'Christ' (or 'Messiah'), however, is not often used in this Gospel because it was a term often misunderstood. His Messiahship was kept hidden from most people till near the end; for the majority of the Jews expected a Christ who would be a political deliverer, who would come and set them free from the Romans who ruled over them. Because Jesus did not want them to think that he had come to be that kind of Christ, he used most frequently the name 'Son of man' when he spoke of himself. People could understand this in different ways. They could think of it as meaning much the same as 'man' (see Ps. 8:4 and Ezk. 2:1; 3:1), though Jesus spoke of himself not just as 'a son of man' but 'the Son of man'. A few times when he used the name he reminded people of how the Old Testament used it in Daniel 7:13–14 (see Mk. 13:26 and 14:62). For those who wanted to understand, it had a deep and wonderful meaning, a meaning not far away from the true meaning of Christ, the One whom God sent to bring in his kingdom.

(c) He is the Son of God. Jesus is truly Man, as Mark tells us. He is the God-sent Messiah. But Mark makes it very clear that he is also the Son of God. At his baptism and at his transfiguration he was proclaimed as God's own Son (1:11 and 9:7). He confessed the fact himself at his trial, although he knew that it would lead the Jewish leaders to condemn him (14:61–62). The centurion who saw him die on the cross spoke words more deeply true than he could have realized when he said, 'Truly this man was the Son of God' (15:39).

2. Mark tells us what Jesus did. Mark's Gospel often tells us that the Lord Jesus Christ spent much time teaching the people and preaching to them (see 1:14,21,27,38–39 and 2:2,13), but most of the Gospel is taken up with telling, with a great sense of wonder, what Jesus did. Then chapters 11–16 (more than a third of the whole) tell us of the events of the last few days before Jesus died and finally of his death and resurrection. The reason for this is that his death and resurrection were at the very centre of the good news that Christians preached, more important than anything else. To check this you need only to look at the way in which the apostle Paul summed up the gospel in 1 Corinthians 15:1–4 (see also 1 Cor. 1:23 and 2:2 and Gal. 3:1), or you may take note of the things which the apostle Peter said in his preaching recorded in Acts chapters 2–5 and 10. When people heard this Christian preaching with its marked emphasis on the death and resurrection of Christ, they would ask how these events came about. They would want to know more of the details. They would also ask why the death of Jesus was so important, and why did Jesus, the Christ, the Son of God, have to die, and to die the terrible death of the cross.

3. Part of the purpose of Mark's book, therefore, and a very important part, was to tell people not only how Jesus died but why he had to die. The reason could be given in two ways:

(a) Jesus died because the Jews rejected him and handed him over to the Romans for them to put him to death. In Mark's Gospel we see the growing opposition to Jesus and the reasons for this. They rejected the claims that he made to be able to forgive sin (2:1–12). They hated the way that he showed himself to be the Friend of tax-collectors and of others whom they thought of as the worst of sinners (2:15–16). They were bitterly opposed to him because of the way he treated the Law of Moses and the rules that they had added to the Law (2:18–28 and 3:1–6). In the end they rejected him because he claimed to be the Christ, the Son of God (14:61–64).

(b) But there was a deeper and more important reason why Jesus died. In the earliest Christian preaching on the day of Pentecost we read that Peter told the people something of tremendous importance. Jesus was crucified not just because of what the Jews and Romans did, but because he was 'delivered up according to the definite plan and foreknowledge of God' (Acts 2:23). That is, it was the purpose of God. Mark makes it clear that Jesus came 'to give his life to set many others free' 10:45, Phillips). His body was broken and his blood outpoured, as he taught at the Last Supper before he died, that a new covenant might be made between man and God (14:22–24). In order to save others from sin, he could not save himself (see 15:31), but he had to give himself to die for our sins, the perfect sacrifice. As soon as the disciples had come to believe in him as Messiah (8:27–29), we read that he taught them that, as Messiah, he must suffer and die and rise again (8:31; 9:30–32 and 10:32–34). Mark tells us that immediately he died the great curtain of the Temple, which blocked off the entrance to the most holy place in the Temple, 'was torn in two, from top to bottom' (15:38). This showed that men could now come freely to God through what Jesus had done by his death on the cross.

4. Mark therefore wanted to tell how the good news all

began by telling who Jesus was, how he lived, and most of all how and why he died. But what he wrote makes clear also what is the true response people should make to this good news of Jesus and to Jesus himself. In fact, Mark's Gospel shows us the different attitudes of people to Jesus Christ.

(a) There were the Jewish leaders who opposed Jesus more and more till they had him crucified.

(b) There were the crowds who were prepared to listen to him, and to be helped by his miracles; but most of them did not continue to follow him, simply because they did not truly believe in him.

(c) There were the disciples who believed in him and were willing to serve him. In the very first words of the preaching of Jesus, we see the response that men should make to him. He said, 'The time is fulfilled, and the kingdom of God is at hand; repent, and believe in the gospel' (1:15). Many times in the Gospel it is shown that the right response to Jesus is repentance (see 2:15–17 and 6:12) and faith (see 2:15; 4:40; 5:34,36; 6:5–6; 8:14–21). In the early part, we read of Jesus spending much time with the crowds; but he also called men to be his disciples, and we see him leading them on to faith in him. So much that goes before leads up to what we read in 8:27–30 of the way that Peter came to confess Jesus as the Christ. From that point Jesus 'began to teach them that the Son of man must suffer many things' (8:31). We have three clear predictions of his suffering and death (8:31; 9:31; 10:32–34); then the Gospel moves towards its great conclusion in the death and resurrection of Jesus Christ. Faith in Jesus is faith in him as crucified and risen Lord and Saviour. Such faith that leads on to obedience and service is the response that men should make to Jesus.

5. There is another purpose of the Gospel which comes out especially in the closing chapters after the disciples have confessed Jesus as the Christ. They are told not only that their

Master must suffer and die; they also must be prepared to suffer (see 8:34–38; 10:28–30; 35–45 and 13:9–13). This is particularly meaningful if we realize the time when Mark's Gospel was written. We have referred to what the second century writer, Irenaeus, said about the connection of Mark with the apostle Peter. The same writer also said that the Gospel was written after Peter and Paul were put to death. This was the time when Nero was the Roman Emperor, and Christians were being persecuted for their faith. This Gospel would remind them that they should not be surprised at this. Jesus told his disciples that they should be willing to bear the cross and suffer, since he had suffered and died for them.

These five things, therefore, about the purpose and the occasion of the writing of Mark, help us to understand how the Gospel came to be written, and help us also to explain its contents and its arrangement.

Structure and contents

With these things in mind we can turn to see the actual contents of the Gospel and how they are put together.

1. Preparation for the work of Jesus (1:1–13)

   (a) 1:1–8 The preaching of John the Baptist.

   (b) 1:9–13 The baptism and temptation of Jesus.

2. The authority of Jesus and the opposition it provoked (1:14–3:6)

(a) 1:14–20 The beginning of his teaching and the call of the first disciples.

(b) 1:21–45 The ministry of Jesus among the crowds. He taught with authority, cast out demons, healed the sick, all in the strength of a life lived close to his Father in prayer.

(c) 2:1–3:6 When he claimed to forgive sins, when he went

to eat with 'tax-collectors and sinners' and when he healed on the sabbath, the Jews were angry and opposed him.

3. Miracles and teaching in Galilee and the mission of the disciples (3:7–6:13)

(a) 3:7–35 Jesus and the crowds, his disciples and his family. Great crowds came to Jesus, but he called twelve men to be his special disciples, 'to be with him, and to be sent out to preach and have authority to cast out demons'. Others opposed him and his own family tried to stop his work. 'Whoever does the will of God', he said, 'is my brother, and sister, and mother.'

(b) 4:1–34 Jesus' teaching by parables. Here we see the methods of his teaching and what he taught about 'the kingdom of God' or God's rule among men.

(c) 4:35–5:43 The mighty works of Jesus show him to be Lord of all, with power over the wind and waves, power over the forces of evil and power over death and incurable sickness.

(d) 6:1–13 The unbelief of those in 'his own country'. The sending out of the twelve disciples.

4. The continued ministry of Jesus in Galilee and the training of the twelve (6:14–8:26)

(a) 6:14–56 The response to the ministry of Jesus recalls the witness and death of John the Baptist. The disciples return to Jesus after their mission, but in spite of his healing miracles and the feeding of the crowd, they are slow to believe and in the storm on the lake they show their lack of faith.

(b) 7:1–23 Jesus and the Jewish law. The law of Jesus concerns inner purity and truth, not just outward rules and cleansings.

(c) 7:24–8:26 Here we have more miracles that Jesus did, helping the faith of those whose eyes and ears he opened and again feeding the crowds. The disciples are still slow to trust in him. He said to them, 'Having eyes do you not see, and having ears do you not hear?'

5. The way to Jerusalem; the cross for Jesus and for his disciples (8:27–10:52)

(a) 8:27–9:50 The faith of the disciples and the lessons they had to learn. Jesus took his disciples apart by themselves and Peter was led to confess him as the Christ. From that time Jesus spent much of his time with the disciples and (as we have seen) he began to teach them how he must suffer and die, and that they too must be prepared to suffer. But he showed them his glory in his transfiguration and taught them further the lessons of faith, humility, forbearance and watchfulness.

(b) 10:1–45 The teaching of Jesus about marriage and divorce, about the preciousness of children, about riches and about service and suffering.

6. Ministry in Jerusalem (10:46–13:37)

(a) 10:46–12:44 The journey to Jerusalem, the triumphal entry, the cleansing of the temple, Jesus' parable about the wicked tenants and the questions asked by the Jews to trap him.

(b) 13:1–37 The teaching of Jesus about the future, about the fall of Jerusalem and about his own second coming in glory.

7. The passion and resurrection of Jesus (14:1–16:8)

(a) 14:1–15:15 The arrest and trials of Jesus.

(b) 15:15–47 The suffering and death and burial of Jesus.

(c) 16:1–8 Risen from the dead.

8. 'The Markan ending' (16:9–20)

Most early manuscripts do not have these verses and it seems that the original ending of the Gospel has been lost, and that later these verses were added, largely on the basis of what we have in the other Gospels. (For further details see the books listed below.)

The writer of the Gospel

Nowhere in the Gospel itself does the writer give his name. He wanted to write about Jesus and not about himself. The early church, however, had no doubt that the writer was Mark, though we have seen that it suggested that Mark, in what he wrote, used the preaching of Peter. We read of Mark in a number of places in the New Testament. We have noted that his home was in Jerusalem and we know that that home was a meeting place for the Christians in the early days of the church (Acts 12:12). He worked with Paul and Barnabas and went with them on their first missionary journey from Antioch (Acts 12:25; 13:5); but he turned back part way (Acts 13:13) and because of this Paul would not take him again to work with him. Instead, he went with Barnabas (Acts 15:36–40). Later, however, Paul received him back as a fellow-worker (Col. 4:10; 2 Tim. 4:11 and Phm. 24). From 1 Peter 5:13 we see that he was also associated with Peter. We do not know in what way Mark was associated with Jesus in the days of his life on earth. Because his home was the meeting place of the Christians in Jerusalem in the very early days, it has been thought that it was the place of the Last Supper. It has also been thought that Mark was the 'young man' with Jesus and his disciples in Gethsemane (14:51–52). We cannot be certain of either of these things, and it does not matter very much. It does matter that Mark was a man who had plenty of opportunity to check and to be sure of the things about the life and death and resurrection of Jesus that he tells us in his Gospel.

The time and place of the writing of the Gospel

We have noted how it was said in the second century that the Gospel was written after the deaths of Peter and Paul. That would be about AD 65–67. We cannot be quite certain of this, because another writer says that Mark wrote before the death of Peter. We are told that the Gospel was written in Rome (and from 1 Peter 5:13, Colossians 4:10 and Philemon 24 we know that Mark was with both Peter and Paul in Rome). It is clear that the Gospel was written especially for Gentile readers. Aramaic words are interpreted and an explanation is given of Jewish customs which Gentiles could not have been expected to understand (see 3:17; 5:41; 7:3–4,11,34; 15:22, 34 and 42).

Ways of studying this Gospel

There are many ways of studying this Gospel. The following are suggested:

1.   Read it section by section, taking just one incident at a time for careful study, and asking in studying each section what it teaches us of our Lord Jesus Christ himself and about the way that we should live as his disciples.

2.   Read it through quite quickly from beginning to end. Do this several times, each time trying to find the answer to a particular question, such as:

(a) How does the Gospel show Jesus to be the Son of God and to be Lord, Lord over men, over the forces of nature, over the powers of evil? How is he shown to be the Christ? to be truly Man? to be the Servant of God who also made himself Servant of men?

(b) Look at Jesus' relationship with the crowds in this Gospel. What does he want to do with them and for them, for all who were willing to come to him?

(c) What was he trying to do with his disciples? Study the stages by which he led them to trust in him, to be willing to keep close to him and even to suffer for him.

(d) Bearing in mind what has been said of the connection between this Gospel and the early Christian preaching, what are the ways in which the content of Mark illustrates and fills out that preaching and indicates the right response of men to our Lord Jesus Christ? (Think of Peter's preaching as recorded in Acts 2:22–24 and 10:36–41 and note the passages referred to above that predict and then describe the Lord's death and resurrection, the passages that show his power as Son of God and Saviour, and the passages that speak of the response of repentance and faith.)

Reference books

NBCR and *IBD; MNT,* ch. 1

Hugh Anderson, *The Gospel of Mark* (Marshall Pickering, 1976; Eerdmans, 1976)

R. A. Cole, *Mark* (IVP, 1961; Eerdmans, 1961)

C. E. B. Cranfield, *The Gospel according to Mark* (CUP, 1963)

A. M. Hunter, *The Gospel according to St. Mark* (SCM, U.K., 1969)

L. W. Hurtado, *Mark* (Harper, U.S.A., 1983)

W. L. Lane, *The Gospel according to St. Mark* (Eerdmans, 1973)

Matthew

We have thought of Mark's Gospel, its purpose, its contents and its structure, and in particular the way in which it presents Jesus as Son of God, Son of man and as the Christ. We have also considered the way that Mark presents the good news of Jesus and what should be man's response to it. Matthew is, in many ways, similar to Mark in these basic things. We are taught similar things about Jesus Christ, though we shall see that this Gospel has its special emphasis in the way it speaks of him. There are many things recorded in Matthew that are in Mark. In fact the contents of more than 600 of the 661 verses of Mark are in Matthew, and often there is the same order of the main events described, so that many people in studying the two Gospels closely have come to the conclusion that Matthew used Mark in writing his Gospel. Matthew, however, is a much longer Gospel, 1070 verses compared with Mark's 661. There are, therefore, many things in Matthew that are not in Mark.

Special features of Matthew

1. Although Mark often tells us that Jesus taught the people, he gives us little of his actual teaching. Matthew, on the other hand, gives us much of the teaching of Jesus. This Gospel is arranged in such a way that we have the teaching of Jesus Christ given for the most part in five great sections each of which ends with similar words (see 7:28, 11:1, 13:53, 19:1

and 26:1). The first of these sections is what we call The Sermon on the Mount (chapters 5–7); then there is the teaching connected with the mission of the disciples (10), a chapter of parables (13), teaching about the life of the disciples in fellowship (18) and finally the teaching of Jesus about the Scribes and Pharisees and about the future (23–25). (See *MNT*, pp. 66–72.)

2. There is much more quotation of the Old Testament in Matthew than in any of the other Gospels. Often these quotations are introduced by such words as, 'This took place to fulfil what was spoken by the prophet . . . ' This gives good reason for placing Matthew first in order among the books of the New Testament. It is a bridge between the Old Testament and the rest of the books of the New Testament, as it shows how the Old Testament hopes and prophecies, history and laws were fulfilled in the coming of Jesus. The first chapter shows him to be 'son of Abraham' and 'son of David', fulfilling the promises made to Abraham and the prophecies of the Messiah of the house of David. The people of Israel in Old Testament days were as God's son, but the life of Jesus on earth was the life of One who was perfectly God's Son, living obediently and entirely as God the Father intended. Like Israel he came up out of Egypt where he had been forced to go (2:15, quoting Hosea 11:1). He had forty days' temptation in the Judean wilderness as Israel had had forty years of testing in the wilderness between Egypt and Canaan. As Israel had had the law given to them from Mount Sinai, so Jesus gave to his disciples a new law from the mountain (5:1). In Matthew there is a greater emphasis than in any other of the Gospels on the fact that Jesus is the *Christ*, the Messiah whom the Jews had hoped for, the King of Israel. (see *MNT*, pp. 64–66 for details of this). What he did among men brought about the beginning of a new Israel, a new people of God. He was greater than the temple (12:6) and greater than all the characters of Old Testament history (12:41–42).

3. Much of what we find in Matthew and do not have in Mark or the other Gospels is teaching that Jesus gave or quotations of the Old Testament. There is also much of what is given at the beginning of the Gospel about the birth of Jesus and at the end of the Gospel about his trials and death and resurrection that adds to what we know from Mark. We also have, for reasons that we shall soon see, teaching of Jesus applied specially to the Jews which is not found in the other Gospels, since they were written for Gentiles for the most part.

The purpose of the Gospel and the people for whom it was first written

1. We have seen that it is most likely that Mark's Gospel was written chiefly for Gentiles and not for Jews. Matthew, however, seems to have been written for Jews or Jewish Christians rather than Gentiles. This would give special meaning to the emphasis on the fact that Jesus is the Christ and the One who fulfilled the Old Testament Scriptures. We also notice that Jewish customs are not explained. Moreover such parts of the Gospel as chapter 23 about the Scribes and Pharisees, would not have direct application to Gentiles, but would have special importance for Jews or those living close to Jewish people. Most probably the Gospel was written in Palestine, or in Syria close to Palestine.

2. Whereas Mark was written chiefly to tell how the good news of Jesus all began, and probably the writer was thinking especially of readers who were not yet Christians, Matthew seems to have been written particularly for Christians. It had in view those who knew the gospel and had believed, but who needed the teaching of Jesus for their Christian lives. We can understand that after people had become Christians, whether formerly Jews or Gentiles, they would soon wish to know more of the details of the life of Jesus, how he lived, what he taught about different aspects of life and how he said that his disciples should act under the many different kinds of circumstances that they faced. This Gospel gives the answers to many such questions.

3. It has also been thought sometimes that this Gospel may have been written specially for public reading when Christians met together for worship. There are some quite good reasons for thinking this but it is by no means certain.

Structure and contents

We have noted already that most of the teaching of Jesus in Matthew is found in five main sections. This fact leads us to divide the Gospel as follows into sections in which narrative and teaching come alternately:

1. The coming of Jesus (1:1–4:25)

(a) 1:1–17   The genealogy of Jesus.
(b) 1:18–25   The birth of Jesus.
(c) 2:1–12   The wise men from the East come to worship him.
(d) 2:13–23   Jesus is taken into Egypt.
(e) 3:1–17   John the Baptist's preaching and the baptism of Jesus.
(f) 4:1–11   The temptation of Jesus.
(g) 4:12–25   The call of the disciples and the beginning of the ministry of Jesus.

2. The Sermon on the Mount (5:1–7:29).

(a) 5:1–16   The Beatitudes (or, as Billy Graham has called them, 'the beautiful attitudes').
(b) 5:17–48   Jesus' teaching and the Law.
(c) 6:1–34   Teaching on prayer and on faith.
(d) 7:1–29   The authority of Jesus' teaching.

3. The power of Christ revealed (8:1–9:38).

(a) 8:1–17   Miracles of healing performed on the leper, the centurion's servant, Peter's mother-in-law and the demon-possessed.

(b) 8:18–22   The meaning of discipleship.

(c) 8:23–34   Christ's power over the storm and the demoniacs.

(d) 9:1–17   His power to forgive and to make men new.

(e) 9:18–34   His power over disease and death, dumbness and demons.

(f) 9:35–38   His compassion for the people.

4. The teaching given to the twelve about their mission (10:1–11:1)

5. The programme and purpose of Jesus (11:2–12:50)

(a) 11:2–19   Jesus' answer to the messenger from John the Baptist.

(b) 11:20–30   Faith in Jesus and unbelief.

(c) 12:1–14   His teaching about the sabbath and healing on the sabbath.

(d) 12:15–50   Those who accept and those who oppose his power.

6. The teaching of Jesus in parables (13:1—52).

7. The revealing of Jesus and the faith of his disciples (13:53–17:27).

(a) 13:53–58   Jesus in his own country.

(b) 14:1–12   Herod and John the Baptist.

(c) 14:13–36 The miracles of the feeding of the 5000, of stilling the storm on the lake and of healing the sick.
(d) 15:1–20 Jesus' attitude to the Jewish regulations.
(e) 15:21–39 More miracles in Galilee.
(f) 16:1–20 The slowness of the disciples to believe, then the confession by Peter of Jesus as the Christ, the Son of God.
(g) 16:21–28 Teaching about the cross.
(h) 17:1–23 The transfiguration and teaching that followed it.
(i) 17:24–27 The temple tax.

8. Teaching about humility and the spirit of forgiveness (18:1–35).

9. The journey to Jerusalem (19:1–22:46).

(a) 19:1–15 Marriage, divorce and the children.
(b) 19:16–30 Jesus and the rich young man.
(c) 20:1–16 The parable of the labourers in the vineyard.
(d) 20:17–28 Sacrifice and service.
(e) 20:29–34 The blind men outside Jericho.
(f) 21:1–46 The triumphal entry and Jesus in the temple.
(g) 22:1–14 The parable of the marriage feast.
(h) 22:15–46 Questions to test Jesus.

10. Warnings and predictions (23:1–25:46).

(a) 23:1–39 Woes on the scribes and Pharisees and warnings of judgment.
(b) 24:1–51 The fall of Jerusalem and the second coming of Christ.
(c) 25:1–46 Parables of judgment; the ten maidens, the talents, the sheep and the goats.

11. The arrest, suffering and death and resurrection of Jesus (26:1–28:20).

    (a) 26:1–56   The anointing, the last supper and the arrest.
    (b) 26:57–27:26   The trials before Caiaphas and Pilate.
    (c) 27:27–66   The death of Jesus and his burial.
    (d) 28:1–20   His resurrection and the great commission.

The writer of the Gospel

As in the case of Mark's Gospel, the writer of this Gospel never mentions his own name. A second century Christian writer, Papias, says that 'Matthew composed the oracles in the Hebrew language and everyone translated them as he was able.' Some people think that by the 'oracles' Papias meant this Gospel and that he was saying that Matthew was thus the writer of the Gospel. Others think that the Gospel itself is not what is called 'the oracles'. It does not seem at any rate that the Gospel was first written in Hebrew. The 'oracles' may have been a collection of Old Testament quotations such as we find used in Matthew, or a collection of the teaching of Jesus that the Gospel used, and hence the name of Matthew came to be linked with the Gospel as we have it.

Study questions

1. Consider the teaching sections of the Gospel (chapters 5–7, 10, 13, 18 and 23–25) and think out whether they are more applicable to Christians or to those who have not yet become Christians. After studying both Matthew and Mark, which do you think would be the better Gospel to suggest to a person who is not a Christian to read? Why?
2. Study the teaching sections of the Gospel mentioned above, and make lists of different parts of our Lord's teaching under such headings as faith, discipleship, riches, obedience, the law, fellowship, *etc.*

3. Make a list of the Old Testament quotations and the references to the Old Testament in Matthew. How important do you think it is for us to see the life and death and resurrection of Christ as the fulfilment of the Old Testament scriptures?

Reference books
NBCR: IBD: MNT, ch. 6
R. T. France, *Matthew* (IVP, 1987; Eerdmans, 1987)
R. H. Mounce, *Matthew* (Harper, U.S.A., 1985)

Luke

It has been said that Luke is the loveliest book ever written. It certainly shows us the amazing beauty and loveliness of the earthly life and teaching of our Lord Jesus Christ. Beauty is shown even in his death, in his care for others as he suffered and in the way he sought the forgiveness and salvation of those crucified with him and those who nailed him to the cross. Then there is the delight of his showing himself after his resurrection to those who had trusted him. It is also a Gospel that is full of joy: the words 'joy' and 'rejoice' are used more often than in any of the other Gospels.

In many ways Luke is similar to Mark and Matthew. About half of the content of Mark's Gospel (320 out of 661 verses) is to be found in Luke. In addition about 250 verses of Matthew and Luke are similar in content (most of these give us the teaching of Jesus). Again, in most essential things, Luke has an order that is similar to that of Mark and Matthew. There is also a great similarity in the way that Jesus Christ is presented in his Gospel. He is 'the Son of God' (1:35), the One who came to be Saviour (19:10); He is 'the Christ' (2:11). He often uses the term 'Son of man' of himself, and there is a great deal of teaching about the 'kingdom of God' in the Gospel. As in the other Gospels, it is emphasized that he, though Son of God, is truly man, but there is a special way in which this is stressed by Luke. We must turn now to consider the things that make Luke's Gospel different from the others.

Special features of this Gospel

1.   Luke is particularly concerned to show that Jesus is the Saviour for all, and that the good news of what he has done is for all people and applicable to all. The genealogy of Jesus is not just taken back to Abraham as in Matthew, but to Adam (3:38). John Stott says, 'It is striking to observe his particular interest in different classes of person, who might have been thought to have been excluded.' Then he lists the following (see *BNT*, pp. 30–37):

(a) *Children*   It was not an uncommon practice in the Roman Empire to discard unwanted children at birth and leave them to die. Even the disciples of Jesus thought their Master did not want to be worried by little children, but he said, 'Let the children come to me, and do not hinder them; for to such belongs the kingdom of God' (18:16). We read in 2:40–52 of the childhood of Jesus and in 8:49–56 and 9:37–43 and 46–48 of his care for children.

(b) *Women*   Among the Jews and in the Roman Empire women were regarded as distinctly inferior to men. Luke shows the place that Jesus gave to women and the part that they had in the purposes of God. The emancipation of womanhood owes more to Jesus Christ than to any other person in history. Luke tells us more of Mary, the mother of Jesus than any other Gospel writer (1:26–56; 2:5–7, 19–20, 34–35). He alone tells us of Elizabeth, the mother of John the Baptist (1:5–7, 24–25, 39–45), of Anna in the temple (2:36–38), of the widow of Nain (7:11–17), of the women who ministered to Jesus (8:2–3), of the woman who had been bent double for eighteen years (13:10–17) and of the women of Jerusalem who wept as he was led out to be crucified (23:27–31).

(c) *The sick*   In all the Gospels we read of the healing ministry of Jesus, but in Luke there is special emphasis on the compassion of our Lord for all in need. We see his concern for lepers. Luke not only has what others record, but he adds the account of the healing of the ten lepers (17:11–19).

(d) *The poor*   There is more teaching on the danger of riches in Luke than in any other of the Gospels. The parables of the rich fool (12:13–21), the dishonest servant (16:1–13) and the rich man and Lazarus (16:19–31) are in Luke only. We see the emphasis on concern for the poor in 4:18; 6:29–31; 7:22; 12:33; 14:12–14 and 18:22.

(e) *The outcasts*   The Pharisees opposed Jesus because he was willing to receive those whom they rejected as sinners. Arising out of this situation Luke gives us the Lord's three parables of the lost sheep (15:3–7), the lost coin (15:8–10) and the lost son (15:11–32). Among the 'sinners' the Pharisees rejected, they specially included tax-collectors. Luke (5:27–32) tells us, as do Matthew and Mark, of the call of Levi (Matthew) to be a disciple. Luke alone tells us of Zacchaeus, that other tax-collector, and the extending of God's salvation to him leads Jesus to say, 'the Son of man came to seek and to save the lost' (19:10). Also Luke is the one Gospel writer who tells the story of the Pharisee and the tax-collector at prayer (18:9–14); and he tells of Simon the Pharisee criticizing when Jesus allowed a woman who was 'a sinner' to anoint his feet (7:36–50). Finally, Luke tells of the salvation of the repentant thief dying on the cross beside Jesus (23:39–43).

(f) *Foreigners*   In John 4:9 we see how the Jews of the time of Jesus would have no dealings with the Samaritans, half-Jewish, half-Gentile people as they were. Luke makes plain that the attitude of Jesus to the Samaritans was a more loving one (9:51–56) and he it is who gives us Jesus' parable of the Good Samaritan (10:25–37). Luke similarly tells us of the faith of Gentiles (4:24–27; 7:1–10; 13:29 and 23:47) and his Gospel is brought to a close with the instructions being given to the disciples 'that repentance and forgiveness of sins should be preached in his name to all nations' (24:47).

2.   Some of the particular points of emphasis of Luke's

Gospel we understand best when we realize that he did not just write a Gospel, but a two-volume work, a Gospel and then the book that we call The Acts of the Apostles. We need to read them together. We shall consider more of the parallels when we study Acts, but one of the points of emphasis of the Gospel is that Jesus lived as One who was truly Man, in the same dependence on the Father and by the same indwelling of the Spirit, as Christians in the early days of the Church could live, and as we today are intended to live. So Luke tells us more about prayer than any of the other Gospel writers; we read of Jesus himself praying in 3:21; 5:16; 6:18; 9:18, 29; 11:1; 22:32; 39–46 and 23:34; we have his teaching on prayer in 11:1–13; 18:1–14 and 22:40–46. We are also told more of the work of the Holy Spirit in the life of Jesus in Luke (in 1:35; 3:22; 4:1,14,18 and 10:21) than in any other Gospel (note also 1:15 and 24:49).

The purpose of Luke and the people for whom the Gospel was written

Both this Gospel and the Acts of the Apostles are addressed to one who, in 1:3, is called 'most excellent Theophilus' (see also Acts 1:1). The address of honour suggests that Theophilus may have been a high-ranking Roman official or governor. Luke's Gospel and Acts were probably written in times when the Roman Empire was beginning to persecute the Christians. Part of the purpose of the two books, therefore, may have been to explain what Christianity was all about and so to show that there was no reason why Roman governors should take action against Christians. This, however, can only have been part of the purpose.

Luke (in 1:1–4) says that many before him had written records 'of the things which have been accomplished among us'. He has checked all the details with 'those who from the beginning were eye-witnesses and ministers of the word', so that he might write 'an orderly account' and that Theophilus, and no doubt many others like him, might 'know the truth' of the things of which they had learnt.

This means that Luke's Gospel was written so that people might have a sure knowledge of the facts on which the faith of Christians was based. Such a record, the result of careful research, is naturally of tremendous value for Christian people at all times, that they may be certain of the truth of who Jesus is, what he did, how he died and rose from the dead, and that non-Christians too may know the facts on which Christian faith rests. Many who have checked details of Luke's Gospel and Acts with writings and inscriptions related to the first-century situation have come to realize what a careful and accurate historian the writer of the two books was. This means that his work is not only one of the most beautiful works ever written but also, from a historical point of view, one of the most important books ever written. (See *MNT*, pp. 50–52 and *NBD* on Luke's Gospel).

Structure and contents

We have given a detailed analysis of the contents of Mark and mentioned how the outline of Mark is followed by Luke, as well as by Matthew. Matthew, we have seen, has the special arrangement of sections of teaching and sections of narrative. There does not seem to be any such special arrangement in Luke. The contents of this Gospel may be set down in very brief outline as follows:

1. 1:1–4   The introduction to the Gospel.
2. 1:5–2:52   The birth and infancy of Jesus.
3. 3:1–4:13   The beginning of the ministry of Jesus.
4. 4:14–9:50   The ministry of Jesus in Galilee.
5. 9:51–19:28   Travelling from Galilee to Jerusalem; teaching and miracles.

6. 19:29–21:38 Jesus' entry into Jerusalem and his ministry there.

7. 22:1–24:53 The trials of Jesus, his crucifixion and resurrection.

The writer of the Gospel

Once again the writer of the Gospel does not mention his name or tell us anything about himself. It is clear, as we have seen, that the Gospel and Acts were written by the same person (compare 1:1–4 and Acts 1:1). It is also clear from Acts that he was a companion of the apostle Paul in many of his journeys (see p. 290 and *BNT*, pp. 27-28). The early church (from the second century) was quite certain that Luke was the writer, the same Luke, the doctor of whom we read in Colossians 4:14, 2 Timothy 4:11 and Philemon 24. In fact as we read this Gospel and the Acts of the Apostles it is often valuable to remember that the writer of these two books, as John Stott puts it (in *BNT*, pp. 23–28), was (a) a Gentile, (b) a doctor, (c) an educated man, (d) a historian, (e) a traveller and (f) Paul's companion.

Study questions

1. Read the Gospel and note the different kinds of people whom Jesus was able to help, to heal or change their lives. Make a list which shows who they were, young or old, men or women, Jews, Samaritans, Gentiles, and what their needs were. What does such a study tell us of the purpose and scope of the Gospel?

2. Study the passages listed above which tell us about Jesus at prayer or that give his teaching concerning prayer. What lessons for our own prayer life can we learn from these?

3. In what ways are the words of 1:1–4 important in telling us of the purpose and the methods of the writing of this Gospel?

Reference books

NBCR and *IBD; BNT,* ch. 2

E. M. Blaiklock, *Understanding the New Testament: Luke* (Broadman, U.S.A., 1982)

E. E. Ellis, *The Gospel of Luke* (Marshall Pickering, 1974; Eerdmans, 1981)

N. Geldenhuys, *Commentary on the Gospel of Luke* (Eerdmans, 1951)

L. Morris, *Luke* (rev. ed. IVP, 1983; Eerdmans, 1974)

John

When we turn over the pages from Matthew, Mark and Luke to John and begin to read this fourth Gospel, we find it to be a Gospel that uses simpler words than any of the others, but full of such deep truth that we can stop and meditate on and ponder a single verse and feel that there is always much more for us to understand. We have seen the differences there are between the first three Gospels in their particular purposes, and in their content and arrangement. We have also seen their similarities and their underlying unity. When we turn to John's Gospel we find greater differences, differences from all the other three, and yet there is still the same underlying unity.

John and the Synoptic Gospels

We can list some of the main differences between John and the other three Gospels as follows:

1. This Gospel begins not with the baptism of Jesus (as Mark), nor with the birth of Jesus (as Matthew and Luke), but with the fact that Jesus, the living and personal Word of God, was 'in the beginning with God' (1:1–2). The other Gospels are arranged in an order which shows how the ministry of Jesus went on, from his baptism and temptation, the call of the first disciples, his preaching and teaching and healing among the crowds in Galilee, to the growing opposition against him, the way that the disciples were led to confess him as the Christ and then were taught of the necessity of his suffering

and death. John does not give us an order of events like this. The purpose of his Gospel seems rather to be to pick out great and important things from the life and ministry of Jesus, which show who he is and what he came to do.

2.   The other Gospels tell us a great deal of what happened in Galilee in the early part of Jesus' ministry, and then of his journey to Jerusalem and his suffering and death there. John's Gospel tells us much more of what happened in Jerusalem and Judea in the early part of Jesus' ministry. To the heart and centre of Jewish life he came, and we are shown what 'the Jews' (often referred to in the Gospel just like this) did to him. Of the Jews first, but then of the world at large, the words of 1:11-12 are true, 'He came to his own home, and his own people received him not. But to all who received him, who believed in his name, he gave power to become children of God.' (We should note that although the other Gospels emphasize his early ministry in Galilee and tell us little of his time in Jerusalem, they do indicate that he taught and worked there. For example see Luke 13:34-35.)

3.   In the other Gospels most of the teaching of Jesus is in short sayings or parables while in John much of it is in long conversations or discourses. We can realize that both were involved in his teaching. There were the short, sometimes poetic, sayings that were easily remembered, and the parables; and John in fact (10:6 and 16:25,29) tells us of his teaching in parables and proverbs. Then there were the long discourses or sermons, and although Matthew, Mark and Luke do not give these in such detail as John, they tell us how he taught the people for many hours at a time (for example, see Mark 6:34-35). The plan of John is very often to tell of a miracle that Jesus did (called a 'sign'), then to give teaching which comes to a climax in a great claim that the Lord makes. For example, in chapter 6 we have the miracle of the feeding of the 5000 (which is also in the other Gospels), then a great deal of teaching about the spiritual food that Jesus offered to men, and

this teaching is then summed up in the tremendous claim that he made, 'I am the bread of life: he who comes to me shall not hunger, and he who believes in me shall never thirst' (6:35).

4. There are important things which the other three Gospels tell us which are omitted in John, the baptism of Jesus, his temptation, the call of the twelve disciples, his transfiguration and his praying in Gethsemane. Perhaps John could assume that such things were known, or that people could easily learn of them from others. For example, he speaks of 'the twelve' (6:67,70), though he does not actually tell us how there came to be twelve special disciples. On the other hand, there are many things added which we do not have in the other three Gospels. We are told how the fishermen disciples came to know Jesus before he actually called them (1:35–42). We are told of Nicodemus (chapter 3), the Samaritan woman (chapter 4) and the raising of Lazarus (chapter 11). We are given details connected with his trials, his death and resurrection that the other Gospels do not tell us. We cannot say that John definitely knew the other Gospels when he wrote his, but he may have realized the kind of things which people could easily learn at that time concerning Jesus and the things they were not as likely to know.

5. The other Gospels show us more of the way that our Lord revealed himself little by little to the disciples, and how they gradually came to the point of believing in him fully and confessing him as 'the Christ, the Son of God'. John's Gospel presents Jesus from the beginning as the One who came to be seen as 'the Christ', 'the Lamb of God', 'the Son of God', and that the right response to him for all who read the Gospel is the response of faith.

Such differences between John and the other Gospels are very noticeable, but we should also remember the great similarities. There are many similarities in little details (e.g., compare 12:12–15 and Matthew 21:1–9). Above all there is great unity in the presentation of Jesus Christ, truly Man, truly

Son of God, in what we are told of the character of his ministry,
the kind of things that he did, the importance and the purpose
of his death, the reality of his resurrection. In all these there
is essentially the same picture given to us by John and the
Synoptic Gospel writers.

The purpose of the Gospel

In 20:31 there is a clear statement of the purpose behind the
writing of the Gospel. John finishes his work and realizes that
many other things might have been said, 'many other signs'
reported, but he says 'these are written that you may believe
that Jesus is the Christ, the Son of God, and that believing
you may have life in his name'.

This shows clearly that the Gospel was written most particularly for those who did not believe, that they might be
brought to faith in Jesus as the Christ, the Son of God, and so
find eternal life in him. We have also the emphasis on the
place of 'the signs' that Jesus did. The 'signs' are miracles,
but they are not just wonderful works that Jesus did. They
show us who Jesus is and what he came to do. Jesus did his
signs (as 2:11 tells us), to show forth his glory, so that people
might come to believe on him. Jesus fed the crowds, and so
they saw his power, and were taught that he had come to give
spiritual food to hungry people (chapter 6). He gave sight to
the blind man, and in this way also his power was seen; they
said, 'never since the world began has it been heard that any
one opened the eyes of a man born blind' (9:32). But it was
shown also that he came to be 'the light of the world' (8:12 and
9:5). He raised Lazarus from the dead, and so showed his
power over death; but also he was able to say, 'I am the resurrection and the life; he who believes in me, though he die, yet
shall he live' (11:25).

This Gospel thus tells us many of the things that Jesus did,
but linked with his actions we have his teaching which ex-

plains what he did, and very frequently, as we have seen, this teaching leads to his great claims: 'I am the bread of life' (6:35), 'I am the light of the world' (8:12 and 9:5), 'Before Abraham was, I am' (8:58), 'I am the good shepherd' (10:11), 'I am the resurrection and the life' (11:25), 'I am the way, and the truth, and the life' (14:6). When we understand these things about the purpose of the Gospel, it helps us to understand the structure of the Gospel, how it is arranged and put together. (See further *NBCR* and *IBD*.)

Contents

There are many ways in which we might sum up or give an outline of the contents of this Gospel. The following outline indicates some of the 'signs' and of the great subjects of the Gospel and the ways in which we are shown the Person and the purpose of Jesus Christ.

9. 8:1–9:41   The giving of sight to a blind man, showing Jesus as the Light of the world.

10. 10:1–42   Jesus as the Good Shepherd.

11. 11:1–57   The raising of Lazarus, showing Jesus as the resurrection and the life.

12. 12:1–50   Jesus comes to Jerusalem to die, showing death as the door to life.

13. 13:1–38   Jesus washes the disciples' feet, showing the meaning of cleansing and the call to humble and loving service.

14. 14:1–31   Jesus as the Way, the Truth and the Life.

15. 15:1–27   Jesus as the true Vine; the way of life for those who believe in him.

16. 16:1–44   The gift of the Spirit.

17. 17:1–26   The prayer of Jesus for his disciples.

18. 18:1–19:42   The arrest, the trials and the death of Jesus.

19. 20:1–31   The resurrection of Jesus.

20. 21:1–25   Conclusion. The one whose witness lies behind the whole Gospel: 'This is the disciple who is bearing witness to these things, and who has written these things; and we know that his testimony is true' (21:24).

The writer of the Gospel

Very many books have been written on the question of the authorship of this Gospel. As in the case of the other Gospels, the writer does not give us his name. He wants to tell us about Jesus and not about himself. He would have felt exactly as John the Baptist did when he said that Jesus must increase in the place that men gave to him in their lives and he, John, must decrease (3:30). Like John the Baptist too, the writer wants simply to be 'a voice' telling of him who is Lord of all (1:23). Several times in the Gospel we have reference to one who is deliberately unnamed, but called 'the disciple whom Jesus loved'. This one was next to Jesus at the Last Supper (13:23), probably the one closest to the Lord at the time of his trial before the high priest (18: 15–16) and he was the one to whom Jesus entrusted his mother at the time of the crucifixion (19:25–27). In 19:35 we read, with reference to the death of our Lord on the cross, 'He who saw it has borne witness, his testimony is true, and he knows that he tells the truth, that you also may believe'. After the resurrection he was the one who, with Peter, saw that the tomb was empty and came to believe in the resurrection (20:1–10). Then he is linked with Peter again as the disciples met with the risen Lord by Lake Galilee (21:7) and the words spoken about him lead to the statement of 21:24 that it is his witness that we have in this Gospel.

It has been felt by many down the centuries that the only person that this could have been was the apostle John, and John is certainly never named in the whole of the Gospel. In recent years arguments have been given against this view, but strong arguments still stand in support of it.

The time and place of the writing of the Gospel

John the apostle has been linked with Ephesus and with the churches of Asia Minor which were founded through the work of the apostle Paul in his third missionary journey (see Acts 19). By many, John is thought to have written this Gospel in Ephesus near the end of his life, perhaps about the year AD 90, or even later. On the other hand, a strong case has been made out for dating the Gospel before the Fall of Jerusalem in AD 70.

Although the Gospel says a good deal about the fulfilment of the Old Testament in our Lord Jesus Christ, it is a Gospel which would speak with a clear message to Gentiles, and probably it was intended primarily for non-Jewish people. We can think of the apostle John in his old age, looking back on the times when he first met Jesus, looking on the events of his ministry, his death and resurrection, and seeing ever more clearly their meaning as he had preached and taught and lived in the light of them and in the service of Christ for so long. So he wrote this Gospel to tell to all who would read it who Jesus really is and what he came to do in this world of ours.

Study questions

1.   Study the importance of the whole subject of 'witness' in this Gospel, especially the different kinds of witness which show that Jesus is the Son of God. Note the example of witness that we have in John the Baptist. Note how the Gospel itself is spoken of as reliable witness to Jesus. The most important passages to study in answering this question are: 1:6–8, 19–37; 3:22–36; 5:30–47; 8:12–20; 10:22–30; 15:26–27; 18:37; 19:35 and 21:24. See also *BNT*, pp. 117–122.

2.   Study the Gospel and note the great personal claims of our Lord Jesus Christ, who he claimed to be and what he claimed to do. (See especially 1:49–51; 2:18–22; 3:13–16; 4:13–14, 25–26; 5:17–18; 6:33–40; 7:37–39; 8:12,51–58; 9:5; 10:7–18,25–30; 11:25–26; 12:31–36,44–50; 14:6–7.) What should these claims mean to Christians today? See also *BNT*, pp. 122–126.

3.   What teaching is given by our Lord in chapters 14–16 concerning the Holy Spirit? Note particularly the significance of the names given to him and what is said about the work that he does or will do.

4.   In the prayer of Jesus in chapter 17 for whom is the Master praying and what are the things for which he asks? Consider what this says to us about our life as disciples and about our own praying.

Reference books

NBCR; IBD; BNT, ch. 6

J. R. Michaels, *John* (Harper, U.S.A., 1984)

L. Morris, *The Gospel according to John* (Eerdmans, 1970)

R. E. Nixon, *Understanding the New Testament: John* (Broadman, U.S.A., 1982)

R. V. G. Tasker, *John* (IVP, 1960; Eerdmans, 1960)

W. Temple, *Readings in St. John's Gospel* (Macmillan, 1961; Morehouse, 1985)

B. F. Westcott, *The Gospel according to St. John* (Baker, U.S.A., 1980)

The Acts of the Apostles

We have already noted that this book is the second part of a two-volume work. Luke purposely wrote to Theophilus a record of the life and death and resurrection of Jesus that he might know the certainty of the things that Christians believed (Luke 1:1–4). Then he followed it with this book, addressed to the same Theophilus, to tell what happened after Jesus' resurrection and when his disciples went out to preach his gospel to the world (1:1).

The purpose

Three things in the first chapter of Acts tell us a good deal about the purposes of the writing of this book.

1. In 1:1 it says that the first book, the Gospel, told of 'all that Jesus began both to do and teach'. This means that this book shows how the work and teaching of Jesus are continued in his church. Of course, there are ways in which what Jesus did was unique, and could never be repeated. The work that he did by his death and resurrection for our salvation was done once and for all. His disciples can only bear witness to that work, and this is emphasized in this first chapter (1:8 and 22). But they continue his work of teaching, preaching, ministering to people in their needs, healing the sick and casting out demons. And just as we have seen that Luke in his Gospel emphasizes that Jesus, as Man, lived by the Holy Spirit filling him and by depending on the Father in prayer (see p. 37) so there is great emphasis in Acts on Christians being filled

with the Spirit and led by the Spirit (see 1:4–5,8; 2:1–38; 4:8,31, *etc.*) and great emphasis on prayer (see 1:14; 3:1; 4:24–31, *etc.*). We also see that Christians have to suffer as Christ himself suffered. Stephen suffered death, praying for his enemies as Jesus did (7:54–60). James was killed and Peter imprisoned at the time of the Feast of Unleavened Bread and the Passover when Jesus had suffered and died (12:1–5). Paul, like his master, set his face to go to Jerusalem, though he knew that this would mean suffering (see 20:22–23; 21:10–14).

2. In 1:8, in the last words of Jesus before his ascension, he gave to his disciples their task. In the power of the Spirit they were to be his 'witnesses in Jerusalem and in all Judaea and Samaria and to the end of the earth'. The story of Acts shows how they were witnesses, and how geographically the gospel spread from Jerusalem till the book ends with the apostle Paul preaching in the great centre of the Roman Empire 'openly and unhindered' (28:31). It also shows us the stages by which it was possible for the Jewish disciples to break out from their Jewish prejudices and feelings and to go out to the Gentile world. The writer of Acts has obviously chosen his material very carefully, so that we can see the key people and the key events that made this spread of the gospel possible.

3. Luke's Gospel and Acts were written at a time when the authorities in the Roman Empire were beginning to persecute the Christians. Theophilus, addressed as 'most excellent' in Luke 1:3, appears to have been a Roman official or governor. It seems that one of the purposes of Luke's work was to show Roman leaders that there was no need or cause for them to persecute the Christians. Jesus was condemned to death by the Roman governor Pilate, only because of the pressure of the Jews on him, since he found no fault in him (Luke 23:1–24). Then in the early days of the church it was usually the Jews who stirred up opposition to the Christians. Roman governors gave them a fair hearing and did not condemn them

or in one case apologized that they were not given a fair hearing. (See 13:6–12; 16:12–40; 18:12–17 and 19:23–41). For further details see *BNT*, pp. 42–51, *MNT*, pp. 52–58, *NBCR* and *IBD*.

Contents

It is helpful to study the contents and arrangement of the Acts of the Apostles from the standpoint of what has been said above of the purpose of the book. What are the things which are chosen to be included? What are the things which are described in detail and so with great emphasis? We may outline the contents of the book as follows:

1. 1:1–26   The command to be witnesses to the end of the earth; the ascension of Christ; the choice of the twelfth apostle and the work of the apostles giving testimony to Christ's resurrection.

2. 2:1–47   The coming of the Holy Spirit. In the power of the Spirit Peter preached to people of many lands who were in Jerusalem for the feast of Pentecost; and in the power of the Spirit Christians lived in fellowship together.

3. 3:1–4:37   The healing of the lame man outside the Temple in Jerusalem; the preaching of Peter and the opposition of the Jewish leaders; Barnabas and others give houses and lands for the support of those in need.

4. 5:1–42   The judgment on Ananias and Sapphira; healing and preaching; the imprisonment and release of the apostles.

5. 6:1–7:60   The appointment of the seven to care for the widows among the Greek-speaking Jews; the witness of Stephen, indicating a different attitude to the Law and the Temple; people were no longer to be restricted by the Law or to cling to the Temple; Stephen's arrest, his defence and martyrdom.

6. 8:1–40   Persecution in Jerusalem; Christians scattered

through Judea and Samaria; Philip's preaching in Samaria
and then to the Ethiopian.

7. 9:1–31 The conversion of Paul; his call to be an apostle
to the Gentiles; his witness in Damascus and in Jerusalem.

8. 9:32–11:18 Peter's work at Lydda and Joppa; his mission to the Gentile Cornelius, who with his family responds to
the gospel and receives the Holy Spirit; Peter, back among the
Christians in Jerusalem, has to defend his attitude to Gentiles.

9. 11:19–30 The preaching to the Gentiles in Antioch and
the growth of a Gentile church there.

10. 12:1–25 The death of the apostle James and the imprisonment and release of Peter.

11. 13:1–14:28 Paul's first missionary journey (with
Barnabas); churches established in Cyprus and Galatia.

12. 15:1–35 The council at Jerusalem; Jews and Gentiles
declared to be one in Christ.

13. 15:36–18:22 Paul's second missionary journey (with
Silas and Timothy); churches in Galatia revisited and new
churches established in Macedonia and Greece.

14. 18:23–20:6 Paul's third missionary journey; three
years' work in Ephesus and visits to Macedonia and Greece.

15. 20:7–21:26 Paul's return to Jerusalem and the Jewish
attack on him there.

16. 21:27–26:32 Paul's arrest and trials.

17. 27:1–28:31 Paul's voyage to Rome and his witness
there.

The preaching of the early church

In the book of Acts we not only have the story of how the
gospel went out from Jerusalem to Rome, and how the
Samaritans and then the Gentiles were brought into the fellowship of Christians. We are also given accounts of what the
gospel was which was being preached. We have Peter's preaching in Jerusalem (2:14–40; 3:12–26; 4:8–12; 5:29–32) and

to Cornelius (10:34–43) and Paul's preaching in Pisidian
Antioch and Athens (13:16–41 and 17:22–31). In every case
what we are given can only be brief summaries of what was
actually said, and there are variations in these different sermons; but we can see what was the essential content of the
early Christian preaching (compare the summaries of it in
1 Corinthians 2:1–5 and 15:1–4), and how this included:

1.   Who Jesus is and what he did in his life on earth.
2.   How he was crucified and raised from the dead, fulfilling
the Old Testament Scriptures and showing him to be Lord and
Christ.
3.   The giving of the Holy Spirit.
4.   The need for people to respond in repentance and faith
(and be baptized) and so to receive God's salvation, the
forgiveness of sins and the gift of the Holy Spirit.
5.   Christ will come again in glory to judge all men.

The writer

It is clear that Luke, the doctor, was the writer of this book
and the third Gospel (see p. 275). When the narrative in Acts
changes from speaking of 'they' and 'he' to 'we' we can understand that Luke was at these times a companion of Paul (see
16:10–17; 20:5–16; 21:1–18, and 27:1–28:16). When we
notice the places that Luke must thus have visited with Paul
we can realize that he had great opportunities of finding out the
facts concerning the things of which he wrote in his book. We
can appreciate also that he would have had a tremendous
amount of information about the life of the early church in all
these places. Therefore it is very important to see what he does
choose to record and how he arranges his narrative. It is also
to be noted that the evidence of archaeology shows how
accurate Luke was as he recorded details of geography, history
and Roman government. (See *NBCR*.)

Study questions

1. Read the book of Acts and note what is said of the power and guidance of the Holy Spirit as the gospel went out into the world. Note also what is said of prayer and of the Holy Spirit in the fellowship of Christians.

2. Trace on a map the different places and countries mentioned in Acts to which the messengers of the gospel went.

3. What do you think of the importance of (a) Peter, (b) Stephen, (c) Philip, (d) Barnabas, (e) Paul and (f) James in the movement to take the gospel out to the Gentile world? (For Peter see 10:1–11:18; for Stephen see 6:8–7:60; for Philip see 8:4–40; for Barnabas see 11:19–26 and 13:1–15:4; for Paul see 9:10–16; 11:19:26 and chapters 13–28; for James see 15:6–21.)

Reference books

NBCR; IBD, BNT, pp. 42-51; *MNT*, ch. 5

F. F. Bruce, *Commentary on the Book of the Acts* (Eerdmans, 1954)

E. F. Harrison, *Acts: The Expanding Church* (Moody, 1976)

I. H. Marshall, *Acts* (IVP, 1980; Eerdmans, 1980)

R. P. Martin, *Understanding the New Testament: Acts* (Broadman, U.S.A., 1982)

D. J. Williams, *Acts* (Harper, U.S.A., 1985)

Paul and the Gospel He Preached

There are thirteen books or letters in the New Testament that bear the name of Paul. They tell us a good deal about the man as well as about what he preached and what he did. Happily, however, we have also the record of the Acts of the Apostles in which we can trace the life of Saul of Tarsus, the persecutor, who became Paul the great apostle to the Gentiles. That story begins with his presence at the martyrdom of Stephen and his continuing determination to use time and strength in the persecution of the Christians (Acts 7:58–8:3). He had been trained in the Jewish law under the great rabbi Gamaliel in Jerusalem (Acts 22:3). He was a member of the strict party of the Pharisees (Phil. 3:5 and Acts 26:5) and had a tremendous zeal to uphold the religious traditions of his people (Gal. 1:13–14). Then, as he travelled to Damascus to take action against the Christians there, he met the risen Christ. His life was changed completely (Acts 9:1–31). Then, and perhaps more deeply as he spent time alone with God in Arabia (Gal. 1:17), he realized three things:

1. That the crucified Jesus was risen from the dead, and that he is the Christ and Lord of all (Acts 9:5).

2. That the way of acceptance with God, the way of forgiveness and salvation, could not be by the law that he had tried to keep. He had broken the law. His salvation, therefore, and the salvation of others could only be by Another bearing men's sins, that is, by the sacrificial death of Jesus Christ. The good news of what Jesus had done by his death and resurrection

was therefore a message to be preached to all (Gal. 2:15–21).

3. That this gospel applied in the same way to both Jews and Gentiles, and God was sending him to preach especially to the Gentiles, whom as a Jew he had previously despised and rejected (Acts 9:15 and Gal. 1:15–17).

Paul bore witness to Jesus as the Christ in Damascus and Jerusalem and then went back to his home in Tarsus in Cilicia (Acts 9:20–30). When preaching among the Gentiles began in Antioch and Barnabas saw the work being done there, we read that Barnabas (who had first introduced Paul to the other apostles in Jerusalem) went to Tarsus and brought Paul to Antioch (Acts 11:25–26). From Antioch Paul went out to his great missionary work that the book of Acts records; three missionary journeys that took him up and down the four Roman provinces of Galatia, Asia, Macedonia and Achaia (see map).

In our study we shall see where the thirteen letters fit into Paul's life and work, and consider the message and teaching of each of them. We shall not study them, however, either in the order in which we find them in the New Testament, nor even simply in the order in which they were written. We shall begin with the two letters which show most clearly the gospel which Paul preached, Galatians and Romans; then go on to the letters which give us an insight into the life and problems of the churches that he was able to establish; finally we shall look at the letters he wrote to his colleagues in the work of the gospel, Timothy and Titus.

Approximate dates of Paul's life and letters

34	Paul's conversion (Acts 9:1–19).	
37	His first visit to Jerusalem after his conversion (Acts 9:26–29).	
48	His second visit to Jerusalem (Acts 11:27–30).	
48–50	First missionary journey, to Cyprus and Galatia (Acts 13–14).	Galatians
50	The council at Jerusalem (Acts 15).	
51–53	Second missionary journey, to Galatia, Macedonia and Greece (Acts 16:1–18:22).	1 and 2 Thessalonians
54–58	Third missionary journey, to Ephesus, Macedonia and Greece (Acts 18:23–21:14).	1 and 2 Corinthians Romans
59–60	His arrest in Jerusalem, trials and imprisonment in Caesarea (Acts 21:15–26:32).	
61–63	His journey to Rome and imprisonment there (Acts 27–28).	Philippians Philemon Colossians Ephesians
	His release and further work (?) final imprisonment and death.	1 Timothy Titus 2 Timothy

Some of these dates and details are uncertain. Sometimes it is not completely clear where and when Paul's letters were written, but the above is an outline which shows where probably they fitted into his life and work.

Reference books

You will find several brief but excellent articles on Paul in standard reference books such as the NBD and IBD. In addition, the NBD and IBD article on "Chronology in the New Testament" considers the dates of different events in his life. In NBCR you will find a general article on "The Pauline Epistles" and BNT, chapter 3, deals with "The Message of Paul."

For a picture of Paul cast in biographical form John Pollock's *The Apostle* (Hodder, 1972; Victor, 1985) makes vivid the life and labors of Paul. In addition, we warmly recommend *Paul* by John W. Drane (Lion, 1977; Harper, 1977) as a clearly written and illustrated presentation of the apostle's life and letters, as well as Donald Coggan's more recent *Paul: Portrait of a Revolutionary* (Hodder, 1984; Crossroad, 1985).

For those who want to trace Paul's thought and ministry in greater detail there is no finer treatment than F. F. Bruce's *Paul: Apostle of the Free Spirit* (Paternoster, 1977, published in the U.S. under the title *Paul: Apostle of the Heart Set Free,* Eerdmans, 1977). In addition, students may want to consult the short but penetrating surveys of Paul's thought by Leander E. Keck (*Paul and His Letters,* Fortress, 1979) and Joseph A. Fitzmyer (*Pauline Theology: A Brief Sketch,* Prentice-Hall, 1967). And for a classic on the preaching and teaching of the apostle we recommend James S. Stewart's *A Man in Christ* (Hodder, 1935; Harper, 1935; repr. Baker, 1975).

Galatians

When Paul and Barnabas set out on their first missionary journey, they went from Antioch in Syria to the island of Cyprus and then to Perga in Pamphylia (Acts 13:1–13). From there they went on and preached the gospel in Antioch in Pisidia, in Iconium, Lystra and Derbe (Acts 13:14–14:23). All these towns were in the Roman province of Galatia (see map).

After the gospel had been preached and churches had been planted in each of these places, Paul and Barnabas returned to Antioch in Syria (Acts 14:24–28). Very soon, however, a special difficulty arose. There were Jewish Christians who came from Judea to Antioch who said that, unless Gentiles who had become Christians accepted the Jewish law and submitted to the covenant sign of circumcision, they could not be saved (Acts 15:1) and they could not belong to the people of God. This teaching caused trouble and unrest in Antioch, and those who brought this teaching went on from Antioch to the churches that had been established in Galatia through Paul's work there.

Paul recognized that this was not just a dispute about details that were of little importance. The central things of the gospel were involved. Action had to be taken. Two things were done to deal with the whole problem that had been raised:

1. Paul wrote his letter to the Galatian Christians; and
2. The council of Jerusalem (of which we read in Acts 15) was called. Both may be dated about the year AD 50.

Contents and argument

1. 1:1–24 After a very brief introduction, Paul expresses his surprise that the Galatians were turning aside from the gospel and accepting teaching that was no gospel at all. Paul reminds them how he himself had been turned to Christ from being a persecutor and how the gospel had been made plain to him by the Lord himself.

2. 2:1–21 Paul had had to strive even with Peter and Barnabas so that the great truths of the gospel might not be compromised in any way. There is one gospel for both Jews and Gentiles. Gentiles do not need to be circumcized in order to be saved. All men may receive salvation by faith; it is God's free gift in Jesus Christ. In him they find life and in him they have fellowship together.

3. 3:1–14 People receive the Holy Spirit by God's grace through faith and not by their obeying the law. They receive salvation in the same way. The principle is shown in the Old Testament. There is no hope of salvation through the law. We are all condemned for failing to keep the law. Our hope is in what Jesus Christ has done to bear our sin. We find acceptance with God by faith in him.

4. 3:15–4:7 The purpose of the law was to prepare the way for Christ. Now that Christ has come we are no longer like servants under the law; Jews and Gentiles alike become sons of God through faith in him.

5. 4:8–5:12 Paul begs the Galatians not to turn back from the freedom of the gospel to put themselves under the law. He illustrates this from the difference in Old Testament days between Ishmael, the son of Hagar, and Isaac, the son of Sarah, who inherited God's promises. A person must choose between the way of the law and the way of grace, but to choose the way of the law is to turn aside from the gospel.

6. 5:13–6:10 The gospel means freedom; freedom from sin and freedom from trying to depend on the law as the way

of salvation. This, however, is not freedom to do whatever
one wishes to do. There is a law of Christ, and this is the law
of love, summing up the old commandments. The Spirit must
rule in the Christian's life and then the fruit of the Spirit will
be found there.

7.   6:11–18   Paul's final appeal to the Galatians; the cross,
not circumcision, is the centre of the gospel. The gospel is the
message of grace, not law. The great confidence and pride of
the Christian is in what Christ has done for him by his death
on the cross.

Study questions

1.   What are the main points of the answer which is given
by Paul (in Galatians 1:6–5:12) and by the Council of
Jerusalem (Acts 15) to the problem raised by the Jewish
Christians? In what ways do you think that we face similar
problems today? (*e.g.* it is often suggested that a person is
accepted by God because he does or does not do certain things).
2.   What is the true meaning of freedom? In what way are
Christians free men and women? What are we free from? How
would you show that this does not mean that we are free to do
what we like? Use Galatians 5:13–6:18 to answer this.

Reference books

NBCR; IBD; MNT, ch. 2

R. A. Cole, *Galatians* (IVP, 1965; Eerdmans, 1965)

D. Guthrie, *Galatians* (rev. ed. Marshall Pickering, 1982;
    Eerdmans, 1981)

A. M. Hunter, *Galatians, Ephesians, Philippians, Colossians*
    (SCM, 1960; Layman's Bible Commentary, Vol. 22 (John
    Knox, 1959)

R. P. Martin, *Understanding the New Testament: 1 and 2
    Corinthians, Galatians* (Broadman, U.S.A., 1982)

Additional note: Another view of the date of Galatians and the people to whom it was written.

The one name of the Roman province of Galatia may cover the different towns mentioned above wherever Paul preached the gospel on his first missionary journey. Some have thought, however, that he is more likely to have used the name 'Galatian' as referring to those who by race were Galatian or Galatic. These people lived further north and Paul may have visited them later. Some think that Acts 16:6 and 18:23 refer to his working among these people. Certainly if *Galatians* was written to them it must have been written a good deal later than we have suggested, some time after the Council of Jerusalem. There are also those who, while thinking that the letter was written to those of the Roman province of Galatia, feel that it was written after the Council of Jerusalem. For further study of these views see *NBCR* and *IBD* and the commentaries of R. A. Cole and Donald Guthrie listed above.

Romans

Paul wrote his letter to the Romans some years after Galatians, probably from Corinth during his third missionary journey, about AD 57 or 58. Because it is very like Galatians in setting forth the central truths of the gospel Paul preached, we shall move on to it immediately. In Galatians Paul met the special difficulty caused, as we have seen, when some of the Jewish Christians said that Gentiles must keep the law and the old covenant (with its sign of circumcision) in order to find salvation and to become members of God's people. Paul replied that Jews and Gentiles are accepted by God ('justified') only by God's grace in Christ, that grace of God which they receive by faith. In Romans Paul no longer writes in the heat of the controversy that led him to write Galatians, but nevertheless he still wants to make very clear the essence of this gospel of God's grace.

Paul had never been to Rome, but there had been Christians there for some years. We do not know who first preached the gospel there or exactly when it was. Since, however, a strong church in Rome would have an influence which could reach into every part of the great Roman Empire, we can understand the way that Paul thought about the tremendous importance of the church there. He looked forward to visiting it to do all that he could to strengthen the Christians in Rome in faith and in a clear understanding of the gospel (1:1–17). This is also the reason why in this letter more than in any other Paul sets out very plainly and methodically the way of salvation in

Christ, God's purpose for man and the duties of the Christian life. No other New Testament letter does this as systematically as Romans does. A. M. Hunter has called Romans 'the most important letter ever written'.

Contents and argument

Because the apostle sets out so carefully in this letter the way of salvation and of life in Christ, it is important that we follow closely the steps of his argument section by section, grasping the main point of each section and the part played by each sub-section with it:

1. Introduction (1:1–17).

(a) 1:1–7 Greetings to the Christians at Rome from Paul who is an apostle, set apart to proclaim the gospel of Jesus Christ, the Son of God.

(b) 1:8–15 Paul tells of his prayers for the Christians in Rome and his eagerness to come to preach there.

(c) 1:16–17 He is not ashamed of the gospel because it shows 'the righteousness of God', the way that men can be right with God by his gift of that righteousness to those who believe.

2. Man's deep need to be set right with God (1:18–3:20).

(a) 1:18–32 The sins of the Gentile world in turning from the knowledge of God that they might have had, putting idols in the place of God, and living in impurity and all kinds of evil.

(b) 2:1–10 The sins and responsibility of those who think they are right with God and who judge others.

(c) 2:11–16 The sins of the Gentiles who have the law of God written on their hearts and consciences.

(d)   2:17–29   The sins of the Jews who have the written law and fail to obey it, and the covenant with God (with its sign of circumcision) and do not keep it.

(e)   3:1–8   The advantages of the Jews, and the way Paul meets the objections to his argument about man's need.

(f)   3:9–20   Jews and Gentiles alike have all sinned and are 'held accountable to God'.

3. The way of being made right with God by faith in Jesus Christ (3:21–4:25).

(a)   3:21–26   The way of forgiveness and freedom through the sacrificial death of Jesus Christ.

(b)   3:27–31   One way for Jews and for Gentiles.

(c)   4:1–15   The way to be set right with God illustrated from the Old Testament (from Abraham and the Psalms), and the relationship of this way to circumcision and the law.

(d)   4:16–25   Faith in God as the giver of life (illustrated from the life of Abraham).

4. The ongoing Christian life as a life right with God (5:1–8:39).

(a)   5:1–11   The peace and joy and qualities of character that come with the life which is right with God.

(b)   5:12–21   Sin and death came to man through Adam, righteousness and life through Jesus Christ.

(c)   6:1–11   The duty to reject sin and do what is right because of the new life received in Christ.

(d)   6:12–23   The duty to reject sin and do what is right because men are no longer 'slaves of sin' but called to the privilege of serving God.

(e)   7:1–13   The effect of the law on a person's life and the way of freedom from the law as a means of trying to be right with God.

(f) 7:14–25 The inner struggle with sin and the way of victory in Jesus Christ.

(g) 8:1–11 Life in the Spirit means pardon and power.

(h) 8:12–17 Life in the Spirit as sons of God.

(i) 8:18–25 Hope transforms suffering.

(j) 8:25–30 The Holy Spirit helps us in prayer.

(k) 8:31–39 God who gave his Son to us will with him 'give us all things' and give victory under all circumstances.

5. The purpose of God for Jews and Gentiles (9:1–11:36).

The apostle could not deal with the whole matter of man being brought into a right relationship with God without dealing with the place of Israel in God's plan and the place of the Gentiles.

(a) 9:1–5 Paul's concern for his own people because they had been given a special place in the purposes of God in the past.

(b) 9:6–13 God chose Abraham, but not all the descendants of Abraham receive his promises.

(c) 9:14–29 God is Lord of all and none may question what he chooses to do. This applies to both Jews and Gentiles.

(d) 9:30–33 Men are made right with God through faith; to try to be right on any other basis is to stumble.

(e) 10:1–4 The misguided zeal for God among the Jewish people.

(f) 10:5–13 The way of acceptance with God is within the reach of all; any one who hears God's word and believes it and confesses Jesus Christ finds acceptance with him.

(g) 10:14–21 Men cannot hear without a preacher, but Israel has heard and rejected the message.

(h) 11:1–10 Many of the people of Israel have rejected the message but some have accepted.

(i) 11:11–24 When the Jews rejected the message, the opportunity was given to Gentiles. Gentiles are warned, however, not to be proud but humbly to rely on God's grace.

(j) 11:25–32 God still has a purpose to fulfil for Israel.

(k) 11:33–36 Paul praises the wonderful wisdom of God shown in his purpose for both Jews and Gentiles.

6. The way to be right with God in daily living (12:1–15:13).

(a) 12:1–2 Paul's appeal for the dedication of the whole of life to God.

(b) 12:3–8 Christians are to live together in love as members of Christ's body, the church, each using the gifts that God has given and serving in the way of his calling.

(c) 12:9–21 The outworking of love in all relationships and under all circumstances.

(d) 13:1–7 The Christian's duty to his country.

(e) 13:8–10 Love sums up the duty of the Christian.

(f) 13:11–14 The hope of Christ's coming again is to affect every part of the Christian's conduct.

(g) 14:1–12 The need of love, and not the spirit of judgment, in relation to fellow-Christians who may hold different opinions on lesser issues.

(h) 14:13–23 The concern of one who loves others is that his actions will not cause his brother to stumble.

(i) 15:1–13 Christian living means the desire to please others and not oneself, to accept and welcome others as Christ himself has received Gentiles as well as Jews to be his people.

7. Conclusion (15:14–16:27).

(a) 15:14–29 Paul's aim to preach the gospel where it had not been preached; so he thought to come to Rome as he travelled further westwards to Spain.

(b) 15:30–33 His request for prayer.

(c) 16:1–16 Personal messages and greetings.

(d) 16:17–20 An appeal to avoid divisions and disunity.
(e) 16:21–23 Greetings from Paul's colleagues.
(f) 16:24–27 Closing doxology.

Study questions

1. Try to put in your own words the main points of Paul's teaching (a) about the judgment of God in 1:18–3:20; (b) about the way of being right with God in 3:21–4:25; (c) about what should be the results of being right with God in chapter 8.
2. What important things does Paul say in 12:1–13:14 about the duties of the Christian in his personal life and in his relationships with others?
3. How do the things that Paul says in 14:1–15:13 help us in the matter of our relationship with our fellow-Christians when we agree with them about the gospel itself but differ on smaller points?

Reference books

NBCR; IBD; BNT, pp. 59-78; *MNT*, pp. 22-33

E. M. Blaiklock, *Understanding the New Testament: Romans* (Broadman, U.S.A., 1982)

F. F. Bruce, *Romans* (rev. ed. IVP, 1986; Eerdmans, 1986)

C. E. B. Cranfield, *Romans: A Shorter Commentary* (T & T Clark, 1985; Eerdmans, 1985)

Paul and the Young Churches

Our study of Galatians and Romans has led us to think of the great essential of the gospel that Paul preached. Now as we study more of his letters we see his relationships with the churches which God used him to plant and to strengthen. Paul's main missionary work covered some 10–12 years (see p. 294). We have seen that in that time he preached the gospel in many places in four great provinces of the Roman Empire, in Galatia, Macedonia, Acharia and Asia (see map). The longest time that he spent in any place was three years; that was in Ephesus (Acts 20:31). Usually he stayed only a short time. He preached wherever possible to the Jews first because of their Old Testament background of belief in one God, and their hope in the Messiah. Then he turned to the Gentiles. People believed and came to belong together in Christian fellowship. Paul taught them the essential principles of Christian living. He saw to the appointment of elders to lead and superintend the life of the young Christian church (see Acts 14:21–23). Then he trusted them to the Holy Spirit and moved on to work in other places. He certainly continued to be concerned for these people who had believed through his preaching and to be concerned for their fellowship together and their witness to others. We know how he prayed for them (see Eph. 1:16–23; 3:14–21; Phil. 1:3–11; Col. 1:9–14; 1 Thes. 1:2). Then sometimes, also, he sent his colleagues to visit them to help and encourage them, men like Silas and Timothy and Titus (see Acts 19:22; 1 Cor. 4:17; 2 Cor. 12:18 and 1 Thes.

3:2). Sometimes the churches wrote to him about their problems (see 1 Cor. 7:1); and he wrote to them. So it is that many of Paul's letters deal with difficulties that the various young churches were facing; difficulties relating both to Christian teaching and to Christian living.

1 and 2 Thessalonians

Probably Galatians was the first of Paul's letters to be written, and 1 Thessalonians was the second. Paul went to Thessalonica, the capital of the Roman province of Macedonia, on his second missionary journey about the year AD 51. We read in Acts 17:1–9 of his preaching there with Silas, and of their being persecuted and compelled to leave. They left, however, only after many people had believed in Christ. Paul went on to preach in Beroea, then in Athens and in Corinth. In Corinth Timothy, who had also been in Thessalonica, came back to Paul (see 1 Thes. 3:6 and Acts 18:5). Timothy's report concerning the church in Thessalonica led Paul to write this first letter to the Thessalonian Christians, probably at most a year after the gospel had been first preached in Thessalonica. 2 Thessalonians followed not much later. (See *NBCR*).

The purpose of 1 Thessalonians

There were a number of things that Timothy must have told Paul about the Thessalonian Christians which led him to write in the way that he did.

1. The Christians in Thessalonica were giving a great example of faith and devotion. People heard of this in all Macedonia and Greece and Paul commends them for what they have done and for the way they were living as Christians (1:2–10).

2. Persecution had continued, but the Christians had stood

fast and Paul says how he rejoices to know of their faithfulness (3:1–10).

3.   There were those at Thessalonica who were saying that Paul and his message were not to be trusted. He had persuaded them to believe his gospel, but they would never see him again. Paul defends himself (2:1–12) and tells what in fact was his great desire, to visit them again (2:17–20 and 3:10–11).

4.   Timothy may have spoken of the temptations that Christians faced as they lived in a pagan society in Thessalonica; so Paul urged them to live in purity and holiness (4:1–8 and 5:22–24).

5.   There may have been a tendency to disunity and disrespect for their elders and a despising of spiritual gifts that led Paul to write as he does in 5:12–13, 19–21 and 27.

6.   The most important thing that Paul had to deal with was their future hope. Some of the Christians were anxious because loved ones of theirs, who had believed in Christ, had died before his second coming which they trusted would take place very soon. Would they miss the joy of that day and life with Christ to follow it? Paul made clear that they would not. True believers, living or departed, will be with the Lord for ever. This hope brings comfort. It should also make them want to be ready, whenever he comes, but not cause them to leave their normal work in excitement (4:13–5:11).

Contents of 1 Thessalonians

6. 4:1–12   Encouragement to purity of life, love and faithful work.

7. 4:13–18   The position of those who have died in the faith of Christ.

8. 5:1–11   The effect that Christian hope should have on life.

9. 5:12–28   Closing exhortations, prayer and greetings.

The purpose of 2 Thessalonians

Even after Paul had written his first letter to the Christians in Thessalonica, they still faced problems in understanding the second coming of Christ. Some were saying that the great 'day of the Lord' had come already (2:2). So the main purpose of this letter, probably written just a short time after 1 Thessalonians, is to show that the second coming of Christ has certainly not taken place and to tell what must happen before it does take place.

The teaching of 1 and 2 Thessalonians about the second coming of Christ

Some people in studying these two letters have felt it a problem that there is a difference of emphasis in the teaching about the future in 1 and 2 Thessalonians.

In 1 Thessalonians the situation in Thessalonica, the concern of some of the Christians for their loved ones who had died, and Paul's challenge to all the members of the church to keep to the highest standards of Christian living, led him to emphasize two things:

1. We must be ready for Christ's coming at any time. He will come as suddenly as a thief in the night.

2. Those who are alive and those who have died will be together with Christ at that time.

In 2 Thessalonians, because of the difficulties created by people saying that the second coming had already taken place, Paul emphasizes the things that must happen before Christ comes. There must be the greatest manifestation of evil; 'the man of lawlessness' and 'the mystery of lawlessness' and 'the activity of Satan . . . with all power and with pretended signs and wonders', before he is finally destroyed by the Lord Jesus at his coming (2:1–12).

The two emphases are not contradictory. Both were necessary for the purposes for which 1 and 2 Thessalonians were written. We should notice that both kinds of teaching are found together in what we are given of the teaching of Jesus himself in Matthew 24 and Mark 13.

Contents of 2 Thessalonians

1. 1:1–2   Greetings.
2. 1:3–12   Thanksgiving for the Thessalonians' endurance of persecution. Their willingness to suffer shows the reality of their faith. Their persecutors show by their attitude that they must come under the judgment of God.
3. 2:1–12   Paul meets their difficulty about the second coming of Christ. It has not already taken place; there must be a greater realization of the power of evil before Christ comes finally to conquer the evil one.
4. 2:13–17   Exhortation and prayer that they may stand firm in faith.
5. 3:1–5   Paul's prayer for the Thessalonians and his request for their prayers.
6. 3:6–15   His words against idleness and laziness.
7. 3:16–18   Final prayer and greetings.

Study questions

1. Read carefully 1 Thessalonians 4:13–5:11 and 2 Thes-

salonians 2:1–12 and see what they say:

(a)   About the time when our Lord Jesus Christ will come again;

(b)   About what should be our attitude because we hope for his coming.

(c)   About what must happen before he comes;

(d)   About what will happen when he comes.

2.   What qualities of Paul's life as an apostle stand out from 1 Thessalonians 2:1–12? How are these relevant to evangelistic and pastoral ministry today?

Reference books

NBCR; IBD; BNT, pp. 72-78

W. Barclay, *Philippians, Colossians, Thessalonians* (Saint Andrew, 1975; Westminster, 1975)

W. Hendriksen, *1 and 2 Thessalonians* (Banner of Truth, 1972; Baker, 1979)

W. L. Lane, *Understanding the New Testament: Ephesians, Philippians, Colossians and 2 Thessalonians* (Broadman, U.S.A., 1982)

I. H. Marshall, *1 and 2 Thessalonians* (Marshall Pickering, 1983; Eerdmans, 1983)

L. Morris, *1 & 2 Thessalonians* (rev. ed. IVP, 1984; Eerdmans, 1984)

L. Morris, *The Epistles to the Thessalonians* (Eerdmans, 1959)

1 and 2 Corinthians

Paul and the church in Corinth

Corinth was the greatest of the cities of Greece (the Roman province of Achaia) and its capital. Because it was important as a port and as a centre of trade, people of many nations gathered there, many different religions were followed, and we know that it was a city noted for the immorality of its life. Paul went to Corinth on his second missionary journey. He stayed there for more than 18 months and in that time many people became Christians (Acts 18:1–18). On his third missionary journey, when he spent three years in Ephesus, on the other side of the Aegean Sea, there were several letters that passed between Paul and the Corinthian Christians.

1. It seems that Paul heard a report (perhaps through Apollos) of the temptations to immorality that the Christians in Corinth were facing. So he wrote a letter telling them 'not to associate with immoral men' (see 1 Corinthians 5:9–11). We do not have that letter now.

2. Later the Corinthians wrote to Paul and asked him questions about marriage, about eating food offered to idols, about spiritual gifts and about the collection for the Christians in Jerusalem. Paul speaks of this letter in 1 Corinthians 7:1 and because, in 1 Corinthians 8:1, 12:1, 16:1 and perhaps 16:12, we have sections of the letter which all begin in just the same way, they may all be references to their letter to him and lead to his answers to their questions.

3. Paul wrote to answer the questions they had put to him but also to deal with other matters that were reported to him (see 1 Cor. 1:11): divisions and disunity among the Christians, immorality, law-suits between Christians in heathen courts, attitudes and actions that were spoiling their worship and fellowship. This letter is what we call 1 Corinthians.

4.   There were difficulties and misunderstandings between Paul and the Corinthian Christians after this. These led him to visit them. He speaks of this in 2 Corinth. 2:1 as a 'painful visit'. Then he wrote them a letter 'out of much affliction and anguish of heart and with many tears' (2 Cor. 2:4).

5.   Later, when Paul heard from Titus that things were much happier in Corinth, Paul wrote again. This is the letter that we call 2 Corinthians.

Finally Paul visited Corinth again at the end of his third missionary journey (Acts 20:1–3).

(For further details see *NBCR* and *IBD*.)

Contents of 1 Corinthians

We have seen that this letter was written, partly in reply to questions raised by the Corinthians in a letter to Paul, and partly to deal with difficulties that had been reported to him as being experienced by the Christians in Corinth. The letter is specially valuable to us as it shows the problems in faith and conduct, faced by new Christians and the way that Paul dealt with them.

1.   1:1–9   Greetings and praise for God's working in the Christians in Corinth.

2.   1:10–17   Report of divisions among the Christians there.

3.   1:18–2:5   Paul's confidence in the message of Christ crucified rather than in the wisdom and power of the world.

4.   2:6–16   The Holy Spirit is the giver of wisdom and understanding.

5. 3:1–23   Paul's rebuke of the divisions and the emphasis on building on the foundation of Jesus Christ.

6. 4:1–21   The tasks and sufferings of an apostle.

7. 5:1–13   Immorality and the way that the church should deal with it.

8. 6:1–11   The wrong of Christians going to law against fellow-Christians.

9. 6:12–20   The Christian's body is the temple of the Holy Spirit; so there must be no sexual immorality.

10. 7:1–40   Matters related to marriage.

11. 8:1–13   Paul's answer to the question about food offered to idols.

12. 9:1–27   The Christian's freedom, but what he or she should do for the sake of others.

13. 10:1–11:1   The Christian should forsake all idolatry.

14. 11:2–16   The dress of women at worship.

15. 11:17–34   The Lord's Supper and the fellowship meal.

16. 12:1–31   The varied gifts of the Spirit; Christians as members together of the one body of Christ.

17. 13:1–13   Love matters most.

18. 14:1–40   Spiritual gifts – prophecy more important than the gift of tongues.

19. 15:1–58   Christ's resurrection and the resurrection of Christians.

20. 16:1–24   The collection for the Jerusalem church. Final messages and greetings.

Contents of 2 Corinthians

Paul wrote 1 Corinthians to deal with problems in the church in Corinth. After the letter was written, difficulties and misunderstandings arose between him and the Corinthian Christians. We do not know for sure the cause of these. They may have been associated with the disciplining of those who were acting immorally. The misunderstandings caused great distress to Paul. We have noted how he had to make a 'painful visit' to Corinth and then to write a letter which he wrote 'with many tears'. Then he sent Titus to Corinth to try to help in the situation there. It was when Titus returned to Paul with better news from Corinth that the apostle wrote this letter with great relief and thankfulness (7:5–7). Whereas 1 Corinthians tells us a great deal about a young church in New Testament days, 2 Corinthians, the most personal of all Paul's letters, tells us what it meant to be an apostle of Jesus Christ.

We may outline the contents of 2 Corinthians as follows:

1. 1:1–11   Paul's thanksgiving for the comfort of good news from Corinth.

2. 1:12–2:17   The difficulties and misunderstanding between Paul and the Corinthian Christians and the way they had been overcome.

3. 3:1–18   Ministry under the new covenant compared with that under the old.

4. 4:1–18   The burdens and sufferings of a minister of Christ, and Christ's enabling power.

5. 5:1–10   The aim to please God.

6. 5:11–6:10   The work and the life of an ambassador for Christ; his message of reconciliation.

7. 6:11–13   A personal appeal to the Corinthians.

8. 6:14–7:1 A call to the Corinthians to reject all impurity.

9. 7:2–16   Paul's concern for the Christians in Corinth and his relationships with them.

10. 8:1–9:15   The collection for the Jerusalem church. Teaching about Christian giving.

11. 10:1–18   Paul faces criticism of his life and work as an apostle.

12. 11:1–12:13   The work Paul had done and what he had suffered.

13. 12:14–13:10   His plan to come to Corinth and what he hoped to find when he came.

14. 13:11–14   Closing greetings and prayer.

Study questions

1. From reading 1 Corinthians note the teaching that Paul gives dealing with
   (a) divisions among Christians (1:10–3:23),
   (b) food offered to idols (8:1–11:1),
   (c) spiritual gifts (12:1–14:40).

In what ways do we face similar problems today? What things that Paul says are specially helpful in dealing with these problems?

2. Study 1 Corinthians 15 and consider what Paul says about
   (a) the basis of certainty about the resurrection of Jesus,
   (b) the link between this resurrection and the resurrection of Christians, and
   (c) the nature of the resurrection life for which Christians hope.

3. From 2 Corinthians 4:1–6:10 make lists showing what Paul said about
   (a) the difficulties, and
   (b) the responsibilities, of a minister of Christ.

How do you think that these apply to those who are called to any kind of Christian ministry and service today?

Reference books

NBCR and *IBD*

W. Barclay, *Corinthians* (Saint Andrew, 1975; Westminster, 1975)

F. F. Bruce, *1 & 2 Corinthians* (Marshall Pickering, 1971; Eerdmans, 1980)

G. D. Fee, *The First Epistle to the Corinthians* (Eerdmans, 1987)

P. E. Hughes, *Paul's Second Epistle to the Corinthians* (Eerdmans, 1962)

C. Kruse, *2 Corinthians* (IVP, 1987; Eerdmans, 1987)

R. P. Martin, *Understanding the New Testament: 1 and 2*

Corinthians, Galatians (Broadman, U.S.A., 1982)

L. Morris, *1 Corinthians* (rev. ed. IVP, 1986; Eerdmans, 1986)

Paul's Letters from Prison

'Paul, a prisoner for Christ Jesus' (Eph. 3:1 and Phm. 1). 'It has become known throughout the whole praetorian guard and to all the rest that my imprisonment is for Christ' (Phil. 1:13). 'Pray also for us, that God will give us a good opportunity to preach his message, to tell the secret of Christ. For that is why I am now in prison' (Col. 4:3 TEV). These words show clearly that the four letters from which they are taken, Philippians, Colossians, Philemon and Ephesians, were written when Paul was a prisoner for the sake of Jesus Christ. From 2 Corinthians 11:23–25 it is clear that Paul was often arrested because he preached the gospel; he endured 'countless beatings'; he was in prison many times. Paul wrote 2 Corinthians, as we have seen, when he was in Ephesus on this third missionary journey. He still had much to suffer after that time, and the Acts of the Apostles tells of his imprisonments in Jerusalem, Caesarea and Rome. Although no place of imprisonment is mentioned directly in any of them, it has usually been thought that all of these four letters, Philippians, Philemon, Colossians and Ephesians were written when Paul was a prisoner in Rome. In any case it is clear that when Paul was not free to continue to preach the gospel in places where it had not been heard before, or to strengthen the churches by visiting them, he still spent his time and energy helping them by his prayers for them and by the letters that he wrote to them. In these letters, moreover, we see how a man, by the power of Christ, can endure intensely difficult circumstances and yet still be full of joy and of concern for others.

Philippians

When Paul set out with Silas on what was his second great missionary journey, they went first through areas where the gospel had already been preached 'strengthening the churches' (Acts 15:41 and 16:1,5). They went through Syria and Cilicia, through Phrygia and Galatia. Then they felt impelled to go further and further west till they came to Troas on the Aegean Sea. It was there that a vision appeared to Paul in the night; a man of Macedonia was standing beckoning him and saying, 'Come over to Macedonia and help us' (Acts 16:9). Obedience to that vision led to the first preaching of the gospel in what we now call Europe. It all began in Philippi which is described as 'the leading city of the district of Macedonia'. It was in fact a 'Roman colony' which meant that its citizens, many of whom were soldiers retired from the Roman army and settled there, had the same rights of citizenship as if they lived in Rome itself.

When Paul and Silas arrived in Philippi, it seems that exceptionally they found no Jewish synagogue, but there was a place of prayer by the riverside where some women met to pray on the sabbath. One of these women, Lydia, believed the message Paul and Silas preached, opened her home to them, and thus missionary work went ahead. When Paul exorcized the demon from a slave girl used as a fortune-teller, her masters stirred up opposition and Paul and Silas were arrested, beaten, thrown into prison and their feet were fastened in the stocks (Acts 16:11–24). In spite of everything, they were able to sing hymns of praise to God in the prison. That night there was an earthquake, and immediately all the doors were opened'. What happened led to the conversion of the jailor and his household. Before Paul and Silas left Philippi it is clear that there were a good many who had become Christians (Acts 16:25–40).

It was probably the year AD 51 when the gospel was first preached in Philippi. Paul kept in touch with the Christians there. From Acts 19:22 it seems likely that Timothy with Erastus, was sent to visit them. More than once, we gather, they sent gifts to Paul to help him (4:15-16) and to show how they desired to continue to share with him in the work of the gospel (1:5). From the references to Macedonia in Acts 20:1-6, we can assume that Paul had two further visits to Philippi about the years 57-58. Then the years passed by and Paul had no opportunity to visit them and they had no opportunity to send to him. Later, when they knew that Paul was in prison, they sent to him again (4:10). They sent gifts, but they also sent one of their members, Epaphroditus, who was to help Paul in every way he could (4:18). Epaphroditus, however, had been sick and the Philippians had been anxious for him. It seemed wise for Epaphroditus to return home (2:25-30). So there was opportunity for Paul to write to the Philippians and there were many things on his heart to write about, some prompted no doubt by the report that Epaphroditus brought of the church in Philippi.

Reasons for Paul's writing to the Philippians

We can see six reasons for Paul's writing as he did to the Philippian Christians:

1. He wanted to thank them for their gifts to him and for sending Epaphroditus to help him (4:10–18).

2. He wanted to explain why he was sending Epaphroditus back to them (2:25–30).

3. He was able also to tell them of his plan to send Timothy to them as soon as there was further news of his own situation (2:19–24).

4. He could tell them what they wanted to know of his own circumstances, how they had turned out for the advance of the gospel and for the encouragement of Christians around him (1:12–26).

5. He desired greatly to encourage the Philippian Christians to live in unity and fellowship, working and witnessing together with one mind (1:27; 2:1–12; 4:2–3).

6. He felt the need to warn them of the danger of making the law more important than the gospel (3:1–11), the danger about which he had written so strongly in Galatians; also to warn them of any claim to perfection on the one hand (3:12–16) and of careless and selfish living on the other (3:17–21).

Contents of the letter

We may summarize the contents of the letter as follows:

1. 1:1–11 Greetings, thanksgiving and prayer for the Philippian Christians.

2. 1:12–26 Paul tells what has been happening to him and what may happen to him in the future. His imprisonment has meant that 'throughout the whole praetorian guard', the Roman soldiers' barracks, it has come to be known that his 'imprisonment is for Christ'. The gospel has been made known. Christians have come to witness more boldly. He does not know whether the end of his imprisonment will be his death or his release, but he can say 'to me to live is Christ, and to die is gain'.

3. 1:27–2:18 He calls on them to act worthily of the gospel, especially by living in unity and fellowship. Humility is the way to fellowship, humility as was shown in Christ's own humbling himself to become man and to die on the cross. Christians, furthermore, should be lights in the world by the way that they live and they should hold out the word of life to others.

4. 2:19–30 Paul speaks of his plan to send Timothy when there is further news for him to tell and he gives the reason why Epaphroditus is coming back to them. He can warmly commend these two men for their unselfish service.

5. 3:1–21 As Paul speaks of the dangers of turning aside to depend on the law rather than on the grace of God in Christ, he speaks of what his ambitions were in the past when he was a Pharisee and a persecutor of the Christians and what his ambitions had become since he had been a Christian. He calls the Philippians to go on in their Christian lives and to remember that they are citizens of heaven and those who look forward to the coming again of their Lord and Saviour Jesus Christ.

6. 4:1–9 Paul's appeal to his readers to stand firm in the Lord, to agree in the Lord, to rejoice in the Lord and to let their thoughts be filled with things true and lovely and good.

7. 4:10–20 As Paul thanks the Philippians for their gifts he shows his attitude to material things and encourages them to realize that God will supply all their needs according to his infinite riches in Christ.

8. 4:21–23 Final greetings and prayer.

Study questions

1. Read this letter and note down Paul's attitude to (a) material things, (b) hardship and suffering, (c) uncertainty about the future, (d) death.

2. What does this letter teach about what our Lord Jesus Christ has done for us and what this means both for our receiving his salvation and for the way that we should live as Christians?

3. What standards and goals for Christian living are presented

to us in this letter in the examples of the lives of Paul, Timothy, Epaphroditus and the Philippian Christians?

Reference books

W. Barclay, *Philippians, Colossians and Thessalonians* (Saint Andrew, 1975; Westminster, 1975)

F. F. Bruce, *The Epistles to the Colossians, to the Philippians and to the Ephesians* (Eerdmans, 1984)

F. F. Bruce, *Philippians* (Harper & Row, U.S.A., 1983)

D. Guthrie, *Exploring God's Word: A Guide to Ephesians, Philippians, Colossians* (Hodder, 1984; Eerdmans, 1985)

W. Hendriksen, *A Commentary on the Epistle to the Philippians* (Banner of Truth, 1973); *Philippians, Colossians and Philemon* (Baker, 1979)

R. P. Martin, *Philippians* (rev. ed. IVP, 1987; Eerdmans, 1987)

R. P. Martin, *Philippians* (Marshall Pickering, 1976); *Commentary on Philippians* (Eerdmans, 1980)

Philemon

The next three letters probably belong closely together. Paul's writing to Philemon led to his writing to the Colossian Christians. His writing of Colossians led to his writing Ephesians. How did this all come about?

Philemon had a slave, Onesimus, who had run away from his master, perhaps taking money from him as he went (Phm. 18). In some way, just how we do not know, he came to Paul in the place of his imprisonment. Onesimus became a Christian and repented of what he had done. It was clearly the duty of Onesimus to go back to his master. Paul wrote a letter to Philemon asking him to take Onesimus back into his home, but now he would be to him not just a slave but a brother in Christ. If Onesimus had taken money from Philemon, or was indebted to him in any way, Paul promised that he would pay the debt. He said that he felt confident that Philemon would do all that he asked. Before he closed the letter he said that he hoped that it would be possible for him, released from prison, to visit Philemon again (Phm. 21–22).

This is a very short letter, but it gives us a wonderful picture of the spirit of early Christianity, especially of the brotherhood of love that bound Christians together. Paul did not openly attack the system of slavery that was firmly established in the Roman Empire in those days. He did not want Christian slaves to think that, because they were Christians, they could rebel against their masters. He urged them to show their faith in the way that they served (see Eph. 6:5–8 and Col. 3:22–25). When, however, a slave can become a brother in Christ to his master, the sting is taken from slavery. In addition the teaching about love and brotherhood and equality that Paul, and other New Testament writers, gave, was to lead in time to the abolition of slavery.

Study question

Read the letter carefully and consider what it implies as to the attitude of Paul to a slave, to his master and to the system of slavery. What has the letter to say in relation to the attitude of Christians to social systems today that are not in agreement with the teaching of Christ?

Reference books
NBCR and *IBD,* and see below on Colossians

Colossians

Philemon, the master of Onesimus, lived in Colossae in the Roman province of Asia, the area which is Turkey on the map today. Paul had never been to Colossae (2:1), but in the time when he was in Ephesus on his third missionary journey, the gospel spread right through that Roman province of Asia (Acts 19:10). Epaphras, of whom we read in 1:7, was the first missionary to Colossae. A strong church grew up in Colossae as in other towns in that Roman province, but at the time when Paul was writing to Philemon and sending Onesimus back there, he knew that the Colossian Christians were facing special difficulties. He was glad, therefore, to be able to write and send a letter to the whole church there.

The purpose of Paul's letter

Paul was pleased to have such an opportunity of encouraging the Colossian Christians and of reminding them of their great calling in Christ. Then, perhaps, the thought of Onesimus returning as a slave to his master led him to write about relationships in the Christian home, husbands and wives, children and parents, masters and slaves (3:18–4:1). Most important of all, however, Paul knew that there was false teaching being given in Colossae; the Christians there had to know how to meet this and needed to be warned not to be led astray by it.

This teaching that was being given in Colossae was misleading people in three ways:

1.   It said that, although faith in Christ was good, people could go on to a higher wisdom and knowledge, to a better philosophy and understanding of life. In answer to this Paul shows that in Christ alone are 'all the treasures of wisdom and knowledge' (2:3). True wisdom is not man's philosophy (2:8) but God's revelation of himself in Christ. In 1:27 and 2:2 he uses the word 'mystery', a word which probably the false teachers were using with their own meaning. Paul uses it to speak of God's truth that men could not know otherwise, but which has been made known in Jesus Christ.

2.   This teaching in Colossae also said that Christ was only one of the spiritual powers through which men came to God. Paul shows, in answer to this, that Christ is not just one of the powers. He is Lord of all and Creator of all (1:15–17). In him is 'all the fullness of God' and all the spiritual powers of evil were conquered by him in his death on the cross (1:19–20, 2:9–10,15).

3.   The teaching being given also made outward ceremonies such as feasts and fasts very important, and set out detailed rules of what people should do and not do. In answer to this Paul said that Christian living is not a matter of outward observances (2:16–23). It is a matter of death to sin and new life, in Christ and with him. We have to set our minds on 'things that are above, not on things that are on earth' (3:1–4). The things contrary to that life in Christ we must 'put away' (3:5–11) and the good things which should be seen in the Christian life must be 'put on' (3:12–17).

Contents of the letter

We may summarize the content of Colossians as follows:

1.   1:1–14 Greetings, thanksgiving and prayer for the Colossian Christians.

2.   1:15–2:7 The greatness and glory of Christ; the call to the Christians in Colossae to live in him.

3. 2:8–23 Warning against the 'philosophy' and 'tradition' that do not give Christ his true place and which make the Christian life just a set of rules.

4. 3:1–4 The real way of life in Christ.

5. 3:5–11 The things that are to be given no place in that life in Christ.

6. 3:12–17 The things that are to be given a place in Christian living.

7. 3:18–4:1 Family relationships.

8. 4:2–6 Encouragement to prayer and witness.

9. 4:7–18 Personal news, greetings and final instructions.

Study questions

1. Go through this letter and note all the things that Paul says about Jesus Christ, who he is and what he has done for us.

2. Note what the apostle says in chapters 3 and 4 about the qualities that should be found in the Christian life. Consider also his prayer in 1:9–14 from the point of view of the qualities that should be seen in our lives; note also the way that it indicates that we can pray both for ourselves and for others.

Reference books

NBCR; IBD; MNT, ch. 3

F. F. Bruce, *The Epistles to the Colossians, to the Philippians and to the Ephesians* (Eerdmans, 1984)

D. Guthrie, *Exploring God's Word: A Guide to Ephesians, Philippians, Colossians* (Hodder, 1984; Eerdmans, 1985)

R. P. Martin, *Colossians and Philemon* (rev. ed. Marshall Pickering, 1981; Eerdmans, 1981)

A. G. Patzia, *Colossians, Philemon, Ephesians* (Harper, U.S.A., 1984)

N. T. Wright, *Colossians and Philemon* (IVP, 1987; Eerdmans, 1987)

Ephesians

We have seen how Paul came to write his letter to Philemon in Colossae and how probably this led him to write his general letter to the Colossian church. There are three things that help us to understand how, in all probability, Ephesians came to be written.

1. If we read Colossians 4:7–8 and Ephesians 6:21–22 together we see that the two letters were written at the same time and that they were carried by the one messenger, Tychicus. When we read the whole of these two letters we see that they deal with similar subjects and often they use the same words and phrases. They have similar sections dealing with relationships in the family (5:22–6:9 and Col. 3:18–4:1). They both speak of Christian living as 'putting off' the old nature and 'putting on' the new (4:17–25 and Col. 3:5–15). They both speak of the duty of thankfulness, to be expressed in praise and song (5:19–20 and Col. 3:16–17). Both speak of Paul's own work and calling as making the gospel known to the Gentiles (3:1–13 and Col. 1:24–29). There are many close links between the two letters.

2. There is the strange fact that, although Paul spent three years in Ephesus (Acts 20:31), there are no personal messages or greetings in this letter, whereas very often he has many such messages in the letters he writes (see, for example, Romans 16).

3. Then we must notice that some of the earliest copies of this letter do not have the words 'at Ephesus' in 1:1. This would mean that there would be no reference to Ephesus or to

Ephesian people in the whole of the letter. With this fact we should notice that Paul, writing to the Colossians, refers to another letter that he wrote at the same time as he wrote to Colossae. In Colossians 4:16 he says that the Colossians should pass their letter on to the church in Laodicea and receive another letter of his 'from Laodicea' and read that.

How the letter came to be written

The three things which we have just noted lead us to think as follows about the letter which we call Paul's letter to the Ephesians. It was written to the Ephesians, but to others as well. It was probably the letter that Paul says that the Colossian Christians were to receive from Laodicea, a town which was not far from Colossae and Ephesus. It seems that when Paul had written his letters to Philemon and to the Colossians, his mind and heart were full of the things that he had said to the Colossians of the greatness of Christ. He thought of the Christians in all the churches of the Roman province of Asia: Ephesus, Colossae, Laodicea and the rest. Without having any special problems to face, any special question to answer, he would write a letter to them all telling them of the wonderful purpose of God in Jesus Christ. His heart is full of praise, and much of the letter is more in terms of thanksgiving and prayer than of actual teaching. He wants them to know more of the greatness of Christ and what it means to live as members of his people. He prays for them, he encourages them, he reminds them of the most important things of Christian living, for their individual lives and even more for their life together with others.

Contents of the letter

These may be summed up as follows:

1. The purpose of God in Christ (chapters 1–3)
(a) 1:1–2   The apostle's greeting.

(b) 1:3–14   Praise to God for all his blessing in Christ. God chose us to be his own. He adopted us as his sons. He brought us redemption, forgiving us our sins. He made known his purpose. He gives us hope of what will be our inheritance at the end, and now we have the gift of his Spirit in our lives. All of these blessings are given so that we may live 'to the praise of his glory'.

(c) 1:15–23   Paul now prays for the Christians to whom he writes and asks that they may know the hope of God's calling, the riches of their inheritance, and the power of God in their lives, the power that God showed in his raising Christ from the dead and exalting him to be Lord of all.

(d) 2:1–10   We were dead in sin, cut off from the life of God and controlled by our own selfish desires; we were in the power of the evil one, but God has given us new life in Christ. By his grace we are saved from sin and brought to live a totally different life, doing the 'good works' which it is God's plan for us to do.

(e) 2:11–22   What God has done for us through the death of Christ on the cross is to give us peace with himself; but this also means that we have peace and fellowship together. Jews and Gentiles, who were separated before, are made one. People of such different backgrounds are one in the people of God, members of his family, parts of his temple in which his Spirit lives.

(f) 3:1–13   Paul speaks of the amazing privilege of being called to be a messenger of the gospel, and especially that he, a Jew, should be sent to be the apostle of the Gentiles.

(g) 3:14–21   Again Paul prays for those who read his letter, that they may have inner strength by the Holy Spirit, and that with lives rooted and grounded in the love of Christ, they may go on to understand more and more of that love and be filled with all God's fullness.

2. The purpose of God for the Christian's daily life (chapters 4–6)

(a) 4:1–6 The unity of the Spirit in the life of the church, and the call to Christians to maintain that unity.

(b) 4:7–16 To all Christians differing gifts of the Spirit are given; all, as different members of a body, have different purposes in the life of the church, but all are to be used for the building up of the whole body in love.

(c) 4:17–5:2 The old way of life is to be put aside by the Christian, all that is evil, selfish, dishonest, impure, unloving in word or thought or action; the Christian has a new nature which means a life in the likeness of God, showing forth his truth and purity and love.

(d) 5:3-14 Immorality must have no place in the Christian's life. We lived in the darkness before, but now we are in the light. Christ has given us light and that light is to be shown in our lives.

(e) 5:15–20 The Christian must not live in ignorance but know the will of God and do it, constantly filled with the Spirit, thanking God in everything and singing his praise.

(f) 5:21–6:9 Relationships in the family; husbands and wives are to pattern their relationship on that between Christ and his church; children and parents both have their responsibilities. Servants (or slaves) are to serve their masters as if they were serving Christ; masters are to remember that they have a Master in heaven to whom they will give account.

(g) 6:10–20 The Christian's warfare against the powers of evil, the armour that God provides and the way of victory through prayer.

(h) 6:21–24 Conclusion.

Study questions

1. As with Colossians, go through this letter and note all that

it says about Jesus Christ and what he has done for us.

2. Note what Paul says about Christian living in this letter, especially seeing the things that involve not just personal life but life in relationship with other people.

3. Briefly summarize the teaching given about the church in this letter.

Reference books

NBCR; IBD; MNT, ch. 3

W. Barclay, *Letters to the Galatians and Ephesians* (Saint Andrew, 1975; Westminster, 1975)

F. F. Bruce, *The Epistles to the Colossians, to the Philippians and to the Ephesians* (Eerdmans, 1984)

F. Foulkes, *Ephesians* (IVP, 1963; Eerdmans, 1963)

D. Guthrie, *Exploring God's Word: A Guide to Ephesians, Philippians, Colossians* (Hodder, 1984; Eerdmans, 1985)

A. G. Patzia, *Colossians, Philemon, Ephesians* (Harper, U.S.A., 1984)

J. R. W. Stott, *The Message of Ephesians* (IVP, 1979)

Paul and His Coworkers

As we read the Acts of the Apostles we see that there were those who shared with Paul in his missionary work. On his first great missionary journey Barnabas worked with him and, for a short time, Mark (Acts 13:2,5,13). Silas was Paul's partner in his second missionary journey (Acts 15:40) and then Timothy came to share with him in the work (Acts 16:1–4). There were others who travelled and worked with him at different times; Luke, we know, was one of them (see p. 290).

When writing his letters Paul linked these colleagues with him: Timothy in the writing of 2 Corinthians, Philippians, Colossians, 1 and 2 Thessalonians and Philemon; Silas (the same as Silvanus) in the writing of 1 and 2 Thessalonians; Sosthenes (who is perhaps the same person as the one we read of in Acts 18:17) in 1 Corinthians. We read of these men in the opening verses of the letters.

There were times when Paul sent these fellow-workers to do special tasks for him in the strengthening of the churches. Sometimes they were left behind when Paul himself moved on to begin new work. It is not surprising to find that Paul wrote letters to them. Perhaps he wrote many such letters. We have just three in our New Testament; 1 and 2 Timothy and Titus.

Timothy

We have seen that Timothy came to share in Paul's work during his second missionary journey. His home was in Lystra and probably he became a Christian when Paul first visited there (Acts 14:6–20). His father was a Greek (Acts 16:1), but his mother and grandmother were Jews who truly served the Lord and taught young Timothy the Scriptures from his earliest years (2 Tim. 1:5; 3:14–15). Timothy would have remembered well the persecutions that Paul faced during that first visit to Lystra. On his second missionary journey we find that Timothy was 'well spoken of' by the Christians there (Acts 16:2–3) and so Paul took him as a colleague in his work.

With Silas, Timothy was left in Beroea in Macedonia when Paul went on alone to preach the gospel in Athens (Acts 17:14). He must have been in Thessalonica also about this time as Paul speaks of this when he writes to the Thessalonians and tells of the good news that Timothy brought back to him from them (1 Thes. 3:1–8). Later, after Paul himself had worked in Corinth (Acts 18:1–18), he sent Timothy to that great city to continue his work (1 Cor. 4:17 and 16:10–11). During his third missionary journey, when Paul himself was in Ephesus, he sent Timothy with Erastus into Macedonia (Acts 19:22). Without doubt Macedonia would have included Philippi (called in Acts 16:12 'the leading city of the district of Macedonia') and so Paul could write to the Philippian Christians (2:19–22), 'Timothy's worth you know, how as a son with a father he has served with me in the gospel'; and could say of him, 'I have no one like him, who will be genuinely anxious for your welfare'.

Timothy went with Paul on that journey to Jerusalem at the end of the apostle's third missionary journey, helping to take the gifts of the Gentile churches to the Christians at Jerusalem (Acts 20:3–4). 1 Timothy 1:3 speaks of Timothy at work in Ephesus, left there when Paul was going to Macedonia. Many believe that this was in a time after Paul's imprisonment in Rome, as recorded at the end of the Acts of the Apostles, when he was released and so was free for further missionary work.

Some of the details may not be clear but we know enough to realize what a trusted fellow worker Timothy was to Paul.

Titus

We know less of Titus than we do of Timothy. He is never mentioned by name in the Acts of the Apostles. In the early days of Paul's great missionary labours he was with the apostle in Jerusalem, and a controversy arose over him, because he was a Gentile (Gal. 2:1–5). Then, in a time of great difficulty in Paul's relationships with the church at Corinth, Titus was his representative and messenger. As he wrote of Timothy to the Philippians he could write of Titus to the Corinthians, speaking of his 'earnest care' for them and telling them 'he is my partner and fellow worker in your service' (2 Cor. 8:16,23). When Titus brought back report to Paul of the Corinthians' zeal, their sorrow for their failures and their generosity, it cheered the apostle's heart more than anything else could have done (2 Cor. 7:6–7, 13–16 and 8:6).

Later Titus was given work to do in Crete (Tit. 1:5) and finally in Dalmatia (2 Tim. 4:10). Both of these may have been after Paul was a prisoner in Rome.

Study questions

1. What kind of picture do you get of Timothy, his good qualities, his difficulties and his work, from reading 1 and 2 Timothy and also Acts 16:1–2, Romans 16:21, 1 Corinthians 4:17; 16:10, Philippians 2:19–22 and 1 Thessalonians 3:1–6?
2. Similarly, what do you learn of Titus from the letter written to him and from 2 Corinthians 7–8?

Reference books

F. F. Bruce, *The Pauline Circle* (Paternoster, 1985; Eerdmans, 1985)

Paul's Letters: 1 and 2 Timothy and Titus

These three letters are very different from Paul's other letters, so much so that in recent years many who have studied them very carefully have wondered whether they could be by the apostle himself. But the situation for which they were written was very different from that for which he wrote his other letters. Instead of being written for churches as all the others were (except for Philemon), they were written for individuals, for his own close colleagues. He had personal encouragement to give them, especially to Timothy, and he had to give them guidance as to how to deal with matters related to the building up of the inner life of the churches. The word 'pastor', of course, means 'shepherd', and so the three letters have come to be called 'The Pastoral Epistles'. Four things had to be the concern of Timothy and Titus in the building up of the churches: their ministry, their fellowship, their teaching and their witness. All of these have an important place in these three letters.

1. The ministers

In some of the letters of Paul that we have studied we have read what is said of the spiritual gifts given to different members of the body of Christ (1 Cor. 12:4–31; Eph. 4:7–16 and Rom. 12:3–8). We have read of the ministry of apostles, prophets, evangelists, pastors, teachers and others. There were those who had responsibility that was not limited to any one church or congregation. There were others whose ministry was in the local congregation. In Acts 14:23 we read that 'elders' were appointed in 'every church'. In Titus 1:5 Paul says that Titus was left to 'appoint elders in every town'. In Philippians 1:1 we read of 'bishops and deacons' in the church at Philippi. Now in these letters to Timothy and Titus we read more of the work of these 'elders or 'bishops'[1] and of 'deacons'. In particular we are told the kind of people that should be chosen for this work.

In 1 Timothy 3:1–7 and Titus 1:5–9 we read of the qualities needed in the elders or bishops and in 1 Timothy 3:8–13 we read of those needed in deacons. In 1 Timothy 5:17–18 we read that some elders were especially involved in preaching and teaching; those were to be supported by the church. From 1 Timothy 3:11 it is clear that there were women who ranked as deacons (see also Romans 16:1), but Paul has more to say about the roles of men and of women in 1 Timothy 2:8–15.

2. The fellowship

Much is said in these three letters that relates to the fellowship of Christians. In particular, Paul faces the problem which the church faced from the very beginning, the problem of the poor who needed supporting (Acts 2:45). Then, in particular, it was the widows (Acts 6:1). Here it is still the widows (1 Timothy 5:1–16). There were some widows who should have been supported by their own families. There were others whom the church should support and who, in their turn, should give of themselves in prayer and service. Paul speaks also of the meeting of Christians for prayer and worship, the vital importance

---

[1] From Titus 1:5–7 and also Acts 20:27, 28 it seems clear that 'elders' and 'bishops' were the same. 'Elder' describes the man's place in the Christian community; the word 'bishop' means 'overseer' and shows that the elder has the responsibility of oversight.

of prayer being led by those who sought to live a holy life 'without anger or quarrelling' (1 Tim. 2:8). 'The public reading of scripture', 'preaching' and 'teaching' were all essential for the churches (1 Tim. 4:13).

3. The teaching

There is great emphasis in all these letters on keeping true in doctrine. In Paul's earlier letters we are taught many things that Christians should believe, *e.g.* the doctrines of salvation (especially in Galatians and Romans), of the resurrection (1 Corinthians), of our hope for the future (1 and 2 Thessalonians). In these letters to Timothy and Titus we do not have so much teaching given to us on such subjects, but it is stressed that Christians must hold firmly to 'the faith', 'the teaching', 'the truth' that has been given and received (see 1 Tim. 2:4; 3:9, 15–16; 4:6,16; 6:20–21, 2 Tim. 2:1–2,8; Tit. 1:1,13).

This emphasis was specially necessary because there were many about who were giving false teaching. There were false teachers who made a wrong use of the law (1 Tim. 1:7) and who said that people should not marry and should not eat meat (1 Tim. 4:1–5). Then there were things that these teachers said that were not so much false as useless, the kind of things that led only to arguments and quarrels and in no way helped Christians to live a godly life (see 1 Tim. 1:4–7; 4:7; 6:3–4, 20–21, 2 Tim. 2:14,16, 23–26; 4:3–4 and Tit. 1:13–14 and 3:9–11). Paul stressed to Timothy that he must 'continue' in what he had 'learned' and 'firmly believed'; these were truths derived from the Scriptures 'inspired by God and profitable for teaching, for reproof, for correction, and for training in righteousness' (2 Tim. 3:14–16). Then he was to be concerned to entrust those same truths 'to faithful men who will be able to teach others also' (2 Tim. 2:2).

4. The witness

Paul also emphasizes that Christians must show the faith that they profess in their lives. As Titus 2:10 puts it, 'in everything ... adorn the doctrine of God our Saviour'. All Christians had to 'behave' in the right way 'in the household of God ... the church of the living God', intended to be 'the pillar and bulwark of the truth' (1 Tim. 3:15). As we have seen, the elders or bishops and the deacons had a special responsibility to live lives above reproach. Timothy and Titus themselves had to be sure that they were examples to all in word and in life, 'in love, in faith, in purity' (see 1 Tim. 4:12; 6:11–16, 2 Tim. 2:15; 3:10–17; Tit. 2:7–8).

Many times it is said that the life of the Christian is to be marked by 'good deeds' (*e.g.* 1 Tim. 6:18; Tit. 2:7,14; 3:8,14). We are to be 'ready for any honest work' in the community, eager to do it (Tit. 3:1). We are to be good citizens, obeying the law and respecting the authority of rulers, and for those rulers we are to pray that there may be peace and that Christians may thus be able to lead quiet lives, 'godly and respectful in every way' (see 1 Tim. 2:1-4).

Contents of 1 Timothy

We have mentioned the possibility of Paul's being released from his imprisonment in Rome, perhaps fulfilling his desire to go to Colossae in the Roman province of Asia (Phm. 22) and Philippi in Macedonia (Phil. 2:24). If so, we can understand how Paul may have gone to Ephesus some 100 miles from Colossae, left Timothy there and gone on himself to Macedonia (1 Tim. 1:3). Then later he could have written this letter to Timothy in Ephesus as he faced many problems in guiding the churches there. We have already commented on the things which gave him greatest concern, and we may put down the contents of this letter as follows:

1. 1:1–2   Paul's greeting to his 'child in the faith'.

2. 1:3–7   The need to oppose false and worthless teaching.

3. 1:8–11   The true purpose of the law, and of the gospel.

4. 1:12–17   The grace of Christ to Paul the persecutor.

5. 1:18–20   Paul's warning to Timothy.

6. 2:1–8   Public prayer; the attitude of prayer and those for whom prayer should be made.

7. 2:9–15   Advice to Christian women.

8. 3:1–13   The qualities needed in bishops and deacons.

9. 3:14–16   The truths for which the church is to stand.

10. 4:1–5   False teaching about marriage and food restrictions to be opposed.

11. 4:6–11   How Timothy should serve as 'a good minister of Christ Jesus'.

12. 4:12–16   The way Timothy should live and teach, using the gifts of the Spirit entrusted to him.

13. 5:1–2   The way of dealing with different groups in the church.

14. 5:3–16   The way of dealing with widows.

15. 5:17–25   Instructions concerning elders and church discipline.

16. 6:1–2   The duties of Christian slaves.

17. 6:3–10   The dangers of love of money.

18. 6:11–16   The things for which Timothy is to aim in his life.

19. 6:17–19   True and false riches.

20. 6:20–21   Final warnings against false teaching.

Contents of Titus

We consider the letter to Titus next, as probably in order of time it was the next to be written. We can imagine Paul, released from Rome, going to the island of Crete as well as to

Ephesus and Macedonia. There Titus was left behind to work and later Paul wrote this letter of advice and encouragement to him. We can summarize its contents as follows:

1. 1:1–4 Paul's work as an apostle and his greeting to Titus.

2. 1:5–9 The qualities needed in elders (bishops).

3. 1:10–16 The false teachers in Crete and Titus's need to rebuke them.

4. 2:1–10 Counsel concerning the life of different groups of people, older and younger, men and women.

5. 2:11–15. The way that all Christians should live in the light of what God has done in Christ and in the light of his coming again.

6. 3:1–3 The life of Christians in the community.

7. 3:4–7 Salvation in Christ and the work of the Holy Spirit in Christian people.

8. 3:8–11 The call to positive Christian living and the avoiding of profitless controversies.

9. 3:12–15 Personal requests and greetings.

Contents of 2 Timothy

As far as we can tell this was the last letter that Paul wrote. If he had been released from prison, he was now a prisoner again. He could say, 'I am already on the point of being sacrificed; the time of my departure has come'. He looked back on the course behind him, 'I have fought the good fight, I have finished the race, I have kept the faith'. The future for him now was on the other side of the river of death. 'Henceforth', he said, 'there is laid up for me the crown of righteousness, which the Lord, the righteous judge, will award to me on that Day' (4:6–8). He had final instructions, encouragements and messages for his 'beloved child' in the faith, Timothy.

1. 1:1–2 Paul's greetings to Timothy.

2. 1:3–7 He thanks God for Timothy's faith and encourages him to be strong in the Spirit of power.

3. 1:8–14 His challenge to Timothy not to be ashamed and in no way to turn aside from his calling.

4. 1:15–18 Those who had turned aside.

5. 2:1–7 Timothy must be willing to face suffering, and, strong in the faith himself, entrust it to others who will in their turn be teachers of the truth.

6. 2:8–13 As Christ suffered and died, his servants must be prepared to suffer for him and to die with him.

7. 2:14–19 The way to deal with false teachers.

8. 2:20–26 The things 'the Lord's servant' should avoid and the qualities of life that should be seen in him.

9. 3:1–9 Warning of troubles to come through men 'holding the form of religion but denying the power of it'.

10. 3:10–17 Paul's example and the importance of the Scriptures, a guide to Timothy's life in the past and of constant value for Christian discipleship.

11. 4:1–5 The call to Timothy to 'do the work of an evangelist'.

12. 4:6–8 Paul at the end of his earthly life.

13. 4:9–12 His personal requests and messages.

Study questions

1. List the occasions in these letters where there is emphasis on the need to guard the truth, teach the truth or persevere in the truth. See 1 Timothy 1:3; 2:4,7; 3:2,9, 14–16; 4:1–7,11, 13,16; 5:17; 6:2–4, 20–21; 2 Timothy 1:11,13–14; 2:1–2,8, 14–19, 23–26; 3:14–17; 4:1–5; and Titus 1:1–3,9–11,13; 2:1,11–15; 3:8–9.

2. From these three letters make a list of the ways in which qualities of Christian living are stressed and the ways in which wrong attitudes and unchristian conduct are to be avoided most strenuously. See especially 1 Timothy 1:18; 4:6–8; 11–16; 2 Timothy 1:6–10, 13–14; 2:1–13, 15–16, 22–26; 3:14–17; 4:1–5; Titus 2:7–10 and 3:9.

3. Consider the instructions given in these letters to different groups in the Christian community; men and women, young and old, elders or bishops, deacons and deaconesses, widows, slaves. What relevance do these instructions have today?

Reference books

NBCR; IBD; MNT, ch. 4

E. M. Blaiklock, *The Pastoral Epistles* (Zondervan, 1972)

G. D. Fee, *1 and 2 Timothy, Titus* (Harper, U.S.A., 1984)

D. Guthrie, *The Pastoral Epistles* (rev. ed. IVP, 1957; Eerdmans, 1957)

W. Hendriksen, *Commentary on 1 and 2 Timothy and Titus* (rev. ed. Banner of Truth, 1983); *Thessalonians, Timothy and Titus* (Baker, 1979)

A. T. Hanson, *The Pastoral Epistles* (Marshall Pickering, 1982; Eerdmans, 1982)

J. N. D. Kelly, *A Commentary on the Pastoral Epistles* (Baker, U.S.A., 1981)

J. R. W. Stott, *The Message of 2 Timothy* (IVP, 1973)

Hebrews

Hebrews ends as a letter with personal messages and greetings, but it does not begin like other New Testament letters, giving the name of the writer and the people to whom it was written. We might think of it more as a sermon for anyone who might hear or read it, and yet we find that there were particular readers in mind. We are told how they loved and served others (6:10), how they had to suffer abuse and persecution for their faith (10:32–33) and how they helped those who were imprisoned for Christ's sake (10:34). The writer said how he hoped to come to see them soon (13:19, 23).

The writers and the readers

Who was the writer of this letter? As is the case with the writers of so many of the books of the Bible, he does not tell us his name or speak at all about himself. In the early days of the church after the New Testament had been written, Christians were not sure who wrote it. Some thought it was Paul; others said it definitely was not Paul and it is certainly true that in all the rest of the letters that we have from Paul his name stands clearly at the beginning. Barnabas, Luke and Apollos have been named as possible writers. There have been many other suggestions. The great Bible teacher of the early third century, Origen, said, 'Only God knows who wrote it'. We may be wise to leave that as the answer to our question.

Who then were the people to whom the letter was written?

We are not actually told. The title 'To the Hebrews' was added later. Yet probably they were Hebrew (that is, Jewish) Christians. As we can see from 2:1–4; 4:1–2; 6:1–12; 10:26–39 and 12:1–17, they were people who were tempted to turn back from following Christ. So much is said comparing the faith of the old covenant with that of the new that it would seem that they were tempted to turn back to the faith of the Jews. The writer repeatedly encourages his readers to keep on serving Christ to the end. We can also see that they were a group of Christians in a particular place. Since at the end (13:24) we have greetings sent to them by 'those who come from Italy', we may be right in saying that the letter was written to people in Italy. When we link all these things together it seems likely that the letter was written to Jewish Christians in Italy, most likely in Italy's capital, Rome.

Purpose and argument of the letter

If Hebrew Christians turned back from their faith in Christ, they would be most likely to go back to their old Jewish faith. In the Roman Empire of those days the Jewish faith was in fact a religion which by law a person was allowed to hold. The Christian faith was not. So one was less likely to be persecuted as a Jew than as a Christian. From beginning to end of this letter, therefore, we find that the writer is trying to do three things:

(a) to show that Jesus is greater than all those people of whom the Old Testament speaks and all the institutions of those days;

(b) to show that Jesus is the One who fulfilled all the Old Testament hopes and promises;

(c) to encourage his readers to keep on in their faith in him.

Following sections of this letter in which teaching is given showing the greatness of Christ and how all the Old Testament is fulfilled in him, we have sections showing how we should go on in our faith in him because of who he is and what he has done for us.

We can trace the steps of the argument of the letter in the following way.

1. 1:1–4 Christ is greater than all the Old Testament prophets. They were messengers of God's word. He is the Son of God.

2. 1:5–2:18 Christ is greater than the angels (1:5–14). If it is important to obey God's word given by angels, it is much more important to obey the word spoken by his Son (2:1–4). Jesus is far greater than the angels, but he humbled himself to become less than the angels for us; he became Man and died for us to bring us back to God and to conquer death (2:5–18).

3. 3:1–4:2 Christ is greater than Moses. Moses was a servant in God's house. Christ is Son in the house (3:1–6). In the days of Moses the people failed to inherit the promised land of Palestine because of their unbelief; we must not fail through such unbelief (3:7–4:2).

4. 4:3–16 Christ is greater than Joshua. In a limited way Joshua brought the people to rest in the promised land, but this was not a full enjoyment of rest. We have 'rest' when we come to enjoy God's salvation in Christ (4:3–10). We need to be sure that we enter the rest that God has provided for us by our coming to God through Jesus Christ our great High Priest (4:11–16).

5. 5:1–7:28 Christ is greater than Aaron (who was high priest in the time of Moses) and all the priests of the house of Aaron. He is Priest-King and in this way resembles Melchizedek of whom the Old Testament speaks in Genesis 14:18–20 and Psalm 110:1–4 (5:1–10). Then a warning is given not to fall away from God's grace, but to go on to the end (5:11–6:12). Christians have the assurance of God's oath and promise (6:13–20). Then in further ways it is shown that Jesus, our great High Priest – Priest and King – is far greater

than the Levitical (or Aaronic) priests (7:1–28).

6. 8:1–13 Christ makes for us a new and better covenant than the old covenant with Israel. This was foretold in Jeremiah 31:31–34 and not fulfilled before the coming of Christ.

7. 9:1–10 Christ has entered into a better tabernacle than the Old Testament tabernacle, that is into heaven itself.

8. 9:11–10:39 Christ has entered heaven and made the way for us to enter through a Sacrifice better than all the Old Testament sacrifices (9:11–14). In Old Testament days there could be no covenant made without sacrifice; now the new covenant is made with the sacrifice of Christ. In those days there could be no forgiveness of sins without sacrifice; now we have forgiveness through the sacrifice of Christ (9:15–28). In those days there had to be many sacrifices. Now that Jesus Christ has offered himself once for all as the perfect sacrifice, the old sacrifices are no longer needed (10:1–18). So readers are encouraged to hold fast to the faith in Christ they have shown in the past and they are warned not to reject God's grace in him (10:19–39).

9. 11:1–40 Old Testament examples of faith. The faith we should have is shown in Abel, Enoch, Noah, Abraham, Isaac, Jacob, Joseph, Moses, Rahab and many others. But the Old Testament men and women of faith could not receive the fulfilment of the promises before the coming of Christ. We have 'something better' in Christ and so should persevere in our faith in him.

10. 12:1–13:25 In these last two chapters we have practical exhortations concerning Christian living. We should run the Christian race with patient endurance and accept God's disciplining of our lives (12:1–13). We should be holy and without bitterness (12:14–17). God's warning at Sinai when the law was given was a serious warning; now God speaks 'from heaven' and we should be very careful not to reject his warning (12:18–29). There is then an exhortation to love and

purity and faith (13:1–9). Because Christ suffered, being rejected by the Jews and put to death outside the gate of Jerusalem, we should be willing to be rejected by men for his sake (13:10–15). We are to 'do good' and obey our leaders (13:16–18). Then the letter closes with prayer and request for prayer, with final messages and greetings (13:19–25).

Going on and going out

The Christians to whom this letter was written were warned not to go back. Christ is so much greater than all that even the wonderful Old Testament revelation could bring. He is the Fulfiller of the Old Testament hope. In the days of fulfilment there must be no turning back to those things which only prepared the way of the Christ and foretold his coming. Christians must not turn back; and they must not stand still. They must go on. They are a pilgrim people on earth. Heaven is their final home. There are many things in this letter (especially in chapter 11) which are similar to what Stephen said to the Jews and to Jewish Christians in Acts 6–7. Christians must be like Abraham leaving his home and like Moses leaving Egypt at God's call and prepared to suffer with the people of God (11:8–16, 24–27). We must be prepared to 'go forth' to Christ 'outside the camp' to suffer for him, 'for here we have no lasting city but we seek the city which is to come' (13:13–14).

Study questions

1. What do we mean when we say that Jesus is our great High Priest? See what this letter teaches, especially in 2:17–18; 4:14–16; 5:1–10; 7:15–28; 9:11–14,23–28; 10:11–22. Notice in what ways his priesthood is said to be like and in what ways unlike that of the Aaronic priests.

2. List the things that we can learn for ourselves from the

practical exhortations in this letter in 4:11,14–16; 10:35–36;
12:1–2,12–16 and 13:1–7.

3.   How do the relevant passages of the Old Testament help
us to understand more the faith of the men and women named
in chapter 11? Abel (Gn. 4); Enoch (Gn. 5:24); Noah (Gn.
chapters 6–9); Abraham (Gn. chapters 12–22); Isaac (Gn.
chapters 24–26); Jacob (Gn. chapters 27–33); Joseph
(Gn. chapters 37,39–50); Rahab (Jos. chapters 2 and 6).

Reference books

NBCR; IBD; BNT, ch. 4; *MNT*, ch. 7

F. F. Bruce, *A Commentary on the Epistle to the Hebrews*
(Eerdmans, 1964)

D. Guthrie, *Hebrews* (IVP, 1983; Eerdmans, 1983)

D. A. Hagner, *Hebrews* (Harper, U.S.A., 1983)

W. H. Griffith Thomas, *Hebrews, a Devotional Commentary*
(Eerdmans, 1962)

R. M. Wilson, *Hebrews* (Marshall Pickering, 1987; Eerdmans, 1987)

James

This is a short letter but very practical. It says little in the way of teaching about Jesus Christ and what he has done for us. It says a great deal about the way that we should live as Christians.

Purpose

James seems to have written his letter for people who knew the gospel and the teaching of the Christian faith and who said that they were Christians, but were not showing it in their lives. They did not control their tongues. They were selfish and quarrelled with one another. The rich among them were hard on the poor. They boasted about what they would do in the future. Therefore James writes about the ways in which their faith, if it is real faith, should show itself in their lives.

Faith and works

When we read this letter we might think at first that what it says is against what Paul says in his letters, especially about 'faith' and 'works'. Paul emphasizes that we are saved by faith and not by works (see Gal. 2:16; 3:10–14, Rom. 3:20–28; 4:1–8 and Eph. 2:5–8). James says, 'faith by itself, if it has no works, is dead'; Abraham was 'justified by works', and 'a man is justified by works and not by faith alone' (2:17,21,24). We can understand the difference between Paul and James and see that one is not against the other when we realize the different purposes for which the two wrote and the different meanings that they gave to 'faith' and 'works'.

1. *Paul* says that a man is not saved by works but by faith, meaning that a person is not saved by the works that he does in obedience to the law. The problem that Paul faced when he wrote his letters was that there were those (especially Jews, like Paul himself before his conversion) who thought that they would be saved if they kept the law. If they did all the works that the law told them to, God would accept them. Paul came to realize that no one had kept the law. All had sinned against it. Therefore no one could be saved by these works of the law. We must be saved by faith, and faith means depending on Christ and accepting his gift of salvation and forgiveness. For Paul 'works' are works of the law and 'faith' is relying on Christ.

2. *James* means something different by 'faith'. Faith may be just belief about God, the kind of belief that even the demons have (2:19). It does not affect a person's life. It is not a matter of depending on God. James says, therefore, that if this faith is real, if it is to be a saving faith, it must show itself in 'works'. Paul, in fact, says the same thing in different words. In Galatians 5:6 he says that what matters in the Christian life is 'faith working through love'. That is really the subject of James chapter 2. Similarly Paul says in Ephesians 2:10 that faith should lead us to do the 'good works' which God planned that we should do (in this verse he uses the word 'works' in the way that James uses it).

Contents of the letter

6. 1:16–18　The good gifts of God.

7. 1:19–27　Doers of God's word and of good works, not hearers only.

8. 2:1–13　The danger of honouring the rich more than the poor; the law is summed up in love and love is to be shown equally to all.

9. 2:14–26　The way that faith should be shown in works and not just words.

10. 3:1–12　The use of the tongue.

11. 3:13–18　Wisdom in the Christian's life means humility and peace.

12. 4:1–10　Quarrels result from selfish desires; the right attitude of the Christian is that of humble dependence on God.

13. 4:11–12　The sin of judging others.

14. 4:13–17　The wrong of boasting about the future.

15. 5:1–6　A warning to the rich who live in luxury and oppress others.

16. 5:7–11　Exhortation to patient endurance.

17. 5:12　Oaths forbidden.

18. 5:13–18　Exhortation to earnest prayer, especially for the sick.

19. 5:19–20　Bringing back a brother who has wandered from the ways of God.

The writer and the readers

The first verse of the letter tells us that it was written by James. There were two apostles whose name was James (Acts 1:13). The one who was the brother of John was the first of the apostles to be put to death (Acts 12:1–2). We know nothing more than the name of the other apostle James, the son of Alphaeus. Then there was a third James, the brother of Jesus, who became leader of the church in Jerusalem (see Acts 12:17; 15:13; 21:18; Gal. 1:19; 2:9 and 12). It has usually been thought that this was the James who wrote this letter.

The letter is addressed to 'the twelve tribes of the Dispersion' (1:1); probably this means that the readers were Jewish Christians living in many different places outside Palestine.

The teaching of this letter and the teaching of Jesus

There are many close similarities between the things that are taught in this letter and what we know of the teaching of Jesus from the Gospels, especially from the Sermon on the Mount in Matthew chapters 5–7. Christians should rejoice in trial (1:2; Mt. 5:10–12). They are called to be 'perfect' (1:4; Mt. 5:48). They should pray in faith without doubting (1:6; Mk. 11:22–24). They should know God as the giver of all good gifts (1:17; Mt. 7:11). They should be doers of God's word and not just hearers (1:22–25; Mt. 7:21–27). The law of love for one's neighbour sums up the commandments that relate to our attitude to others (2:8; Mk. 12:31). We are not to judge others (4:11–12; Mt. 7:1). In fact those who are merciful to others find mercy (2:13; Mt. 5:7; 18:33–35). As a tree is known by its fruit so a person's life is known by what is seen to come from it (3:12; Mt. 7:15–20). Christians are called to be those who make peace (3:18; Mt. 5:9). They should ask from God in prayer and thus receive (4:2; Mt. 7:7–8). They should humble themselves before God and so be lifted up (4:6,10; Lk. 18:14). They should seek the lasting riches and not those which perish through moth and rust (5:1–3; Mt. 6:16–21). They are not to make their word stronger by oaths but be content with a clear 'Yes' or 'No' (5:12; Mt. 5:33–37).

Study questions

1. Look up the references given and try to put in your own words what Paul means when he says that we are saved by faith and not by works, and what James means when he says

that we are not saved by faith but by works. How do both teachings apply in your own situation?

2.   What does this letter teach us about (a) the words that we speak, (b) prayer, (c) riches.

Reference books

NBCR; IBD; BNT, ch. 5; *MNT*, ch. 9

J. B. Adamson, *The Epistle of James* (Eerdmans, 1976)

W. Barclay, *Letters of James and Peter*, Daily Study Bible (Saint Andrew, 1976; Westminster, 1976)

P. H. Davids, *James* Harper, U.S.A., 1983)

D. J. Moo, *James* (IVP, 1987; Eerdmans, 1987)

E. M. Sidebottom, *James, Jude, 2 Peter* (Marshall Pickering, 1982; Eerdmans, 1982)

1 Peter

This letter comes to us as written by the apostle Peter (1:1) with the help of Silvanus (5:12). This is almost certainly the same Silvanus or Silas who was Paul's colleague on his second missionary journey (see Acts 15:40), and perhaps the way that it is said that Peter wrote, literally 'through Silvanus', may mean that Silvanus did not simply write down Peter's words but put in his own words what Peter expressed to him. Peter wanted his message to reach Christians in a wide area, in the five Roman provinces of Pontus, Galatia, Cappadocia, Asia and Bithynia (1:1). We do not know whether Peter had visited all these provinces, but from 1 Corinthians 1 it would seem that he had been in Greece at Corinth and so he may have visited the places in these other provinces on the way to or from Greece. They are spoken of as 'exiles of the Dispersion', words that normally were used of the Jews who from the time of the Fall of Jerusalem in 586 BC had been 'dispersed', scattered into many countries. From what is said in the letter it would seem that many of the readers were not Jews, but they were the 'new Israel', God's people under his new covenant in Christ, and so could be spoken of as his scattered people, living in these provinces but 'exiles' from their permanent heavenly home (compare Philippians 3:20).

The purposes of writing

Two purposes account for very much that is said in this letter.

1. The Christians in this area were being persecuted or in danger of being persecuted for the fact that they were Christians. They needed encouragement with the reminder of Christ's own sufferings (2:21–24), the fact that their fellow Christians throughout the world were suffering (5:9) and that God used trial and suffering to refine his people (1:6–7). Even if they died for their faith, it did not matter, because they had eternal life and 'a living hope through the resurrection of Jesus Christ from the dead' (1:3). They must not be surprised that they have to suffer (4:12) but rejoice to be called to 'share Christ's sufferings' (4:13). Nevertheless, they needed to be very sure that they were really suffering for Christ's sake and not because of their own wrongs or foolishness (3:13–18 and 4:13–19).

2. These Christians had also to live out their lives in a hostile non-Christian world with standards very different from theirs. Christ had set them free from the worthless manner of life that they and their people had lived from generation to generation in the past (1:18). They must not go back to those old ways (1:14). They had lived by them long enough (4:2–3). Now they must obey their Lord who had redeemed them and be holy as he is holy. Truth and love and purity must mark their lives. Those who have become part of God's own people must show forth 'the wonderful deeds of him who called (them) out of darkness into his marvellous light' (2:9). This must affect the way that they live as citizens (2:13–17) and as wives and husbands (3:1–7). It must affect all their relationships (3:8–12). Christ is their Lord whom they serve and to whom they bear witness (3:15). If they are slaves they will think of serving and honouring him even when they have to submit to cruel earthly masters (2:18–25). If they are leaders they will know that they still must act with great humility and with the highest ideals of service (5:1–6).

Contents of the letter

ministry; younger Christians are to submit to their elders.

17. 5:6–11   The call to humility, prayer and watchfulness; the reminder of the fellowship of suffering.

18. 5: 12–14   Conclusion.

The time and place of writing

In 5:13 it is said that the church in Babylon sends greetings to those to whom this letter is written. It is almost certain that it was not literally Babylon that was meant. Rome was the equivalent in the first century of ancient Babylon of Old Testament times, the capital of the great empire that oppressed God's people. We can feel confident that this letter was written in Rome. Writers from the second century tell us that Peter suffered death in Rome in the time when Nero was emperor (AD 54–68). The letter may thus have been written about AD 66 or 67. It is sometimes said that Christians in the provinces of the Roman Empire did not have to suffer death for their faith in Christ as early as the times of Nero. But when Nero began to cause Christians to be thrown to the lions, crucified and burnt to death in Rome itself, who could tell what might soon happen in the provinces?

Study questions

1.   Study especially the verses in this letter that speak of the suffering and death and resurrection of Christ (1:2–4, 10–11, 18–21; 2:21–25; 3:18–22; 4:13; 5:1) and note what meaning they are said to have for the Christian. Notice the use of Isaiah 53 in what is said of the sufferings of Christ in 2:22–25.

2.   Read the letter and note all the qualities of Christian living that we are called to show in our lives. Contrast with these the things that are said about non-Christian living.

Reference books

NBCR; IBD; BNT, ch. 7

W. Barclay, *Letters of James and Peter* (Saint Andrew, 1975; Westminster, 1975)

J. N. D. Kelly, *The Epistles of Peter and Jude* (Black, 1969; Baker, 1981)

A. R. C. Leaney, *The Letters of Peter and Jude* (CUP, 1967)

E. G.. Selwyn, *The First Epistle of St. Peter* (Baker, U.S.A., 1981)

A. M. Stibbs and A. F. Walls, *1 Peter* (rev. ed. IVP, 1983; Eerdmans, 1983)

2 Peter and Jude

These two letters are rightly studied together since chapter 2 of 2 Peter is very similar to Jude. At many points the similarities are so close that it seems that one must have been written using the other, or both must have used a letter or sermon written earlier than either. There are quite strong reasons for thinking that Jude wrote his letter first. Then much of what he wrote was used in the writing of 2 Peter chapter 2.

Jude

Jude, after the greetings with which he begins his letter (verses 1–2) says that he had wanted to write about the salvation that all believers share in Jesus Christ. He was troubled, however, because of those who were denying Christ and giving wrong teaching. Christian people had to be warned and needed to be called to strive for the faith entrusted to them (verses 3–4). In the past, judgment had come on those who had turned away from God, the angels, the heathen of Sodom and Gomorrah: even Israel as God's chosen people had turned aside (verses 5–7). The false teachers about whom Jude was concerned spoke against the truth and opposed those who held to it. They must be prepared to face the judgment of a holy God (verses 8–16). True believers must be watchful, remembering the warnings concerning false teaching given by the apostles. The way to keep themselves true is plain. 'Build yourselves up on your most holy faith; pray in the Holy Spirit; keep yourselves in the love of God; wait for the mercy of our Lord Jesus Christ unto eternal life.' In other words, 'watch and pray', and in addition, convince the doubters, lead others into the way of salvation. These are the things that matter most (verses 17–23). Then with one of the most beautiful doxologies in all the New Testament, a doxology most meaningful for those under pressure from the world, Jude's letter closes: 'Now to him who is able to keep you from falling and to present you without blemish before the presence of his glory with rejoicing, to the only God, our Saviour through Jesus Christ our Lord, be glory, majesty, dominion and authority, before all time and now and for ever. Amen' (verses 24–25).

2 Peter

This letter is very different from 1 Peter and in fact the three chapters form three very different parts of the one little book.

1. *Chapter 1*, after its greetings (verses 1–2), is an encouragement to Christians to live fruitful and faithful lives. Qualities are listed which should mark the Christian's life: faith, virtue, knowledge, self-control, steadfastness, godliness, brotherly affection, love (verses 3–11). It was Peter's life-long duty, as he understands it, to remind his fellow Christians of these essentials of Christian living (verses 12-15). For Christians live their lives in the service of the Son of God and in obedience to the Word of God. He knew very well himself, since he had been with the Lord on the mountain at the time of the transfiguration when the voice had been heard from heaven, 'This is my beloved Son'. Though that vision faded and was not repeated, and in any case was experienced only by a few, all Christian people have the word of Scripture, given by the Spirit of God and understood as the Spirit gives understanding. It is like 'a lamp shining in a dark place' until the day of eternity dawns (verses 16–21).

2. *Chapter 2* begins with the kind of warning that the

New Testament often gives, of false teachers who will try to make financial gain out of their religious teaching and so lead many people astray. These false teachers are described as they are in Jude and their judgment spoken of in similar terms. Truth and error, right and wrong, are not alternatives to be played with. When once the truth is known it must be held. When the way of righteousness has been followed there must be no turning back; 'for it would have been better . . . never to have known the way of righteousness than after knowing it to turn back from the holy commandment' (verse 21).

3.   *Chapter 3* begins with reminder of the words of prophets and apostles. They had spoken of the false teachers who would come; they had also spoken of those who would express doubts about the second coming of Christ. Such people would ask 'Where is the promise of his coming?' They would say that everything goes on just as ever before, despising the certainty that he will come, and 'He will come to judge the living and the dead' (verses 1–7). The time of that coming and of that judgment is uncertain; the fact is sure. Time with man is not as time with God. To him 'one day is as a thousand years, and a thousand years as one day'. If he delays, it is that more may turn to him in repentance before it is too late (verses 8–10). Since judgment is sure and this present order will come to an end to be replaced by 'new heavens and a new earth', Christians constantly should live 'lives of holiness and godliness' (verses 11–13). The letter closes (verses 14–18) with the call to zeal and watchfulness, the challenge not to turn aside from the truth but to 'grow in the grace and knowledge of our Lord and Saviour Jesus Christ'.

Writers and readers and dates

1.   *Jude* speaks of himself as 'a servant of Jesus Christ and brother of James', and he writes 'to those who are called, beloved in God the Father and kept for Jesus Christ'. In other

words, it is a truly general letter, written for any Christians who may read it. The name Jude is the same as Judas, and, apart from Judas Iscariot, we know of two Judes in the New Testament, Judas, the son of James, who was an apostle (Acts 1:13), and Judas the brother of Jesus (Mt. 13:55). Perhaps the writer of this letter was one of these two, more likely the second because we know from Matthew 13:55 that he had a brother James.

2. *2 Peter* was also a general letter 'to those who have obtained a faith of equal standing with ours in the righteousness of our God and Saviour Jesus Christ' (1:1). The name of Simon Peter, the apostle, stands at the beginning. There is reference to his being an eye-witness of the transfiguration (1:16–18). This letter is spoken of as the second letter he has written (3:1). Many people have doubted whether the letter as it stands came from the hand of the apostle Peter. There were doubts in the early centuries of the church and people asked whether it should be in the New Testament Scriptures; but it was accepted. Today people ask whether an apostle would use the writing of Jude as seems the case in chapter 2 of this letter. They ask whether the time after the death of the early Christians ('since the fathers fell asleep' as it says in 3:4) may indicate a time later than the death of Peter about 66 AD. They ask also whether the reference to Paul and to his writings as Scripture (3:15–16) may indicate similarly a later time than Peter's life-time. Neither of these references could prove beyond all doubt a later date. Some feel that to a letter that Peter wrote, encouraging his fellow Christians and recalling the transfiguration, other important things were later added, the warnings of Jude's letter, the emphasis on the second coming of Christ and the reference to Paul's letters. We can certainly value this letter for what it brings us, its truth for faith and life, its warnings and encouragements, its reminders of him who has come and will come and who is always present with his own.

Study questions

1. What do we learn about Scripture in 2 Peter 1:19–21?
2. In these two letters what qualities of Christian life are we encouraged to show?
3. What does 2 Peter 3 teach us should be the effect on our lives of our hope of the second coming of Christ?

Reference books

NBCR; IBD; MNT, pp. 93-95

The commentaries on 2 Peter and Jude listed under 1 Peter

M. Green, *2 Peter and Jude* (rev. ed. IVP, 1987; Eerdmans, 1987)

E. M. Sidebottom, *James, Jude, 2 Peter* (Marshall Pickering, 1982; Eerdmans, 1982)

1, 2 and 3 John

Although none of these letters gives us the name of the person who wrote them, there are many things in them which link them together. They all have a great deal to say about 'love' and 'truth', about 'keeping God's commandments', about 'joy' and about believing that Jesus is the Son of God who has come 'in the flesh' (that is, truly as man). 2 and 3 John are written to particular people. 1 John, like Jude and 2 Peter, is a general letter, though there were readers in mind who were passing through particular difficulties.

All of the letters are very like John's Gospel in many of the things that they say and the words that they use. In the early centuries of the church they were accepted as being by the apostle John. In recent years some have doubted whether the apostle wrote them in much the same way as they have doubted whether he wrote the Gospel (see pages 46–47). If he did not write them, we frankly do not know who did. The similarities between all four writings cannot be denied. Obviously they were very relevant to the times when they were written, the latter part of the first century AD. They have also a special relevance to our own times.

The purpose of 1 John

We have seen that John's Gospel expresses its purpose very clearly. The writer tells his readers that it was written 'that you may believe that Jesus is the Christ, the Son of God, and that believing you may have life in his name' (John 20:31). The Gospel was written, in other words, that those who had not believed might come to believe and to find life in Christ. This letter has a different purpose, but it is as clearly expressed as is the purpose of the Gospel. It was written for Christians that they might be sure of their life in Christ. 'I write this to you that believe in the name of the Son of God, that you may know that you have eternal life' (5:13).

The times when this letter was written were difficult for Christians. There were many people who professed to know God and to have fellowship with him but in their lives they did not show forth such faith at all. So the letter gives three tests of the reality of the knowledge of God in a person's life, three tests whether a person can rightly claim to have fellowship with God. In the course of this letter we have first one, then another of these tests. They are given once, they are given again, and when we come to the end of the letter they are all linked together, as the three things together must be seen in a Christian's life.

1. *The test of obedience.* To be sure that we know God we must 'keep his commandments'. If we do not set out to obey God, we cannot profess to belong to him and to be his children. See 2:3–6; 2:28–3:10 and 5:1–3.

2. *The test of love.* If we do not have love for others, we do not know the love of God in our hearts and we are in the darkness. See 2:7–11; 3:10–18; 4:7–12, 16–21; 5:1–3.

3. *The test of belief.* The Christian must also believe the right things about Jesus (such belief is the foundation of saving faith); that he is the Christ, the Son of God and that 'He has come in the flesh'. See 2:18–27; 4:1–4,14–15; 5:1–5. This test was necessary because there were false teachers who said that the Son of God did not really become man; God was not really born into our life and did not really die on the cross. They said that he came into the human life of Jesus at his baptism and left Jesus before he died on the cross. This helps

us to understand what is emphasized so much in 4:1–6 and the way that it says in 5:6 that he came 'not with the water only' (his baptism) 'but with the water' and 'the blood' (his death). We may compare with this the great emphasis on the reality of the death of Jesus in John 19:33–35.

So John says that by these three things you can know whether people are true Christians: if they want to obey God, if they love others and if they believe the right things about Jesus Christ. It is still true that these three things together are the most important things for the individual Christian and for the church today: obedience, love and faith. Our aim should be not just to be strong in one and perhaps weak in the other two, but to grow stronger and stronger in all three.

Structure and contents of 1 John

We can divide this Epistle helpfully into five parts, an introduction, three main sections where the tests of obedience and love and faith are applied, applied again and then brought together; and finally a conclusion.

1. Introduction (1:1–2:2).

   (a) 1:1–4   The eternal Word of God has become man, and through him we have eternal life and fellowship with God.

   (b) 1:5–2:2   God is light and we can have fellowship with him only as we confess our sins and receive forgiveness through the death of Christ for us.

2. The first application of the tests of a person's knowledge of God and fellowship with him (2:3–27).

   (a) 2:3–6   The test of holiness.

   (b) 2:7–11   The test of love.

    (c) 2:12–17   Warnings against love of the world.

    (d) 2:18–27   The test of right belief.

3. The second application of the same three tests (2:28–4:6).

    (a) 2:28–3:10   The test of obedience.

    (b) 3:11–18   The test of love.

    (c) 3:19–24   The Christian's assurance.

    (d) 4:1–6   The test of right belief.

4. The third application of the three tests (4:7–5:5).

    (a) 4:7–12   The test of love.

    (b) 4:13–21   Love and faith in Jesus as Son of God and Saviour of the world.

    (c) 5:1–5   Faith and love and obedience all linked together.

5. Conclusion (5:6–21).

    (a) 5:6–12   God's witness to his Son Jesus Christ.

    (b) 5:13–21   The Christian's assurance in the knowledge of Jesus Christ as Son of God.

2 John

This little letter is written 'to the elect lady and her children'. This may be a particular lady who is addressed, but more likely it is a church or congregation. Similarly another church or congregation would be referred to in the last verse where it is said, 'The children of your elect sister greet you'. John speaks of the way that he rejoices in those who are following the truth. He encourages them to continue in love and obedience; and he warns them of the false teachers who deny that Jesus, the Son of God, has become Man. Christians must not help or support such teachers by what they do.

3 John

This letter is written to a Christian called Gaius, but we do not know where he lived or anything about him except his name. John speaks of the way he rejoices that Gaius is walking in the truth (verses 1–4) and has shown hospitality to strangers (verses 5–8). He criticizes Diotrephes who wanted to make himself important and showed no love for his fellow Christians (verses 9–10). He also speaks of Demetrius who is a faithful Christian (verses 11–12). In the end of his letter he says how he hopes to come to see Gaius soon (verses 13–15).

Study questions

1. Make a list of the things which 1 John says about the love that Christians should show others. See especially 2:7–11; 3:10-18; 4:7–21 and 5:1–3.

2. What are the different ways in which 1 John speaks of obeying God or following in his ways? See especially 1:5–10; 2:1–6; 2:27–3:10; 4:21–5:5.

3. What things are taught about prayer in 1 John 3:19–24 and 5:13–17?

4. Read through 1 John and note down all that the letter tells us about who Jesus Christ is and what he has done for us.

5. How do 2 and 3 John show that in a Christian's life love and truth must be bound together?

Reference books

NBCR; IBD; MNT, pp. 95-99; and *BNT,* pp. 126-131

W. Barclay, *Letters of John and Jude* (Saint Andrew, 1976; Westminster, 1976)

F. F. Bruce, *The Epistles of John* (Marshall Pickering, 1978; Eerdmans, 1978)

J. R. W. Stott, *The Epistles of John* (rev. ed. IVP, 1983; Eerdmans, 1983)

Revelation

We have studied the four gospels, followed by the story in the Acts of the Apostles of the way the gospel went out into the world, and then the 21 letters that we have in the New Testament. The last book in the New Testament is different from all the others. It is called the Revelation or sometimes the Apocalypse. 'Apocalypse' is a word from Greek that means the same as 'revelation', but it reminds us that the Jews had a number of what we call apocalyptic writings, writings which reveal what God will do in the end when he again breaks into history (see *MNT*, pp. 83–84). The book of Revelation was written for Christians who were suffering persecution in the Roman Empire, especially in the province of Asia, where there were the seven churches of Ephesus, Smyrna, Pergamum, Thyatira, Sardis, Philadelphia and Laodicea. The book begins with a vision of the risen Christ (chapter 1). It then has messages for the Christians of the seven churches (chapters 2–3). The rest of the book tells of the final triumph of Christ, his judgment of all humanity and the blessing of life in heaven for the faithful (chapters 4-22). We can realize how a book with such subjects would help persecuted Christians and strengthen them by the hope that there is in Christ.

Understanding the book

The book of Revelation is hard to understand, and Christians have explained it in many different ways. We need to realize that the book is full of symbols. That means that many things are not literal descriptions of times and numbers and events, but numbers and colours and many different things in the descriptions stand for truths of God and of what God has done or will do.

It helps us to understand the book of Revelation if we remember also that many, many times the book quotes or refers to the Old Testament. It is specially valuable to read it with a Reference Bible that points back to the Old Testament. Often when we turn to the Old Testament passages, we are helped to understand what the writer is saying in Revelation.

Then the numbers used have meanings: three often speaks of heaven, four of earth; seven (three plus four) is the perfect number. When we have three and a half years, half of seven, or the equivalent 42 months or 1260 days (11:2–3; 13:5) we have half of perfection; we have half the full time from beginning to end, that is, the time between the first coming of Christ, which is the mid-point of human history and the second coming of Christ which is the end of our history. In six we have a human number (one short of perfection) and so 666 is the number of 'the beast', the enemy of the people of God (13:18). The number of God's people is twelve. There were 12 tribes in the Old Testament and 12 apostles in the New Testament. The 24 elders are thus the representatives of the people in Old and New Testaments (4:4).

In all our study of the book it is most helpful to remember what the very first verse of the book says it is. It is a revelation that God gives to his church and it is 'the revelation of Jesus Christ'. In other words the greatest purpose of this book (as in fact that of every other book in the New Testament) is to show us Jesus Christ. John Stott says, 'What a persecuted church needs is not a detailed forecast of future events . . . but a vision of Jesus Christ to cheer the faint and encourage the weary' (*BNT*, p. 158). We see Jesus Christ standing in the midst of the churches. We see him as the Lamb of God who died for us. In the end he takes his church (as his bride) to live and reign with him for ever in the new heavens and the new earth that he makes.

Structure and contents

There is a clearly and carefully worked out structure of the book in which the number seven is most important. Sometimes the seventh of one series leads into the next group of seven. The contents of the book may be summarized as follows:

1. Introduction (1:1–20).
   (a) 1:1–8   John's greetings and praise of Christ.
   (b) 1:9–20   His vision of the risen Christ in his glory.

2. The letters to the seven churches of the Roman province of Asia (2:1–3:22).

3. Worship in heaven (4:1–5:14).
   (a) 4:1–11   John sees the throne of God in heaven and hears all creation joining in worshipping him as Creator of all.
   (b) 5:1–14   Now there is the worship of Jesus as the Lamb of God. There is a scroll with seven seals which only he can open. This means that only he, who has died to be the Saviour of the world, can bring the world's history to its close.

4. The opening of the seven seals (6:1–8:5).
   (a) 6:1–17   When the first six seals are opened, warfare, famine and death follow, the sufferings that there must be in the world before the end comes.
   (b) 7:1–17   There is now a break before the opening of the seventh seal as the safety of all the faithful from every tribe and nation is assured.

(c) 8:1–5   The opening of the seventh seal, in preparation for the sounding of the seven trumpets.

5. **The sounding of the seven trumpets (8:6–11:19).**
   (a) 8:6–9:21   As the trumpets are sounded we have God's warning through his judgments on the earth. 'God's warnings and the Church's witness go hand in hand' (Stott).
   (b) 10:1–11:14   Again there is a break before the sounding of the seventh trumpet and we are shown how, in spite of all opposition, the church is to witness faithfully until the final triumph comes.
   (c) 11:15–19   The seventh trumpet is sounded and the end of warfare is announced. 'The kingdom of the world has become the kingdom of our Lord and of his Christ, and he shall reign for ever and ever.'

6. **The seven signs (12:1–14:20).**
   (a) 12:1–17   The first three signs in which are shown the forces that oppose the kingdom of God.
   (b) 13:1–14:5   The next three signs. The 'beast rising out of the sea' (13:1) is probably the Roman Empire, persecuting the Christians. Then there is 'another beast which rose out of the earth' (13:11), probably representing the forces that tried to make people worship the Roman emperor as Lord and God (13:12).
   (c) 14:6–13   Again there is a break before the final sign; and in these verses the 'call for the endurance of the saints'.
   (d) 14:14–20   The seventh sign; the angels with the sickles of judgment.

7. **The seven bowls; the last plagues (15:1–16:21).**
   (a) 15:1–8   Those who have conquered the powers of evil sing the song of Moses and the song of the Lamb.

(b) 16:1–12 The first six plagues. God's judgments in which the powers of evil are overthrown.

(c) 16:13–16 The preparation for the final conflict.

(d) 16:17–21 The seventh bowl.

8. The final judgment and the triumph of God (17:1–20:15).

(a) 17:1–18 The judgment of the great harlot, Babylon (Rome).

(b) 18:1–24 The destruction of Babylon and the laments over her.

(c) 19:1–5 The praise of God for the overthrow of foul Babylon.

(d) 19:6–10 The joy of 'the marriage supper of the Lamb'.

(e) 19:11–21 Final victory.

(f) 20:1–10 The reign of 1000 years.

(g) 20:11–15 The judgment of the great white throne.

9. The church's union with Christ (21:1–22:5).

(a) 21:1–9 The church as the bride prepared for her husband.

(b) 21:10–27 The church as the heavenly city, the new Jerusalem.

(c) 22:1–5 Paradise restored, the river of life and the tree of life. The Lord is the perfect light there and his people 'shall see his face . . . and reign for ever and ever'.

10. Conclusion (22:6–21).

The final words of Christ to his persecuted church, 'Surely I am coming soon'; and they reply, 'Amen. Come, Lord Jesus'.

The writer of the book

Who was the writer of this strange and wonderful book, so

different from any other book in the New Testament? Four times his name is given clearly in the course of the book – John (1:1,4,9; 22:8). He had close links and deep concern for the churches of the Roman province of Asia to whom the little letters of chapters two and three are addressed. Not far away from them he was in exile on the island of Patmos 'on account of the word of God and the testimony of Jesus' (1:9). Second-century Christian writers seemed to be clear that it was the apostle John. Later, questions were asked and there was hesitation about ascribing it to the apostle. We have noted the difficulty that some feel about ascribing the fourth Gospel and the three Epistles to the apostle John. Now this work is very different again from any of those four writings, different in style and even in grammar. At the same time there are great similarities. Jesus is the Word of God (19:13), the Lamb (although a different word is used in the Greek). He gives to the thirsty 'the water of life' (21:6; 22:17). There are many similar expressions used.

If the John who wrote Revelation was not the apostle, he might have been John Mark, but we have no strong reasons for thinking that. He might have been another contemporary John whom the second-century writer Papias speaks of as John the Elder, but we know nothing more of this man. He might have been a John completely unknown to us. His work means more than our attempts to identify him. Like the writer of the Gospel, and the Epistles that bear the name of John, he is more concerned to give us the 'revelation of Jesus Christ' than to tell us of himself.

The date of the book

It is easier to speak of the conditions of the times in which Revelation was written than to give it a precise date. As we have seen, they were times of persecution, especially in that Roman province of Asia, and the persecution was to increase

(2:10). When chapters thirteen and fourteen speak of worshipping 'the image of the beast', it is probably the worship of the Roman emperor that is in mind. Because it is known that emperor worship flourished especially in the days of Domitian's rule as emperor (81–96) it has been customary to date the book to his reign. The legend that the emperor Nero would rise from the dead, perhaps reflected in 17:8,11, is thought to have impressed people especially in Domitian's time. On the other hand, there have been strong reasons put forward for an earlier date, perhaps in the reign of Nero (54–68) when, in all probability, both Peter and Paul suffered martyrdom, or a little later than Nero's time but before the fall of Jerusalem in AD 70.

Study questions

1. What things said about the life of the seven churches in chapters 2–3 do you think especially apply to the life of the church today?

2. From chapters 1, 4, 5 and 7 what message of comfort could you take:

    (a) for a person suffering persecution,

    (b) for a person who is sad because a Christian friend or relative has died?

3. In chapters 11–15 what are the ways in which God's victory in the battle against Satan and his forces is made clear?

4. Read Genesis chapters 1–2 and then write down the ways in which you see that the last two chapters of Revelation show us God's new creation and the condition of Paradise restored.

Reference books

W. Barclay, *The Revelation of John*, 2 vols. (Saint Andrew, 1976; Westminster, 1976)

G. R. Beasley-Murray, *The Book of Revelation* (Marshall Pickering; Eerdmans, 1981)

G. B. Caird, *A Commentary on the Revelation of St. John the Divine* (Black, 1966; Harper & Row, 1966)

G. E. Ladd, *A Commentary on the Revelation of John* (Eerdmans, 1971)

L. Morris, *Revelation* (rev. ed. IVP, 1983; Eerdmans, 1987)

R. H. Mounce, *The Book of Revelation* (Eerdmans, 1977)

M. Wilcock, *The Message of Revelation* (rev. ed. IVP, 1984)

Conclusion

We have taken a bird's-eye view of the 66 books of the Bible. Such a view is little more than a glance. There is far more to be seen. We need to come much closer to each book and examine it in far greater detail. We have realized how different the books are in presenting what is called in Ephesians 3:10 the "many-sided" or "multi-colored wisdom of God." Taken together the 66 documents that make up the Bible give us the wonderful balance of what Paul spoke of as "the whole counsel of God" (Acts 20:27). All of the facets are needed to make up the drama, the drama of redemption that has at its center the Lord Jesus Christ. Sometimes we may fix our gaze on one scene or even the one climactic moment in that drama, but we will often need to step back and take in the whole.

Because truth is eternal, because it is the revelation of God, we can never know it all. We can never exhaust its meaning, its significance and its application to our lives that must be made every day afresh and more deeply. The fullness of the truth is, as a great preacher once said,

as if a miner, working away at the primary vein of ore, should continually discover equally precious veins stretching out on every side, and overwhelming him in rich embarrassment. . . . It is as if a man were tracking out the confines of a lake, walking its boundaries, and when the circuit were almost complete should discover that it was no lake at all, but an arm of the ocean, and that he was confronted by the immeasurable sea!" (J. H. Jowett)

As rich and boundless as that are the treasures of wisdom and knowledge contained in the Scriptures. Or, to change the metaphor again, the springs of truth that we have here will never dry up. They are ours for the taking and we will find that the springs of truth are indeed the springs of life.

Suggestions for Further Study

There are many ways that the student may go on from an initial look at individual books of the Bible. The study course *Search the Scriptures* (IVP, 1949) has proved its worth in nearly forty years of use. It takes each book of both Old and New Testaments and divides them up into sections for each day, providing two or three study questions on each section. It is also valuable to take a book of the Bible and, with the help of a commentary and a good reference Bible, try to grasp the meaning of it, verse by verse, section by section. Alternatively, it can be very illuminating to follow a theme or word of particular significance through the New Testament, or the whole Bible. You can do this with a good Bible concordance, but be sure your concordance is based on the particular Bible translation you are using. Books such as Stephen Neill's *Bible Words and Christian Meanings* (SPCK, UK, 1970) and Lawrence O. Richards's *Expository Dictionary of Bible Words* (Marshall Pickering, 1985; Zondervan, 1985) illustrate the helpfulness of such study.

Of course, studying the Bible is a lifelong process and you will often find yourself looking for new and creative approaches to the Bible. A good place to begin is *How to Understand Your Bible* (IVP-USA, 1974) by T. Norton Sterrett. From another angle, *How to Read the Bible for All Its Worth* by Gordon Fee and Douglas Stuart (Zondervan, USA, 1982) has proven very helpful in providing strategies for reading the various types of literature in the Bible. Along these same lines, IVP's How to Read Series devotes individual volumes to particular types of biblical literature. For tackling the Gospels or Acts, Joel Green's *How to Read the Gospels and Acts* (IVP, 1987) is a reliable guide, or his *How to Read Prophecy* (IVP, 1984) can orient you to the foreign world of biblical prophecy. If you want a fresh perspective on studying the Psalms, Tremper Longman's *How to Read the Psalms* (IVP, 1988) is the place to begin. And finally, for a variety of approaches, strategies, tips and plans for Bible reading, A. J. Conyers' *How to Read the Bible* (IVP, 1986) is a valuable resource.

The World of the New Testament Churches

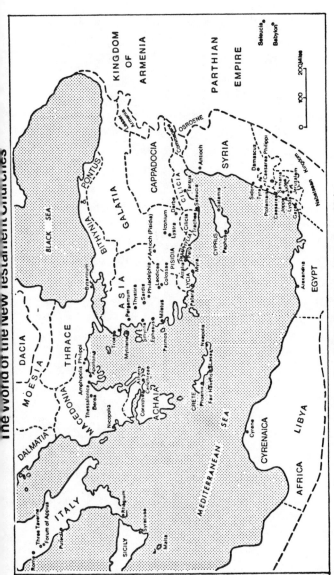

Reproduced by kind permission of Scripture Union.

Index